Also by Juliet Eilperin

Fight Club Politics:
How Partisanship Is Poisoning the House of Representatives

DEMON FISH

JULIET EILPERIN

DEMON FISH

Travels Through the Hidden World of Sharks

Pantheon Books, New York

Copyright © 2011 by Juliet Eilperin

All rights reserved. Published in the United States by Pantheon Books,
a division of Random House, Inc., New York, and in Canada
by Random House of Canada Limited, Toronto.

Pantheon Books and colophon are registered trademarks
of Random House, Inc.

Library of Congress Cataloging-in-Publication Data

Eilperin, Juliet.
Demon fish : travels through the hidden world of sharks / Juliet Eilperin.
p.   cm.
Includes bibliographical references and index.
ISBN 978-0-375-42512-7
1. Sharks. 2. Sharks—Anecdotes. I. Title.
QL638.9.E43 2011   597.3—dc22   2010030264

www.pantheonbooks.com

Jacket photograph © Hermanus Backpackers
Jacket design by Brian Barth

Printed in the United States of America
First Edition

2   4   6   8   9   7   5   3   1

To my mother, Sophie C. Cook, my father, Stephen F. Eilperin,
and my husband, Andrew Light, all of whose
parenting skills put sharks to shame

Contents

Introduction: Shark

The sharks are almost glowing as they pass by, gently nudging each other as they jostle for the bloody pieces of barracuda that the ichthyologist Samuel "Sonny" H. Gruber has thrown in the sea minutes before. Their whitish underbellies reflect the beaming Caribbean sun above. They are shimmering, even as their steel gray upper bodies dull the light and provide them a measure of camouflage. The pearly glow and stealth of these creatures confirm what I have long suspected: sharks operate in a separate universe.

They glide, these lemon sharks, Caribbean reef sharks, blacknose sharks, and nurse sharks. But unlike the pretty tropical fish beside them, which travel in neat, compact schools, these sharks swoop in from all directions. They display no attempt at coordination: each one is out for itself.

Before I enter the water, a researcher warns me I should rely on peripheral vision to make sure I can sense whether a shark is approaching me from the side. Unlike a character in the movies, I cannot scan the surface for the telltale fin that juts out right before the cinematic climax: sharp points appear from an array of angles, making such clear distinctions impossible. While I'm no expert in scuba maneuvers, I do my best to keep moving in this rapidly shifting underwater feeding frenzy so as not to collide with one of the sharks by accident. I am more alert than a highway driver checking her blind spot while cruising at seventy-five miles per hour. It's as if I have crashed an amazing, bizarre party with several friends and need to be on my best behavior at all times, for fear of offending our intriguing but menacing hosts.

———

This is the first time I've entered the surreal world of sharks. It's the summer of 2005 off the shores of Bimini, a small island fifty miles from the Florida coast. I am viewing sharks as a journalist, venturing out with several researchers from the Bimini Biological Field Station. In the Bahamas this pastel-colored institution is better known by its longtime nickname, the Shark Lab. This moniker gives it the same casual feel as the rest of the island: many locals are bemused by the fresh-faced, budding marine biologists who rotate in and out of its cramped quarters with clocklike regularity. The entire enterprise seems more like a *Real World* episode than a real science mission. In Gruber's boat I'm surrounded by about a dozen tanned—in some instances pierced and tattooed—twentysomethings from various countries in skimpy bathing suits. They all appear unfazed at the prospect of taking a dip with creatures that terrify most sane swimmers. These young men and women don't appear to be geeks who have temporarily traded in their polyester white lab coats for black neoprene wet suits: they're casually chatting about their evening plans as we prepare to enter the water, not arguing about the finer features of elasmobranchs—a subclass within Chondrichthyes—or shifting water currents.

Unlike my companions, however, I cannot adopt the same casual pose this summer afternoon. I have painstakingly developed several rationales to keep myself from panicking before scooting off the boat at Triangle Rocks, a gathering place for several shark species:

1. All the biologists on this trip have an interest in keeping me alive, since they'll never get their message out if I die here and fail to publish my work.

2. I'm among the skinniest folks on this outing, so surely I'm less appetizing than the chunkier divers.

3. As long as I act as if I know what I'm doing, and don't deliberately pick fights with these hulking animals, they'll leave me alone.

Calm for the moment, I jump into the water without much fuss and focus on keeping my wits about me as I slip down below the surface.

But my feigned nonchalance dissipates the moment my eyes open, as I see dozens of the kinds of mythical creatures that have dominated the human psyche for millennia, long before *Jaws* hit American movie screens in 1975. Swarming the area looking for food, the sharks come within a few feet of where I am swimming. I don't need to worry about being eaten, it turns out, much to my relief. They are more focused on their catered mealtime than on the human in their midst. Mingling in this congregation are some nurse sharks— among the most harmless sharks divers typically encounter—which only latch onto humans if they're deliberately provoked, in which case their jaws can remain clamped on for some time. But for the most part these are not namby-pamby sharks, the kind that pose no harm. So I gently circle these ancient creatures, thrilled at the idea that I'm surviving on their turf.

Humans—regardless of their culture, era, or geographic location— have been fascinated with sharks from the beginning of time. They predate us by so many hundreds of millions of years but are a remote cohabitant of this earth rather than a familiar one. Sharks were swimming our seas before the continents took their current shape, when oceans covered Bolivia, South Africa, and Montana. Despite their considerable numbers, they remain elusive. Many of them don't travel in schools: they roam the seas on their own, as adventurers. Their murderous power, their ancient lineage, their aloofness—all these attributes have given them a place within human culture where they are simultaneously worshipped and loathed. It's an unenviable position, one that is helping propel their rapid decline.

Historically, sharks represented gods in ancient societies, where their power to destroy us demanded respect. Sharks played a role in these cultures' rituals and their creation stories, helping explain humans' relationship to the natural world. In Fiji the people had a shark god called Dakuwaqa that was seen as the direct ancestor of their high chiefs; the Japanese paid homage to a shark they considered the God of Storms; the Hawaiians still view the shark as an animal deity that serves as their most powerful guardian angel, *'aumākua*.[1] But just as sharks are beginning to vanish from our oceans, these tales are start-ing to fade from human memory. Panama's Kuna Indians used to worship Tío Tiburón, or Uncle Shark; now they view sharks solely as a threat. The Maori people of New Zealand no longer discuss the shark legends they used to prize. Fijians on Beqa Island still respect their shark god enough to insist his name only be written, rather than uttered aloud, but their marine protected areas serve more as a tourist attraction than as a place of worship.[2] As these societies have mod-ernized, they have forgotten why they prized sharks in the first place.

There are still some places left around the globe, like a few small island villages in Papua New Guinea, where this sort of worldview continues to hold sway. In these remote outposts a select group of men are trained in the ritual of shark calling: after performing elabo-rate rituals, they hunt them by hand, bring them home for feasts, and end up earning more respect than anyone else. But even here rela-tions between humans and sharks have undergone a shift, because it is shark conquerors who hold a special place in these societies. Wor-shipping sharks alone is no longer enough.

Over time sharks have become a commodity to be consumed and a threat to be contained. Those who succeed in these efforts see their status among their friends and colleagues rise: In China, the business-men who can afford to order shark's fin soup are the ones who can impress their clients. And in southern Florida, athletes and celebrities such as Shaquille O'Neal pay the tour operator Mark "the Shark" Quartiano hundreds of dollars so they can take a cruise and catch a hammerhead or two.

Killing sharks conveys status to those who slay them (or, by infer-ence, to those who can afford to buy the fruits of these battles) because they inherently pose a mortal threat to us. This shift has enormous implications, since humans have been able to harness technology to destroy sharks in unprecedented numbers. The way we deal with sharks pushes the boundaries of how comfortable we are with dan-ger and taps into our tendency to view the wild as exotic. But it also underscores how globalization and scientific inquiry are transforming our understanding of the sea.

Ironically, we now pose the primary threat to sharks' existence, rather than the other way around. We are helping banish them from the earth at the very time we're learning more about them and their vast seas, which cover two-thirds of the globe. While humans have engaged in deepwater exploration for only the past sixty years, we've barely made a dent in the ocean: 75 percent of its massive terrain remains largely unexplored. About 80 percent of marine life also remains uncataloged. It is the last frontier. When scientists began focusing on marine creatures in the first place, moreover, they didn't pay much attention to sharks, because at the time they lacked the commercial value of other species, like tuna. Until a few decades ago most fishing records didn't even make a distinction between the different species of sharks that were caught in a given batch, as if all sharks were the same. In the words of Enric Cortés, a scientist who helps oversee sharks at the National Oceanic and Atmospheric Administration, they are the "ugly ducklings" of the sea.

Now scientific revelations about sharks have begun to emerge, frequently raising as many questions as they answer. Just a few years ago researchers discovered that great white sharks leave the California coast and journey as far away as Hawaii, spending time in an area between Baja California and Hawaii that scientists now call the "White Shark Café." But they still have no idea what sharks do there, aside from possibly meeting members of the opposite sex, eating, and socializing with other sharks (that's why they call it a café). It wasn't until the mid-1990s, when Taiwanese fishermen pulled up a whale shark, the world's largest fish—with a few hundred eggs inside it at different stages of development—that scientists began to grasp how many offspring this enormous fish can reproduce at any one time. But they still can't comprehensively describe how a whale shark mates and reproduces, or where this takes place. And while researchers can examine a Galápagos turtle's shell and declare how long the creature has been roaming the earth, no one can make the same confident estimate when it comes to sharks. They do have bands in their vertebrae, and it appears this is a good way to measure whale sharks' longevity, but species such as the Atlantic angel shark apparently lay these bands down at random. Even when we possess them, sharks can still manage to elude us.

Scientists can track sharks by embedding them with satellite tags and attaching underwater cameras, technology that captures for the first time their enormous migrations across entire ocean basins. Other researchers are using DNA analysis to determine not only how sharks breed and reproduce but what species are ending up on the global fin market. Another set of scientists, moreover, are cataloging new species of sharks in areas of the world that have been off-limits to researchers for years. In other instances they have captured their behavior with exacting precision. A. Peter Klimley, a professor at the University of California at Davis who has spent years tracking great whites, can tell you how rarely great whites eat—they can survive for as long as a month and a half on a single bite—as well as how they warn away other potential food competitors by slapping their tails.

We are beginning to unravel the mystery of sharks, at just the moment when some of them are in danger of disappearing altogether.

Sharks are fish, but they differ from bony fish in many respects. All sharks belong to the taxonomic class Chondrichthyes, which signifies they have skeletons made from cartilage. Unlike bony fish, which have teeth attached in sockets, sharks have teeth that are connected to their jaws by soft tissue. Their teeth continually fall out or break off and are replaced. Every shark is a carnivore. But not all of them eat other fish: some of them consume tiny plankton, or invertebrates.

Many fish have swim bladders that provide them with neutral buoyancy. Sharks stay afloat by other means. Much of their buoyancy comes from the oil in their liver, but different species use an array of techniques to suspend themselves in the water. Sand tiger sharks suck in air when they reach the ocean's surface and then hold it in their stomachs, allowing them to float. Many sharks gain lift from the pairs of pectoral and pelvic fins they have on their undersides, in the same way that planes rely on their airfoil wings. They can also use their pectoral fins for braking and to move up and down or to the right or left, but they cannot manipulate them to swim backward or hover. With a few exceptions—the gigantic whale and basking sharks stand out in this respect—these animals have torpedo-like bodies that allow the fastest of them to move at speeds up to thirty miles per hour. The short-fin mako ranks as the swiftest shark, with the blue shark, clocking in at roughly twenty-four miles per hour, as the second fastest. When they're not pursuing prey, however, sharks often swim at the pace of a human engaged in a brisk walk.

Bony fish have an easy mechanism that lets them breathe underwater: they can use muscles attached to a bony plate covering their gills, known as an operculum, to bring water through their mouths and across their gills. This mechanism provides them with oxygen while allowing them to expel carbon dioxide through their gills. Some bottom-dwelling sharks can imitate this effect by moving their fins so as to create enough current to bring water in and over their gills, or by operating a pumping system where they suck in water with their gills closed and then force the water out through them. These methods allow them to rest on the seabed. But most of the largest sharks have no choice but to swim at all times, with their mouths agape, in order to obtain the oxygen they need to survive. This is one of the reasons people see sharks as so scary: cruising along as they display their sharp teeth, they look as if they're poised to attack at any moment.[3] This phenomenon—technically called ram ventilation—is what Woody Allen was referring to when his character Alvy Singer famously told Annie Hall in his 1977 classic: "A relationship, I think, is like a shark. You know? It has to constantly move forward or it dies. And I think what we got on our hands is a dead shark."

While humans tend to fixate on the most obvious things they can observe about sharks—their constant movement, their sharp teeth, and their dorsal fins that jut out of the water—these creatures' unique skin and extraordinary senses allow them to dominate the sea. All sharks boast an armored skin covered with denticles—a.k.a. skin teeth—made of the same material as their teeth, crowns covered with hard enamel. This amazing material, which reduces friction by forcing the water to flow in channels, has scales that flex separately from one another, and in general the cusps of the denticles' crowns point toward the tail. This feature, which makes shark skin feel smooth when stroked from one direction and scratchy when stroked from the opposite one, allows sharks to move swiftly through the water. Even before people understood their purpose, they marveled at denticles' scratchiness and exploited it for their own purposes. In August 1869, *The Brooklyn Daily Eagle* reported on an eight-foot shark that washed up into a pool of water near Fifteenth Street and Hamilton Avenue, describing how bystanders had killed it and dragged it onto dry land. According to the paper, "The animal was skinned by some boys, the skin being said to make excellent sand paper."[4]

The types of denticles sharks have depend on the species, allowing for specialization: basking sharks have crowns that point in all directions, while short-fin mako sharks—some of the fastest swimmers in the sea—have smaller, lighter denticles than other sharks. The varying composition of these suits of body armor reflects their respective purposes: lighter denticles maximize a shark's speed while providing slightly less protection against a predatory attack. Like sharks' teeth, these denticles fall out routinely over time and are subsequently replaced, providing them with constant protection. They are as strong as steel and carry an added benefit: by minimizing water turbulence, they allow sharks to hunt better by moving through the sea in near silence.[5]

Humans have done their best to replicate denticles: the swimsuit manufacturer Speedo has made clothing out of an imitation material, Fastskin, and NASA has explored using denticles as a model for the material it could use on airplanes. Ralph Liedert, a researcher at the University of Applied Sciences in Bremen, Germany, informed his colleagues at an annual meeting of the Society for Experimental Biology that covering ships with artificial sharkskin would help them move smoothly because the material would dramatically reduce biofouling. Biofouling, which occurs when barnacles, mussels, and algae latch onto ships, increases a vessel's drag resistance by as much as 15 percent. Liedert has produced an imitation sharkskin from elastic silicone that would reduce this fouling by 67 percent, and he estimates that once a ship reached four to five knots, nearly all of these critters would fly off the hull's surface.⁶ After researchers from Mote Marine Laboratory's Center for Shark Research and Boston University's marine program discovered that sharks hunt prey by sensing the differences when their smell hits each nostril—they call it "smelling in stereo"—scientists have started exploring whether they can apply this same steering algorithm to odor-guided robots that track oil plumes and chemical leaks underwater.⁷

In recent years the concept of biomimicry has become increasingly popular: venture capitalists have started eyeing everything from whales' circulatory systems to the way leaves photosynthesize as a model for commercial products. Sharks' unique adaptive qualities, honed over millions of years, offer a range of possibilities that we've only begun to explore.

I didn't grow up obsessed with sharks, as many small children do. But once I got in the water with sharks in Bimini, I started to think about them quite a bit. Part of my interest stemmed from the fact that they were incredible to look at: the muscular power they can convey just moving through the water makes them formidable swimming companions. The dizzying array of shark-related scientific papers that flooded my e-mail in-box at *The Washington Post* also piqued my interest. As I learned about how researchers are beginning to piece together how sharks live and operate, it became clear that their work is far from complete. But just as significantly, I began to see how sharks' lives reveal much about the ocean: how it functions, and why it is now in peril.

Some like to describe sharks as "the lions and tigers of the sea," while Rachel Graham, a Wildlife Conservation Society scientist who works in Belize, Guatemala, and Mexico, calls them "jaguars" to appeal to Central Americans' pride. Sharks are the kinds of predators, not unlike masters of the savanna and grasslands, that are beginning to tell us about a largely invisible world to which our lives are inextricably tied. Their ancient lineage teaches us how creatures, including ourselves, have adapted to changing environments over millions of years; the toxins that now pervade their bodies show us how what we emit from industrial smokestacks permeates the air and water throughout the globe. They show us not just how we may be heading toward the abyss but also how the natural world functioned before we started undermining it. As one of the most dominant forces underwater, sharks help maintain the balance of marine ecosystems by keeping midlevel predators in check. One of their most valuable qualities, from a strictly human perspective, is that they hint at how the ocean would look if we invested in its resilience instead of plundering its depths.

While it sounds odd, for much of the twentieth century humans saw sharks—along with most other fish—as meat. They were something to be caught in a net or by hook, hauled overboard, and shipped off to market. Even scientists saw them as static creatures, for the most part: they might dissect them to examine their stomach contents, but they didn't observe their underwater lives and contemplate how their actions affected the rest of the ocean over time. But in the same way researchers and land managers now understand that reintroducing gray wolves into Yellowstone has a slew of cascading effects along the region's food chain, experts now understand that healthy shark populations restore the historic balance of marine life. Rather than selectively picking apart the ocean's natural system—blasting corals in one area, fishing out tasty large fish like groupers in another, and pulling up sharks in another—we could commit ourselves to repairing this ravaged system. We have declared less than half of 1 percent of the ocean off-limits, compared with the roughly 14 percent of the planet's terrestrial surface that enjoys protection.[8] We set aside more land for conservation than for farming,[9] but marine reserves don't begin to compete with the areas where fishing lines stretch and trawlers scrape.

Plenty of evidence now exists that if we curb our worst excesses—overfishing, trawling, and polluting—when it comes to the sea, we can give it at least a chance of resisting the broader environmental threats that are well under way, such as climate change. While it's impossible to restore the entire sea to health, protecting the most eco-logically rich areas will produce diverse pockets of the sea in which a range of creatures and plants can thrive. And sharks represent an essential part of the mix.

To better understand sharks, and the men and women whose lives are inextricably tied to them, I ventured across the globe to examine places best described as the water's edge: the areas where humans mingle with sharks. Sometimes this place was literally the land-sea boundary: the place where a Mexican shark fisherman is pulling his catch of mako and blue sharks up onto the beach, or where a Papua New Guinean elder is shoving his canoe off the shore to search for the fish that reconnects him to his ancestors. Other times the water's edge is abstract. The place where I crowd in with shark fin traders to get a better look at the wares at a Hong Kong auction, a Fort Lau-derdale lab where I examine the results of a genetic analysis of shark samples in Mahmood Shivji's office, or the New Orleans bar where I listen to aides to a prominent American politician joke that sharks deserve to be wiped out before they claim another human life all rep-resent different intersections between our lives and those of sharks. In some cases these moments show how we are slowly disassembling the natural world; at other times these incidents exemplify our fight to understand it and preserve it. The extent to which these individuals recognize their dependence on these creatures, of course, dictates the extent to which they are invested in sharks' survival.

In every instance, however, I began to see how we are coming nearer to the monsters of the sea that have terrified us for centu-ries. This is an actual fact: because of recent advances in technology, some researchers are discovering that sharks live much closer to us than we've ever suspected. And the relentless push toward our coasts, whether it's to live full-time or to spend our holidays, drives us into even closer contact. But that doesn't mean we understand sharks bet-ter, or appreciate them more, than we did before.

Often we value things in the natural world because we see ourselves in their reflection: in how they sing, raise their babies, or travel across the countryside. On rarer occasions—when we marvel at the improbable journey of the albatross or the way male lions live apart from females—we prize them because we define ourselves by how different they are from us. But sharks matter because they exist apart from us, not because of how they stand in relation to us. Henry Beston, writer and naturalist, put it best when he wrote of animals, "They are not brethren, they are not underlings. They are other nations, caught with ourselves in the net of life and time, fellow prisoners of the splendor and travails of the earth." Sharks, and their surroundings, merit as much exploration as the moon, but we only devote a fraction of the same resources to them. Not for reasons of conquest, or even because our fate is in part linked to theirs. Sharks are worth understanding in their own right, a source of revelations about a foreign world that abuts ours.

For the most part we still see the sea as a source of valuable commodities we can extract, whether it's the fish we eat or the oil we drill. And for all of the modern techniques we now use to conduct it, the act of fishing itself is pre-agrarian: it's hunting and gathering. Sharks and other commercial fish are something for humans to capture, not cultivate. We seek to defeat their wildness, rather than admire it.

Ancient myths about sharks are fascinating, mainly because they reveal how we—rather than the animals—have changed over time. They underscore how we used to be closer to the natural world, and were more invested in it. We have doggedly viewed sharks through our own prisms, immune to the revelations that have emerged in recent years, and our popular view of them has become more, not less, simplistic over time. This book looks at how humans began by worshipping sharks and grew to hate them, then started to hunt them en masse, before deciding it might be worth fighting to keep them around. This evolving relationship between humans and sharks illuminates how we have sought to submit wildness to our will, with varying degrees of success. But these beasts themselves, and the subterranean world they inhabit, are affecting human society even as it seeks to shunt them aside.

Sharks' power over us has always stemmed from the fact that they are largely unseen. They can strike at any time and can disappear just as easily as they can arrive at the surface. This book is an effort to explore the mystery that surrounds them and decipher it. It attempts to discover what these sea monsters are at their core, the complex and contentious community they help rule, and whether they can continue to exist alongside us. If we pay attention, sharks can tell us about their watery world and its implications for the land we inhabit. How we negotiate sharing the planet with sharks could help determine what our own future looks like, not just theirs.

DEMON FISH

THE WORLD-FAMOUS SHARK CALLER

Sun come up, my shark come up.
> —a shark caller's chant in Dennis O'Rourke's
> 1982 film, *The Sharkcallers of Kontu*

For a brief moment, I despair that we'll ever get to Tembin.

Three of us—myself, my friend Laura Berger, and our driver, Paul Vatlom—had successfully made the trek from Kavieng, the biggest city in the Papua New Guinean province of New Ireland, to the outskirts of Tembin, one of the three most renowned shark-calling towns in the world. The problem: a storm had washed away the bridge to Tembin several years ago, and no one had ever bothered to fix it.

Some of the villagers had heard we were coming, so they decided to pile onto the back of our white Toyota 4x4, further complicating our task. Now we are facing crossing a river and navigating a swamp, all without tossing several uninvited hitchhikers over the side.

Luckily, Vatlom happens to be one of those people who manages to be fearless, deft, and cheerful at the same time. "We will do it," he says, nodding, speaking as much to himself as to Laura and me. And then by shifting gears, gunning the engine a bit, and weaving back and forth, he manages to coax the truck through first water and then mud. The truck rocks slightly, but no one falls off, and within minutes we have arrived in a settlement that looks like a throwback in time, the sort of village in which a Peace Corps volunteer would have arrived in the 1960s.

As the hitchhikers leap off the truck, our welcoming committee comes out to meet us. It is led by Selam Karasimbe, a lean, wiry man sporting a broad smile, a single piece of cloth wrapped around his hips, and a black sweatshirt emblazoned with the words "New York." Trailed by a few women, several small children, and an assortment of pigs, Karasimbe looks like the kind of man who has answers. He is the strongest living connection to the way humans used to see sharks hundreds of years ago. And despite an array of modern-day pressures, he has kept this worldview intact, in a place that seems much closer to our past than our present. It is one of the best ways to understand how the worlds of sharks and humans intersect, and what happens when this relationship is thrown off balance.

Karasimbe is, in his own words, "the world-famous shark caller" of Kontu. "World-famous" may be a bit of an overstatement: most people have never heard of either shark calling or the remote island province, New Ireland, where it is practiced. But the Australian filmmaker Dennis O'Rourke did feature Karasimbe in his 1982 documentary, *The Sharkcallers of Kontu,* an anthropology cult classic. And when it comes to Papua New Guinea, that qualifies for global exposure.

In a world where most humans view sharks with a mix of fear and loathing, Papua New Guinea is one of the few places where people embrace them. For the villagers in Tembin, Mesi, and Kontu—the three towns that still practice shark calling—sharks are an integral part of their creation story, a religious faith that has endured for centuries.

In many ways, New Ireland—the province that is home to shark calling—is a microcosm of Papua New Guinea itself. At least seventeen distinct languages are still spoken there, and while humans have lived on the islands for at least thirty-two thousand years, it was only colonized by the West when Germany claimed it as a colonial protectorate in 1885. Charted in 1767 by the British navigator Philip Carteret, who named it on the basis of its relationship to another, larger nearby island (New Britain), New Ireland served as a port for

American whaling ships in search of water and provisions during their voyages.

Missionaries have worked relentlessly to make Papua New Guinea into a Christian country: according to the 2000 census, 96 percent of the populace identifies itself as Christian. While missionaries are a rare sight in much of the South Pacific at this point, they are still ubiquitous in even the most isolated of Papua New Guinean villages. They often provide basic services, including schooling. And in exchange, they demand fealty to a Christian god.

Many Papua New Guineans have reconciled this Western religion with their traditional ancestor worship. In this traditional faith, the spirits of their ancestors inhabit the current natural world, offering them a way to connect to those who preceded them in their everyday surroundings. These spirits communicate to them, watch over them, and guide their choices: it's a much more immediate connection than the one that typically defines Christian faiths.

But faced with this contrast to Christianity, Papua New Guineans like Karasimbe have deftly fudged the difference. Going to church while also maintaining ties to his ancestors through shark hunting, Karasimbe reasons, is not contradictory. He and others can do this in part because the traditional Papua New Guinean faith has a creator, Moroa, who is from their perspective essentially synonymous with the Judeo-Christian God. While the myth of Moroa predates Papua New Guineans' contact with missionaries, it bears a strong similarity to Christianity. Moroa created the world in a series of steps just like the Judeo-Christian God did, for example, but his instructions are a bit more detailed than some of the early guidance contained in the Old Testament.

Take sharks, for instance. According to legend, Moroa made Lembe the shark before he made man but after he had made the sun and the moon and put fish and dolphins in the sea. Moroa made Lembe "in the time of *tulait,* the time between the end of the night and the beginning of the new day," and in doing so, he divided the shark's belly into two parts.[1] The left side of the belly could sense danger, but the right side would let the shark approach a canoe without fear.

After creating this divided creature, Moroa held Lembe by his tail (Papua New Guineans say you can still see the mark of Moroa's thumb and forefinger on every shark in the sea) and explained to the shark the conditions on which he could approach man. He said he would tell man to catch the shark, and that if man broke any of the *tambus* (taboos) set out for him, Lembe must listen to the left side of his belly and stay away.

As one might imagine, at this point Lembe was getting tired of Moroa's lecture. So he jumped in the sea, just as Moroa was going to tell him about the bait fish man would use to try to lure him. In retaliation, Moroa threw white sand at Lembe, which has given him rough skin until the end of time. "Moroa threw his hands in the air and yelled after the disappearing shark he was truly stupid," Glenys Köhnke recounts. "For now that his skin was rough man would be able to snare him in a specially prepared noose which Moroa would show him how to make."[2]

When Moroa created humans, he went through the elaborate rules for catching sharks and the mechanics of making special equipment for the task, such as the coconut rattle Karasimbe uses today. And when he was done, Moroa had given the shark callers of Papua New Guinea something no one else on earth possesses: the ability to communicate with the scariest creatures in the sea. On a certain level, shark calling is a form of resistance against Western colonizers, since these authorities told Papua New Guineans they could not worship Moroa any longer. The missionaries tried to discredit locals' traditional beliefs altogether, telling them they needed to renounce their old faith and accept Christ instead. But many Papua New Guineans see no reason to abandon ancestor worship. Karasimbe wears a rosary with white disks and black beads and considers himself a Christian, but he points out that when the missionaries argued ancestor worship was essentially godless, they failed to grasp the fact that villagers viewed Moroa as an overarching deity the same way Christians view their own God. Missionaries, he recalls, suggested that the faith traditions they had practiced for centuries were contrary to Christianity and were "fucking up people" because "they don't know about God." But they overlooked an obvious point, he says: "Moroa is God."

At this point many Papua New Guineans see shark calling as a divine right, one of the few skills they boast that no other civilization can offer. They argue that their ability to lure sharks from the deep—and catch them by hand using snares—represents a unique culture that should not be snuffed out by either colonization or modernization. Just because outsiders might not understand the practice, they say, doesn't mean it lacks value. Henry Bilak, a retired soldier living in Mesi, says outsiders don't fully appreciate what his people can do when it comes to connecting with sharks. "This is the oldest form of human communication with sharks," he says, sitting in a village garden blooming with yellow, white, red, and pink hibiscus. "The bottom line is this is what human beings can do. This is what God has given us."

Spending time with Karasimbe, I realize that he and other shark callers hold on so tightly to this part of their faith because it differentiates them from their colonial conquerors. The Germans and the Australians may have brought currency, modern goods, and other advances to Papua New Guinea, but shark calling is something that cannot be replicated by the West. It delineates roles within Papua New Guinean society and anchors these people's conception of the universe.

Not everyone in New Ireland has the divine power to catch sharks. It's an elite club. Only men can practice the tradition—legend has it that the scent of a woman prompts sharks to flee. And these select shark callers pass their secrets on to their sons and nephews. Like most things in Papua New Guinea, a person's *wontok,* or clan, allegiances are paramount: clans zealously guard their particular shark-calling practices, and sometimes men end up as shark callers by virtue of whom they married. While men hold the upper hand in Papua New Guinea, it remains a matrilineal society, so land and other privileges are passed through women rather than men. While this sometimes appears contradictory, given how much influence men wield in Papua New Guinean society, it is the one form of power reserved to women.

Aeluda Toxok, a veteran shark caller in Mesi, took on the calling when he married a woman belonging to the Nako clan. Now in his late sixties, Toxok still goes out regularly in search of sharks. In a given season, he may go out to sea thirty times. Toxok was thirty when he first learned shark calling. By practicing the same rituals as those before him, he sees himself as a sort of shark tamer who calls upon his ancestors for aid in order to corral such a fierce predator. Even with his frizzy white hair and well-lined visage, Toxok is an impressive figure, lean and ready for battle.

One of the most striking aspects of shark callers is their supreme sense of confidence. When I happen on Toxok on the beach, he is preparing his canoe because he has an instinct that he is poised to catch a shark for the first time this season. "Because I have prepared myself, I can go out there and do it. I've got a feeling when the shark is coming. I'm going to catch it," he says. "It's like a game, because I have prepared all the rituals. I have caught sharks, and I know every time I will go out, I will catch a shark."

Toxok's surety is particularly impressive given that once he lures a shark to his outrigger canoe, he must subdue the fish by hand. Shark calling is practiced in three sets of islands along the Bismarck Archipelago—New Ireland, the Duke of York, and the Tabar islands—and in each case they use a contraption to catch sharks that is used nowhere else. To trap a shark, the caller submerges a noose made of plaited cane, which is attached to a wooden propeller float. When the shark is through the noose up to its pectoral fins, the fisherman jerks up on the propeller's handle, which in turn tightens the noose around the shark. At this point, the shark struggles to break free, and the shark caller must resist the animal's force to keep it from escaping. Once the shark is exhausted, the fisherman can relax for a few moments and let the float bring it to the surface. At this point the caller stabs the shark in the eyes, to debilitate it further, clubs it into submission, and brings it aboard his canoe.

Each aspect of a shark caller's equipment is meticulously designed to maximize his ability to subdue a predatory animal. The canoe, for example, must be light enough to paddle for long distances but strong enough to withstand the tussle between man and shark that takes place during each outing. The canoe's seats consist of narrow slats that are uncomfortable to sit on, but that makes the overall vessel lighter, and the trip easier. While this is an efficient design, it's not perfect: the Tembin shark caller Robert Muskup acknowledges during one of our chats, "When I sit there for a long time, I feel that it hurts."

Conserving energy on the trip out to sea is crucial because if the trip proves too exhausting, the caller won't be able to physically battle the shark once he catches it. Toxok admits that he's often tired by the time a shark lodges itself in his noose, "because of the paddling." But he also believes he is better off fighting hand to hand when he's offshore, because he thinks he possesses powers on the water that don't extend to land: "That particular job, I can do it on one hand. I can do it out there, on the sea."

For an activity that comes down to such a basic contest between man and shark, it carries an elaborate nomenclature. Consider the names Papua New Guineans have for the different sections of a shark caller's canoe paddle, a piece of equipment that stretches between two and three feet. There is the *leganbanane,* the top of the canoe paddle that resembles the bud of a baby coconut; the *lebinos,* the leg, or handle, of the paddle; the *lebelik,* the small, V-shaped carving at the paddle's base; the *legiptas,* the broadest part of the paddle; and finally the *lembiros,* the tip of the paddle that, according to Karasimbe, calls out underwater to wake up the spirit of the sharks in the sea, the *sixilikbe.*

To assess their chances of success, shark callers—like fishermen everywhere—divvy up species by their level of ferocity. Karasimbe and his clan have four names to describe the sharks they catch: *lumnummus* is very fierce, *latixon* is fierce, *lasinabi* is friendly, and *lutino* is very friendly. While some of these names correlate to specific species—*lumnummus* often refers to tiger sharks, among the most combative sharks that troll the shores of Papua New Guinea—these categories are aimed at characterizing the animal's spirit rather than what it looks like, or even the class of sharks to which it belongs. In the folk religion of shark calling, spirit matters more than science.

———

A few days before they go out to sea, shark callers observe strict dietary and social restrictions. According to tradition, men cannot eat pig, prawn, crab, lizard, or *kapul,* a small marsupial that lives in Papua New Guinea. Shark callers cannot have sex with their wives, on the grounds that the sharks will be able to detect a woman's scent and will stay away. They cannot step on animal feces for the same reason.

Not surprisingly, some of these prohibitions can prove irritating. Philp Taput, a shark caller from Tembin in his forties, says he's no longer afraid of confronting the sharks, but "the hardest part of it is to keep away from some of the *tambus* [taboos] like staying away from lying with the ladies, sleeping in the *houseboy* [a small building where shark callers gather], and not stepping on excrement." But Taput would never think of violating these admonitions: it helps give him the steeliness he needs to confront sharks, single-handed, in the water. He does look for signs in the natural world that plenty of sharks are in the water, such as seagulls flying above the ocean, but he places more faith in the elaborate, time-honored practices he performs before heading for sea. Paying homage to tradition will deliver the sharks. "When we are preparing our rituals to go out, then we have to ask the power of the creator, the spirit, to go with us. It applies to both our ancestors and being a Christian."

While shark hunting is usually a practical exercise—it supplies the village with food for funeral rites and other special occasions—callers also use their rituals to find answers to the questions that arise from life's tragedies. In this way, they are seen as wise men who can get answers from the sharks even when they're not seeking to catch them. Karasimbe's older brother Mangis Hari, who is in his late seventies, will often perform this sort of divining ceremony for bereaved villagers. As he describes it, speaking in Tok Pisin, it is an extraordinarily precise set of procedures.

"When one of my villagers dies, I collect hair from the dead body. I take that [and put it near a particular tree], and there it remains for three days. After those three days I collect that and I wash it with some magic, some leaves, and then I go down to the beach one afternoon and sit down. I go to a clear place and put it down. With the conch shell, I start doing some magic. I prepare it for the next day. I go out to the beach, I get two different branches and perform magic, I sing some magic songs. When I finish one song, I take one branch and throw it out to sea. I do the same with the second branch, but I strike the conch shell before throwing the branch out to sea. I tie a branch and the hair together. Then I bring it to the cemetery where the deceased was buried. The spirit of the ancestors comes."

Hari then needs to return to the reef just off the beach, to communicate with sharks and other fish in the sea. "I will put my foot on the reef. Three types of fish will appear—two out of the three are dangerous. Then I will ask, 'How did he die, because of a land dispute, or something else?' Then the fish will appear and make signs. The fish will be where I put my foot."

Hari performed this very ritual when his own father died, and says it revealed to him that someone had killed his father with magic. He and his family did not seek retribution for what they perceived as their father's murder, but it settled a question that had plagued them for days. Karasimbe describes this as the other purpose of shark calling: "It is important also if you want to know about your beginning, or your mother or father when they're dead, and you want to find out, 'Why did my father die?' " Shark calling is not just hunting: it is a way of making sense of the world.

As Hari explains his traditional practice, it becomes clear he and his brother have turned the common conception of sharks on its head. While sharks represent the terrifying unknown to most of us, Hari and Karasimbe believe they can sense the sharks at all times. And that form of "seeing," even if it's not literal, erases the fear that dominates our view of them. But not everyone can lay claim to this sort of vision.

While shark callers are a small group within Papua New Guinean society, there are distinctions within this elite. Karasimbe is known as a skilled hunter, and since he has connections to two villages—he grew up in Tembin but settled on his wife's property in Kontu, a five-minute drive from his hometown—he commands respect from a wide swath of New Ireland society. Among living shark killers, Karasimbe may rank as the most prominent in his entire region. But from a historical perspective, few people sit as high in the shark-calling pantheon as Alois Kiput, the legendary Mesi villager who died at the age of ninety-six (give or take a year) in 2003.

Kiput's story matters for several reasons. It shows how a shark caller can anchor a community during his lifetime, giving everyone in the village a sense of possibility and place. But it also shows the fleeting nature of this kind of tradition, especially when faced with strong Western influences. If a religious practice is limited to a select number of individuals—who don't lead a congregation, but merely perform rituals on behalf of an entire community—it is especially vulnerable to erosion. Few experiences exemplify this historic arc better than Kiput and his tribal members.

What made Kiput special was his ability to help other shark callers by performing magic on their behalf. The shark callers of Mesi would approach Kiput and tell him of their plans to go to sea. He would perform the rituals in private, and the callers would go on their way, taking heart from the fact that a master had bestowed some of his magic upon them.

Kiput's *houseboy*—an enclosure where callers seclude themselves before heading to sea—still stands, an unassuming structure made largely of cane. At the back sits the panoply of shark-calling tools, including the *larung* that a caller shakes underwater and the *taur,* or conch horn, that he sounds to announce a successful catch. "He did all the magic here," says Mary Kalasim, Kiput's eldest daughter, peering around her property. "The power and magic, it stays back here." At her instruction her children bring out the seven stone sharks that Kiput used as he performed his prayers: these gray stone carvings of varying sizes remain valuable property.

Stone sharks are one of the most complicated aspects of shark calling. According to callers like Karasimbe and Toxok, these rough-hewn sculptures, complete with carved mouths that glare menacingly, contain spirits that communicate with both a villager's ancestors and the sharks that roam the ocean. By appealing to the stone sharks on an altar—usually at the base of a revered tree—a caller can lure sharks closer in and enlist his ancestors' aid in bringing one back to a village. In Kiput's case, his daughter says, he would use the spirit sharks to give other villagers "the power to do the shark calling."

When a shark caller dies, however, the status he once conveyed upon his family dissipates. While people remember Kiput with affection and respect, his daughter is bitter at how things have deteriorated since his death. Her own daughter, Jacinta, had to drop out of school to support the family. Shark calling may be prestigious, but it doesn't produce a trust fund. Kiput did pass on several rituals to his eldest daughter, such as the *lamaxalum,* which gathers the sharks from the outer reefs closer to shore so a caller can catch them. "When I sing the song, I am sure that the sharks are coming," Kalasim says, displaying the same sort of confidence as Toxok. But as a woman Kalasim could never perform the song in public, so she stays in her dark hut, largely secluded from the village. The sharks' power has little resonance for Kiput's family now that he's gone, and Kalasim has receded from public view.

The one time it reemerges is when one of Kiput's three sons, with whom he shared his secrets, returns to Mesi. When the village needs a shark, this son comes back to help. "When there is a feast, they call him," Kalasim recounts. But it's not how it was when her father was alive, she rushes to add, when the youth of the village used to surround Kiput and his shark paraphernalia. "Now that he has passed away, they have left it, because there's nobody like him . . . Nowadays, no, nobody uses the stone sharks."

Papua New Guinea has changed since Kiput first came of age, and that helps explain why shark calling has lost some of its cachet. Long insulated from the Western world, Papua New Guinea operated for centuries on a barter system and used kina shells—small, circular shells found on the seashore—as a form of currency. (Even now, the official currency is called kina.) People in rural areas tend to talk about aspects of daily life, including meals, in fairly utilitarian ways. Rather than referring to meat, chicken, or fish, they refer to all of these substances as "protein," as in "We will have protein for dinner tonight" or "I am going out shark calling to get protein." These are the ways the vestiges of missionary teaching still surface here: the missionaries have lectured villagers so much about the importance of basic food groups that abstract nutritional categories have earned their place in everyday conversation.

But after enduring colonial rule since 1884 under the Germans, British, and Australians, and having achieved their independence in 1975, Papua New Guineans are struggling to find services and goods that can generate sufficient cash for them. It remains one of the most rural societies in the world, with only 18 percent of its citizens living in cities. As everyday goods have become more expensive, and drinking and drug use among Papua New Guineans have increased in recent years, it's understandable why some village elders might long for a previous era, and why Karasimbe feels so protective about his profession. "The culture, it's about to die," Karasimbe says. "Young males of today, they're focusing on getting drunk and modern culture."

Father John Glynn, an Irish priest, has spent years ministering in Papua New Guinea, witnessing both its gloried past and its less than idyllic present. "New Ireland, like much of Papua New Guinea, has lost an enormous amount of its culture, its traditions, over the past century," Glynn says. "The current generation doesn't even know how much it's lost."

Yet shark calling still carries some prestige in New Ireland: Taput, one of Tembin's shark callers, says the practice transformed him from "an ordinary person" to one with authority once he caught his first shark at the age of nineteen. "Since then, the community has seen me as a shark caller. They treat me as a shark caller. They see me as a big man in the community."

The divvying up of a shark once it's brought to shore also serves as a way of marking the social status of different villagers. A shark caller like Taput expects the liver, the dorsal fin, and the belly once he brings a shark to his village, both because these choice parts pay homage to his skills and because they will ensure him good luck when he ventures out to sea again. In the old days shark callers hung up their fins to dry in their *houseboys:* the gray triangles served as proof of the men's hunting prowess. But now they bring them to Kavieng to sell them to fin traders. Money matters more than status at this point, and fins bring cash.

In June 2007, Alois Solen's brother died. Solen—Karasimbe's nephew—had watched his brother struggle with illness for a long time, and as soon as his brother was buried, he started preparing his canoe and watching for auspicious signs like seagulls circling in the air.

"I saw the sea, and my brother was there," Solen recounts as we sit in front of the Tembin *houseboy* one night. "It took me two days to go out shark calling. The first day I went out, I tried to catch two, but there was some problem with the loop [that serves as the noose to trap the shark]. The second day it took me ten minutes to find the shark. There was a lot of rubbish in the ocean, so I paddled all the way through it and shook the rattle. Three sharks came up: I caught one, brought it into the canoe, and I killed it with the club."

The shark Solen caught was nine feet long, enough to feed at least twenty people. "At that point there was no protein for the people," he explains. "I was happy to give the people something to eat."

But after taking the belly and dorsal fin that were due to him, Solen headed to the offices of Emirau Marine Products in Kavieng, where he got 20 kina, or about $7, for the fin. What started as a traditional funeral rite ended as a business deal in Emirau's air-conditioned office, a place where an iPod sits precariously perched in its docking station near a set of dingy appliances.

Brian Green, the general manager of Emirau Marine Products, is a compact man of modest height who bustles with energy. He seems wired to explode at any moment—but in a good-humored sort of way, as if his anger at the outside world were a mix of resentment and affection for his fellow man. A self-described "Cockney from the East End of London" who has spent a decent chunk of his life in Australia and New Zealand, Green sees his business as a form of rape and pillage that will wipe out the oceans in a matter of time. It's simply a question of supply and demand, he explains, sitting before his standard-issue desk.

"The market is voracious. Shark is under threat, shark fin is in very short supply, and the demand is getting bigger," he says. "I think something drastic has to be done to protect the sharks. But nothing will."

There are only three fin-trading outposts in Kavieng—in addition to Emirau Marine Products, there's Tsang Sang and Darima Marine Products—and all of their managers are watching as fin supplies become scarcer. Like shark fin traders in Hong Kong and elsewhere, Green has noticed how the business has changed in recent years: "You don't get nearly as much on offer, and what you get on offer is small." As overfishing is depleting shark populations, the animals are getting smaller, and that's translating into smaller fins. At this point Emirau trades less than a ton of shark fin a year because of the dwindling supply, while it annually sells sixteen tons of sea cucumber, another Chinese delicacy that hasn't completely collapsed yet.

While men like Solen and Karasimbe might earn respect at home for their shark calling, Green pays little deference to the villagers who come into his Kavieng office to proffer the fins they've caught. He pays them anywhere from $28 to $100 for a kilo of dried fins and sends them on their way. He suspects most of them have abandoned their traditional fishing methods, using larger boats rather than the small, individual canoes that are required to comply with their long-held customs. And even if they do adhere to tradition, it doesn't mean anything to Green. The idea that shark calling has religious significance, and that these men have mystic powers, is ludicrous to him. Instead, he suggests, they're just in business like any other fishermen across the globe.

"Shark calling is bullshit," he says, practically sputtering. "I can take you down to the wharf right now and rattle a Coke can, the sharks will come. The sharks come for the noise." And when it comes to the boats his suppliers use to catch sharks, "it's traditional to use canoes. It's not traditional to use banana boats and motorboats. They're killing them because there's a demand for a product, and the product's fin."

There are moments when Green feels a twinge of conscience, like when Papua New Guinean authorities—in a rare instance of enforcement—confiscated an illegal Chinese shipment of marine life, depriving the smugglers of their profits. Instead, the Papua New Guinean officials put the cache of sea cucumbers, turtle shells, sea horses, and shark fins—"all this stuff that nobody ought to have," in Green's words—up for auction, and Green bought it. "I burned the turtle shells as an example to everybody," Green says, with a modicum of pride. The rest he destroyed privately.

It's unclear why Green makes this sort of distinction, that turtles and sea cucumbers deserve to be saved and sharks do not. To some extent this is the kind of contradictory reasoning many individuals and governments use when they make environmental decisions. Warm and cuddly animals should be spared; scary ones should die. But it's also something I observed time and time again with people who make their living from the sea, whether they're fishing it or trading in the goods that stem from fishing. None of these people can ignore the fact that the sea's resources are dwindling, but they need to reconcile this knowledge with their own conscience. So they come up with some sort of rationalization: their own activities are making just a modest dent in the ocean; they're not the ones driving the demand; or some other excuse. In each case, the final conclusion is the same: they're not to blame for the ocean's decline.

That's why after Green burned the turtle shells he had purchased from authorities, he could go back to his office and continue trading other animals plundered from the sea, on the grounds that his company is different. Since Papua New Guinean law dictates only native residents can trade in shark fins, Emirau Marine Products' principal owner is a Papua New Guinean. This, in Green's mind, makes the business acceptable. "I work for a national company," he says. "They do it because if not, someone from China will come in and do it anyway."

And when it comes down to it, Green adds, the Chinese are to blame for putting the world in this fix: "You've got an emerging middle class, and they are demanding the products they think they need. It's going to totally fuck the world as it is . . . It's only getting worse. It's a voracious demand that the world will never be able to satisfy."

In fact, there's evidence that artisanal fisheries across the continents—from Asia to Africa and North America—are collapsing as foreign, larger vessels come in and swoop up as many sharks and other fish as they can catch. According to the conservation group WildAid, coastal communities in the Indian states of Andhra Pradesh and Tamil Nadu have experienced major declines in catches since 2001, which locals describe as ranging between 50 and 70 percent. In the Kenyan shark-fishing village of Ngomeni, industrial long-liners and shrimp trawlers have hampered local fishermen's ability to feed their own village, let alone sell sharks for profit. In Papua New Guinea, a similar phenomenon is taking place. O'Rourke's film charted the beginning of this trend in the early 1980s: the final scene captures a Chinese trader haggling with shark callers over the quantity of fins they have brought him. "You must supply at least half a ton or a ton, and then I can give you the world market price," the trader tells them. As O'Rourke relates, the fins that once served as trophies the men kept in their communal shark-calling quarters have been gathered up and taken to traders in town, as the villagers adjust to a modern, cash-based society: "The fins have come down from the traditional place in the man's house, because there are taxes and school fees to pay, and new pleasures that only money can buy."

Cassie Rose, an Australian conservationist now based in Port Moresby, agrees with Green's assessment. As we sit over drinks at Port Moresby's Royal Papua Yacht Club (members only, with a portrait of Queen Elizabeth II just to remind guests it is, in fact, a royal yacht club), she looks glumly out at the port that gives Papua New Guinea's capital its name. "There's so much illegal fishing in this country it's outrageous," Rose says. "Vessels from Asian waters come in, pay a pittance to some locals, rape and pillage, and then they're out of there. This nation has no chance."

Men like Karasimbe are less gloomy, because for them shark calling still possesses a sense of magic. Speaking by lamplight one night at his sister's house, where Laura and I are staying, he tries to explain to me why he goes through so many rites before heading out to sea. "You are paying homage to Moroa, to ask him to give you something," he says. "You will feel something in your body, and your heart."

As the sun sets during his traditional offering rite the night before he hunts, Karasimbe prepares a fire into which he throws a piece of taro root or fish. "You will call your ancestor and say, 'That's your piece of taro, that's your piece of fish.' You tell him, 'I want one shark tomorrow, you will give me a shark tomorrow.' And you will be successful. When I make magic, every shark in the sea must come."

This spiritual connection, Karasimbe suggests, is what sets him apart, both from other villagers and from the few Westerners who come to learn about his practice. "I'm the power maker. I'm the man; I can do something. The power is in me," he says, pointing to his chest.

There is no question in my mind that Karasimbe believes he's endowed with special powers and that it is central to his identity. It's key not just to his self-esteem but to how everyone else views him here. When Karasimbe orders a community viewing of a foreign documentary on shark calling that has a few shots of him in it, everyone in Tembin shows up. They see him as a sort of spiritual medium: it's not as if he's a religious authority who tells people how to behave, but he connects them to the departed in a way few others can.

Karasimbe does not use shark calling as an escape from the travails of everyday life. To the contrary: he sees it as something that orders his world and that of others. And he views it as critical to the survival of a culture that is eroding.

As we talk, I stare at his chest: its gray hair is reflecting the light from the coal-fired lamp. Like many Papua New Guineans, Karasimbe does not know his exact age, and estimates he was born around 1945. "Sorry, I don't know," he says. He is still physically fit, but his eyes are clouding over with glaucoma, and he spends a lot of time thinking about how he and the handful of remaining shark callers can train younger men to take their places. "It's our main job," he says, even more important than catching sharks for the villagers.

But Karasimbe is also trying to make a buck. I am paying him to stay in his sister's home and for his services as a translator. And he has the improbable dream of running a sort of rustic B&B in Tembin, where tourists would pay to come and witness shark calling for themselves. It's understandable that he's trying to cash in on his most marketable skill, given the fact that Papua New Guinea has shifted from bartering to a cash-based economy. In the unlikely event that he succeeds, it will exact a much lighter toll on sharks than the Asian vessels that come and troll the waters off New Ireland.

Karasimbe, like Toxok and others, worries the underwater mineral mining that is likely to commence soon, along with the Taiwanese trawlers that already fish off the coast, will kill many sharks. But as long as there are shark callers, he insists, the sharks will survive. "We will call out all the sharks in the province and bring them together, and we will have many sharks again," he predicts.

The next day we are headed out to sea.

It is just after 7:00 a.m. when Selam Karasimbe pushes off from shore in the narrow, bleached-wood canoe he had borrowed from a neighbor. Karasimbe has his own boat, complete with the outrigger that gives him crucial balance when he is fighting a shark hand to hand. But a recent storm damaged his *lesim*, so he is paddling in a newish one, pointed paddle in hand.

Having performed his rituals onshore, Karasimbe moves rapidly through the water, going farther and farther because the water is rougher than he'd like on this summer morning. Sitting in separate canoes with different shark callers, Laura and I keep a respectful distance. Since women are considered bad luck when it comes to shark calling, we're hoping to avoid tainting the process by staying as far away as possible from Karasimbe's canoe. As we make our way out to sea, we can hear the beating of drums and young voices in the distance: a group of local children are practicing a musical performance, unaware of our expedition.

After several minutes of paddling, Karasimbe finds a place to stop. He takes out his *larung,* a rattle composed of two hoops of cane strung with coconut half shells in alternating concave and convex positions. The rattle is surprisingly loud as Karasimbe begins the ritual he has performed hundreds of times before, twisting the rattle from side to side as he bangs it against the boat. The coconut shells dance together, swaying back and forth hypnotically. Then Karasimbe plunges the *larung* into the water in short bursts, its sound reverberating throughout the ocean. This is the noise that is meant to lure the sharks: Papua New Guineans believe it resembles the sound of a school of fish in trouble.

No sharks appear. Karasimbe repeats the rattle ritual more than half a dozen times in different spots, each time going farther and farther away from land. At one point he plunges his hand into the water, pulls up something, and calls me over. Once I catch up with him, he holds out his palm, and I peer into it. There's a tiny hermit crab lying on his calloused hand, and this creature, Karasimbe tells me, has come to convey a message.

"This is the little hermit crab that lives on the skin of the shark," he explains. "She came up to tell us the shark is below but will not come up because there is a problem with someone in the party."

"Is it because there are women in the party?" I ask, bracing for a lecture.

"Maybe a woman jumped over the canoe," he replies, citing one of the more common explanations for why shark-calling expeditions fail.

It's a polite excuse. For whatever reason, the world-famous shark caller has come up empty.

But a few hours later, I get my hopes up when I hear the strangled bellowing of a conch coming from the beach. Maybe someone's caught a shark after all, I think to myself, and I rush down to the beach to see whether a canoe's coming onshore. But I find only Solen's ten-year-old son, who's named Alois Talin, breathing into the pinkish shell. It's just a game for him, his small cheeks swelling with air as he imitates his elders.

Together, the boy and I walk across the road, back to the hut of Karasimbe's sister. I ask him if he wants to be a shark caller when he grows up. Solen's son hesitates for a moment, and in that instant Karasimbe places his hand on his arm. The boy's father has already been instructing him on how to carve a canoe, how to paddle, and how to spear fish in the river. Karasimbe is confident the tradition will survive him.

"I will learn him, and he will be a shark caller," the shark caller says, smiling.

From my perspective, it's hard to believe that Karasimbe actually exercises magic over the sea. Despite my inherent skepticism, before setting out, I was rooting for him to prove me wrong and summon a shark. But our fishing trip did not produce one, underscoring the real-world factors that determine what happens at sea. It could have been anything from current weather conditions to the increasing number of foreign fishing vessels that now cruise Papua New Guinea's waters. It is the sort of moment when scientific realties clash with magical beliefs, and over time these differences could prove irreconcilable. If the sharks here become so scarce that shark callers come up empty time after time, a faith tradition that has sustained these communities for centuries will begin to unravel.

That would represent a loss of enormous proportions. Karasimbe may be overhyping his abilities at times, but he remains gifted nonetheless, and he's worked for years to maintain a practice that came under assault from colonizers that saw dismantling local culture as a path to economic and political domination. It seems incredible to think that the simple act of overfishing may be able to succeed where colonial powers have failed, robbing Papua New Guineans of the spiritual legacy they've held on to for generations. It is one of the most ancient human traditions connected with one of the world's oldest creatures, and it now teeters on the precipice. If it disappears, it will not only cut off a handful of isolated tribes' connections to the past. It will destroy one of the last bastions of a unique culture and advance in human understanding, where we figured out how to coexist with sharks.

2

AN ANCIENT FISH

The sharks were around before almost everything . . . It was probably pretty lonely for them when they were king.
—Stephen R. Palumbi, Stanford University marine biologist

If you ask anyone to imagine the world's most ancient creatures, the
image of dinosaurs automatically leaps to mind. In fact, sharks predate dinosaurs by roughly 200 million years. Their fossils are buried
as far north as Montana, where a tropical sea once stretched for more
than ten thousand square miles. And unlike dinosaurs, this species
has managed to survive despite the massive changes that have occurred to the ocean over hundreds of millions of years: only a handful
of creatures on the earth today are as old as sharks.

The chimpanzee and prehuman line diverged just 6 million years
ago, according to genetic and anthropological evidence. The *Aus-
tralopithecus afarensis* skeleton known as Lucy, which many think of
as one of our most ancient ancestors, walked on the ground of what
is now Ethiopia 3.18 million years ago. The first toolmakers appeared
2.5 million years ago in Gona, Ethiopia, but even these human ancestors don't classify as *Homo erectus*. The humans that can be classified as "anatomically modern" only emerged 200,000 years ago,
judging by skulls found near Kibish, Ethiopia, in the 1960s. *Homo
sapiens* may have coexisted with Neanderthals until 20,000 or 30,000
years ago.[1]

By contrast, sharks emerged nearly 400 million years ago in the
Devonian period, when they diverged from bony fish, evolving with-

out swim bladders and lungs. They enjoyed a prolific burst in the Carboniferous period, between 360 and 286 million years ago, when an array of different shark species evolved. While several decades after the end of this age intense volcanic activity wiped out many of them along with most other marine life, two groups of sharks came out of this period. Between 200 and 145 million years ago the first modern sharks emerged, at the same time that dinosaurs began roaming the earth.[2]

From a historical perspective, we're the new arrivals, not them.

In our current era, when sharks are viewed as "the other," it's important to recognize that during earlier periods of human civilization, they were seen as more intimately connected to us. While some communities simply viewed them as a part of the natural world to be observed, several coastal societies saw them as either playing a critical role in their creation or serving as ongoing arbiters of human activities and disputes. One of the remarkable aspects of shark calling in Papua New Guinea is that it has preserved this sort of worldview to this day, where other traditions have collapsed. But in the overall context of human history, Karasimbe and his cohorts are not unique.

From the earliest moments in which humans developed language, art, and other forms of communication, they began to chronicle the presence of sharks in their surroundings. Phoenician pottery dating back to 3000 B.C. displays images of sharks,[3] while a vase from 725 B.C., discovered at Ischia, Italy, shows a fish resembling a shark attacking a man.[4] The ancient Greeks wrote and painted images of Ketea, sharklike creatures that the Greek poet Oppian described as a species that "rave for food with unceasing frenzy, being always hungered and never abating the gluttony of their terrible maw, for what food shall be sufficient to fill the void of their belly or enough to satisfy and give a respite to their insatiable jaws?"[5] A few hundred years later, the Roman writer Pliny the Elder made his own lasting contribution to the popular scientific conception of sharks when he described their attacks on pearl divers and named them, as a group, "dogfish." This term—a classic example of how humans defined sharks in relation to themselves—started as a generic label for sharks and persisted that way in Europe and America for hundreds of years. For centuries fishermen have cursed dogfish, seeing them as worthless: the July 26, 1864, log entry from the ship *Rozella,* sailing in Broken Ground on Frenchman Bay in the Gulf of Maine, reports, "Dogfish plags us much."[6] Now, however, dogfish refers to a specific set of species.

While most ancient thinkers provided anthropocentric accounts of sharks, Greeks such as Aristotle also studied the animals, and their close relations, for themselves. Aristotle dubbed them, collectively, *selache,* a name that still defines these animals more than two thousand years later. In one of his most vivid accounts of shark behavior, Aristotle described their mating rites: the cartilaginous fishes in copulation "hang together after the fashion of dogs, . . . the long-tailed ones mounting the others, unless the latter have a thick tail preventing this, when they come together belly to belly."[7]

The Islamic world offered its seminal account of sharks in 1270, when the Iraqi judge Zakariya Qazwini compiled an illustrated compendium titled *The Wonders of Creation and the Oddities of Existence.* The book, which was popular reading for hundreds of years, described how some residents lived in fear of the freshwater sharks that swam in the Tigris River. Matthew McDavitt, who practices law for a living in Charlottesville, Virginia, but spends much of his free time documenting how ancient cultures viewed sharks and other elasmobranchs, commissioned a translation of the book's folio 71v, its section on the Persian Sea:

> This is a great evil in the sea. It is like the crocodiles in the Nile River. Also it comes at a specific time mainly into the Tigris River. Some [other fish that ascend the Tigris River] are well-known: Al-Arabian, Al-Dahi, Al-Adaq, Al-Barak, and Al-Kubrij, all different species of fish. Each type comes at certain times, known to the people of Basra. One of them is known as Al-Tin [literally, "the dragon"; also known as Tinin]. It is worse than Al-Kusaj [shark]. It has teeth like spearheads. It is as long as a palm tree. Its eyes are like fires of blood. It has an ugly shape; all other species run away from it.

While these early scientific accounts by Greeks, Romans, and Iraqis detail the real-world interactions between sharks and other species, many ancient island and coastal cultures elsewhere focused on sharks' more mythical aspects. They constructed elaborate and abstract belief systems in which the animals represented different core values: sharks and rays symbolized law and justice to tribes and clans in Australia, Papua New Guinea, and central Africa, while they embodied aquatic fertility and warfare in the Yucatán. These stories portrayed sharks with greater complexity and helped explain the world in which these people lived. While aboriginal Australians developed very different beliefs about sharks compared with the Mayans, native Hawaiians, and men and women living on the Niger Delta, all of these societies saw their lives as intimately connected to sharks and their close relatives rays.

McDavitt became interested in ancient societies' perceptions when he was an undergraduate anthropology major at the University of Virginia in the early 1990s and he saw sawfish snouts depicted repeatedly in Aztec art. "No one could explain what they were," he recalls. He decided to learn the Aztec language in order to delve into the question, but it took years of research to unravel the puzzle.

McDavitt focused on a little-known figure in Aztec mythology called Cipactli, a sea monster who wrestled with four gods who were busy creating the world. The gods ripped the monster in half, according to Aztec lore, making the heavens from her upper body and the earth from her lower half, leaving Cipactli in a paralyzed state where she took on the identity of Tlaltecuhtli, or Earth-Lord. Cipactli is depicted in a number of ways in Aztec art: while the monster's body resembles a crocodile, it boasts a sharklike tail, and at times what McDavitt calls "a strange, toothy appendage" that conjures up a sawfish's rostrum. The sawfish rostrum frequently represents a sword in Aztec iconography, and in the case of Cipactli it was known as the monster's "sword" or "striker."

In the late 1970s archaeologists discovered the ruins of the Aztec Great Temple underneath Mexico City's central plaza, unearthing the remains of sharks, swordfish, and crocodiles among their finds. Piecing together the images he had seen as an undergraduate, McDavitt hypothesizes these remains represent "the personified earth, at once fertile and destructive." The sharp objects could have belonged to ritual implements that were used in human sacrifice, he notes, or could have been offerings to the gods in themselves. Either way, he writes, they show that Cipactli—part shark, part sawfish—clearly played a central role in Aztec cosmology by providing a transition between sea and land. "By cyclically defeating *Cipactli* and entombing her beneath the Great Temple, perhaps the Aztecs hoped to ensure that their living, hostile earth never again found the strength to submerge."[8]

Sharks and rays also played a key role in the way Australian aboriginals living along the coast viewed the creation of their world and their own ancestors. The Yolngu peoples—who live in northeastern Arnhem Land—are divided into some clans, but many of these clans claim to have descended from a whaler shark known as Mä<u>n</u>a. ("Whaler shark" is an Australian colloquialism for sharks they believed attacked whales; in this case the Yolngu are referring to freshwater bull sharks.) Mä<u>n</u>a plays the role of an avenger: attacked by the ancestor of another clan, he left the sea and invaded the land, carving up rivers with his sharp teeth and leaving the teeth behind to take the form of pandanus trees that line these rivers' banks. The leaves of these trees have serrated edges. According to McDavitt, "These trees represent both *Mä<u>n</u>a*'s anger at being speared and the stingray-spine tipped spear that *Mä<u>n</u>a* carried to avenge his death."[9]

A consistent theme of intimate connection emerges across several shark-worshipping cultures: the shark gods take a tribal approach to picking winners and losers, rather than bestowing their largesse over a broad population. In this sense they operate as an extension of family, just more powerful. It's a parochial vision of a deity, where a supernatural shark is akin to a Mafia godfather, to whom individuals can appeal for favors as long as they have paid regular dues to the don over time. Loyalty and familial ties matter above all; it is not a question of the gods making an impartial judgment about what is right.

Native Hawaiians took this practice to the extreme, creating a series of traditions based on the belief in supernatural helpers who are half-human, half-god, and use another medium to communicate their advice. Known as *'aumākua,* these spirits had a single human keeper (*kahu*) who tended to them, and they would pass on their service from one generation to the next. Not all these *'aumākua* were sharks: some were birds or even plants. But many Hawaiians were proud to claim a shark *'aumākua* as part of their familial heritage, and these supernatural beings had a clear, practical purpose: they were supposed to help fishermen haul in significant catches and protect them from drowning.

In an essay, Martha Warren Beckwith recounts how she visited a village where two brothers from a family named Puhi, or Eel, inspired fear among their neighbors because they had an *'aumākua* at their command. A native clergyman named Kawai from a nearby village explained to Beckwith how the Puhi brothers benefited from this arrangement: "When the Puhi go fishing, the shark appears. The *'aumākua* obeys the voice of the man; name the kind of fish you want and it will bring it. The men give it some of the first catch, then it disappears, and they always come back with full nets." The villagers, including the Puhi brothers, were confident that their ability to haul in fish was solely due to their having a divine shark on their side.[10] And the *'aumākua* not only delivered financial rewards to the Puhi brothers, the clergyman told Beckwith, but also kept them alive despite their dangerous profession. "Besides this, the Puhi family can never be drowned. If there is a storm and the boat capsizes, the shark appears and the man rides on its back."[11] A similar tradition lives on in Vietnam, where some fishermen still build altars on beaches to the whale shark, which they call Ca Ong, or Mister Fish, to stay safe while on the water.

In some cases, these *'aumākua* represented a reincarnation of a dead relative, whether it was an aborted fetus or an elderly family member whose bones were wrapped in a cloth and cast out into the sea. One account dating from 1870 describes how a few days after relatives performed such a ceremony, they could "see with their own eyes that the deceased had become a shark, with all the signs by which they could not fail to recognize the loved one in a deep ocean."[12] This intensely personal connection to sharks not only provided comfort at a time of grief but also gave an entire family confidence that they now had someone defending them when they went out to sea.

At the same time many Hawaiians relied on these familiar, ancestral gods for everyday guidance, they also worshipped the *akua,* much more powerful shark deities that influenced the weather and other forces of nature. The shark Kalahiki, one of the more powerful gods, could predict when the wind and currents would be rough and could marshal a company of sharks to bring seafarers safely in to shore.[13] In fact Beckwith describes the *'aumākua* as "ranked as kauwa, or of the servant class, because bound to obey those whom he serves."[14] Even the most powerful shark deities were viewed as having regional allegiances, however. When a dry dock built by American forces collapsed in 1914, many Hawaiians attributed the disaster to the female shark god Ka'ahupāhau, who reportedly protected local residents from the man-eating sharks that lurked offshore. In this case Ka'ahupāhau was defending locals from the Americans, rather than from threatening ocean predators.

According to legend, Ka'ahupāhau was willing to fight off her own kind as well in defense of the humans who had treated her well over the years. At one point, the tale goes, sharks from another area came upon Oahu and started eyeing what they referred to as "delicious looking crabs." Knowing that that amounts to a code name in the shark language for humans, Ka'ahupāhau and her brother Kahi'ukā (the Smiting Tail) devise a particularly clever way to dispatch these hostile visitors: through fishing. Ka'ahupāhau turns herself into a net and, with the aid of her brother, catches the sharks so they can be hauled in by fishermen and left to die in the heat.[15]

The sharks that populate Hawaiian lore frequently mete out justice, protecting some humans while consuming others. In many cases these beings blur the line between human and animal: Ka'ehikimanō-o-pu'uloa is the child of humans who is born a shark, nursed on his mother's milk and *'awa,* the alcoholic drink humans often offered the sharks they worshipped. Ka'ehikimanō-o-pu'uloa embarks on a sightseeing trip in which he pays homage to the shark gods of several islands; while they initially suspect him because of his human origins, Ka'ehikimanō-o-pu'uloa manages to lead them and conspires to kill a man-eating shark. In the end the young shark returns to his human parents, where he "conveyed the greetings of the various distinguished sharks, and told of his victories and honors."[16] Ka'ehikimanō-o-pu'uloa serves as a bridge between the world of humans and that of sharks, demonstrating that the two species can coexist if each one acknowledges the distinct role of the other.

Unsurprisingly, several stories about these supernatural sharks provide explanations for why humans fall prey to sharks at sea. Kauhi, a suspicious lover who wrongly concludes his betrothed has betrayed him, is executed after repeatedly trying to murder his fiancée. But one of his relatives, a shark god, saves him by wiping him away in a tidal wave and transforming him into a shark. When his former fiancée, Kahalaopuna, can't resist surfing with her friends, "he bit her in two and held the upper half of the body up out of the water, so that all the surf-bathers would see and know that he had at last obtained his revenge."[17]

The fact that the best-known Hawaiian shark tale, "Nanaue the Shark Man," has so many variations highlights how ancient Hawaiians were fixated on the danger they faced in the water. The basic outline of the story is as follows: The king-shark god of Hawaii and Maui, Kamohiali'i—who is popularly credited by Hawaiians with inventing surfing—seduces a beautiful human called Kalei. Together they produce a child named Nanaue, who looks normal aside from the fact that he has a shark's mouth between his shoulder blades, which he is forced to cover with a cloak. Kamohiali'i warns Kalei she should never feed their son animal meat, lest he develop a taste for human flesh. But Nanaue's human grandfather ignores this admonition, and over time the boy grows ravenous for human flesh. After being uncloaked by his fellow villagers, Nanaue manages—with the help of his god-father—to escape to sea as a shark, reclaiming his human form once he lands on another island, Moloka'i. Nanaue finds himself pitted against a demigod known as Unauna, or Hermit Crab. With Unauna's aid the villagers manage to tie up Nanaue and burn him, in a place that still bears the name Shark Hill. There are many variations on this theme—in one tale the shark man is Kawelo o Mānā, a sorcerer; in another it's Pau-walu (Many Destroyed)—but in each case the attacker warns his victims in advance of the risks they take by entering the ocean.[18]

This nuanced portrayal of sharks highlights a central tenet of these ancient belief systems: sharks are neither pure evil nor pure good, but something of a mix. McDavitt attributes this to the fact that these islanders, coastal tribes, and river dwellers saw sharks on a regular basis. "If you have a society that's not very engaged with them, it tends to be a monolithic and negative view," he reasons. "If they're engaged, you might see a more balanced view of them."

The Ijo peoples living along the Niger River delta in southern Nigeria also believe in water spirits that are both dangerous and beneficial. According to their legend, these spirits used to play along the beach in masked dances and left their masks on the shore. In late December the Ijo summon the spirits by wearing large masks showing sharks and rays, becoming possessed in an effort to get rid of illness and misfortune. In this tradition, the dances provide a way for the water spirits to "play" with their human friends, but there remains an element of risk in this exchange. As Martha G. Anderson and Philip M. Peek write in their book, *Ways of the Rivers: Arts and Environment of the Niger Delta,* a masked dancer "can interrupt a dance sequence to dive at the drummers through the pole fence provided for their protection or dart around it to attack them. He might go crazy, slashing wildly at his own supporters until others join forces to restrain him, only to follow this by locking one of his human friends in an affectionate embrace."[19] Other societies in the region channel water spirits differently. The Bidjogo of Guinea-Bissau stage dances with shark, sawfish, and stingray costumes as well, but these are used for young men's coming-of-age ceremonies. For them, harnessing these sea creatures' powers allows them to become men at last.[20]

These ancient societies used sharks for practical purposes as well. Aborigines living along Australia's coasts have eaten stingrays and sharks for years, often in the form of a round cake that combines shredded meat with the animal's heated or raw liver. (The Lardil people living on Mornington Island, in fact, use a fist lying on a cupped hand as the sign-language symbol for sharks and rays, mimicking the shape of this rounded cake.[21]) Australian aborigines used other shark and ray products for weapons and ornaments as well: the vertebrae became necklace beads, while the Wik from Cape York fashioned the tails of rays into circles they sported as knuckle-style hand weapons, in the same way Hawaiians made ones out of sharks' teeth.[22] Australians, like Hawaiians, used sharks' teeth to create both cutting implements and war clubs. Their skin served as a sort of sandpaper and was even used for drums.[23]

Thousands of miles away in New England and Florida, American Indians were using sharks for many of the same purposes—sandpaper, tools, and ornaments. It appears sharks' teeth became a commodity used in trading, since a Native American burial site in Ohio included teeth from a great white shark among its finds. The fact that shark remains have surfaced in a range of such burial sites, in locations throughout southern New England and Nova Scotia, suggests that these peoples viewed sharks as deities even as they hunted them in prehistoric times. They used the teeth from some of the fiercest sharks—great white, short-fin mako, and sand tiger—as grave gods, even as they targeted the spiny dogfish for their dinner.[24] And in a sign of how New England waters have changed over time, evidence from American Indian middens in the region show these societies consumed cod and different species of sharks, but not the lobster that defines much of the Gulf of Maine today.

Some societies also used shark worship as an excuse for human sacrifice on earth, as well as for their own entertainment. In the Solomon Islands villagers viewed sharks as good but demanding deities, for whom they constructed worship caves along with stone altars nearby. To pay tribute to them, the villagers selected human victims to lay upon those altars. Several Pacific island tribes also occasionally sacrificed a man, woman, or child, but these cultures viewed the shark gods as hostile. They observed a ritual in which a high priest would approach a crowd along with an assistant wearing a mask whose nose resembled a shark's snout—when the priest instructed the assistant to point his nose at the assembled throng, the person who became the target of the assistant's gaze would be offered up to the sea.

Hawaiian kings used to engage in a particularly gruesome ritual in which they ordered gladiators to fight a shark to the death in a circumscribed, watery arena. To lure the sharks into battle, Hawaiians tossed both fish and human bait into the water; once the fight began, the rules of engagement favored the fish. Not only did the human competitor have to let the shark lunge toward him before he could attack, but his only weapon was a single shark's tooth mounted on a piece of wood that he could hold clenched in his fist. Faced with those odds, few gladiators survived.[25]

While several cultures in the Pacific and Latin America incorporated sharks into their everyday and spiritual lives, an odd thing transpired in Europe as it entered the Middle Ages: people forgot sharks existed. Europeans at the time believed in a large, ill-defined group of sea monsters, but they stopped generating any literature that referred specifically to sharks. Medieval Christian accounts of animals included whales, panthers, and plenty of other wild creatures, but the "dogfish" that caught the attention of Greek and Roman philosophers had no place. Even once the Renaissance began, Europeans used shark artifacts without knowing what they were. A ceremonial practice began of dipping *glossopetrae*, or dragon "tongue stones," into wine—these were sharks' teeth, but the men and women who fetishized them didn't have a clue.[26] This historical break, where Europeans lost their connection to sharks altogether, had profound implications for how the West views sharks today. Severing that historic tie helped ensure that going forward, sharks would become humans' outright opponents.

Sharks returned to the Western consciousness once Europeans began seafaring in earnest and entered tropical waters. The academic debate over the origin of the word "shark" continues to this day—some posit it evolved from the Anglo-Saxon term *scheron,* meaning to cut or tear, while others say it came from either the English term "search" or the French version, *chercher*. However, there's strong evidence that it stems from the Mayan word for shark, *xoc*. The Humboldt State University geography professor Tom Jones argues that the men credited with introducing the word "sharke" to Europe—sailors who served under the British captain John Hawkins—picked it up during a problem-plagued trading expedition to the Yucatán in the mid-sixteenth century. During that expedition, Hawkins lost five ships in a fight with Spanish warships and had to turn to the pilot of a Spanish wine ship, who made his home in the Yucatán port of Campeche. Jones reasons that this man, Bartolomé Gonzales, was likely to have used the term *xoc* when piloting one of Hawkins's vessels, *Jesus of Lübeck*. There's no question that the Maya used the word *xoc* frequently: it even became incorporated into the name of a mythological creature called alternately Ah Xoc, Ah Kan Xoc, or Chac Uayab Xoc, which Jones describes as "an ominous demon that killed and devoured women, children and animals, a were-shark whose anthropomorphic tendencies finally, among the Lacandon, lost all connection with the rarely seen shark that had been its source and inspiration."[27] By contrast, the Spaniards and the Portuguese who had sailed to the tropics had developed two different but related words: *tiburón* and *tuburão*, respectively.

The Romans had already labeled sharks generically as "dogfish," but the English apparently considered the sharks they witnessed in the New World so alien, so vicious, that they classified them as a new species: a *sharke*. According to *The Oxford English Dictionary*, this word emerged in 1569 when Hawkins's sailors returned from their traumatic expedition with a specimen of what they called a *sharke* to London; one account later described the preserved creature as "a marueilous straunge Fishe."[28] For years British writers used the words "shark" and "sharke" interchangeably. Over time, as Europeans became more familiar with sharks' behavior, they came to apply its name to a slew of unsavory human activities. "Shark" became synonymous with the word "predator," as when in 1713 *The Guardian*, in its issue number 73, referred to "the sharks, who prey upon the inadvertency of young heirs." By 1806 it had become another term for lawyers; in 1828 a writer used it to describe a gang of reporters. Americans picked up these slang terms without hesitation and added a new twist in 1946 by applying the word to anyone who displayed lechery when seeking a liaison.[29] The German word for villain is *Schurke*. In every instance, "shark" has had negative connotations.

For much of the sixteenth, seventeenth, and eighteenth centuries, European and American seafarers were on the front lines with sharks. At times, they were grateful for the sustenance sharks gave them. The British captain William Dampier—who explored parts of what later became Australia as well as Papua New Guinea in the late seventeenth century—delivered several enthusiastic reports about them in his writings. While sailing south of Sierra Leone in 1683, Dampier wrote, "While we lay in the calms we caught several great Sharks; sometimes 2 or 3 a day, and eat them all, boyling and squeezing them dry, and then stewing them with Vinegar, Pepper, &c. for we had little flesh aboard."[30] Sixteen years later Dampier and his crew found even more eating opportunities off the coast of Australia (then New Holland), where, he wrote, "There are Abundance of them in this particular Sound, that I therefore give it the Name of Shark's Bay." (The name persists to this day.) The sailors not only munched on sharks there; they dissected them in gruesome detail: in one eleven-foot-long shark, they "found the Head and Boans of a Hippopotomus; the hairy Lips of which were still sound and not putrified, and the Jaw was also firm, out of which we pluckt a great many Teeth, 2 of them 8 Inches long, and as big as a Man's Thumb, small at one end, and a little crooked; the rest not above half so long. The Maw was full of Jelly which stank extreamly: However I saved for a while the Teeth and the Sharks Jaw: The Flesh of it was divided among my Men; and they took care that no waste should be made of it."[31] At times sailors even sought sharks out for their own amusement, as the log of the *Leopard*, a ship that sailed the Gulf of Maine's Frenchman Bay in 1861, makes clear. "Catch a shirk with pork had some fun," it recorded. From Dampier's utilitarian perspective, sharks were a marine resource like any other, which could help his crew survive. While the captain was not above saving part of his catch as a keepsake, laying claim to one shark's teeth and jaws, he neither glamorizes nor demonizes the animals. And with enough vinegar and pepper, they made for decent rations.

But most sailors came to view sharks with hostility, seeing them as a mortal threat. It's not an accident that the first detailed eyewitness account of a shark attack—which now ranks as the earliest record in the International Shark Attack File—involved a sailor. The 1580 *Fugger News-Letter* report describes a seaman falling off his ship somewhere between Portugal and India in vivid detail. While he grabbed a line his shipmates tossed him, "there appeared from below the surface of the sea a large monster, called *Tiburon;* it rushed on the man and tore him to pieces before our very eyes. That surely was a grievous death."[32] For Westerners who had been largely shielded from sharks for centuries, these animals suddenly emerged as an unseen threat that could hurt them without warning, and this fear only grew as ocean exploration intensified.

Historical accounts make it clear those riding on slave ships were particularly vulnerable to attack because these overcrowded ships released their waste—and even some of their slaves—into the ocean, which drew sharks to the vessels. Samuel Robinson, a Scottish teenager who worked on his uncle's slave ship at the turn of the nineteenth century, wrote a memoir decades later in which he recalled the sharks that would follow the trail of waste and trash thrown from the vessel on which he sailed: "The very sight of him slowly moving round the ship, with his black fin two feet above the water, his broad snout and small eyes, and the altogether villainous look of the fellow, make one shiver, even when at a safe distance."[33]

While Robinson was able to keep his distance, not all the slaves aboard the ships did. Sailors frequently discarded the bodies of dead African captives overboard, and occasionally threatened to do the same to their live cargo. At times slaves who jumped into the ocean to escape their captors fell prey to an equally gruesome fate.[34] These seafaring tales were so grim that an abolitionist named James Tytler used the prospect of this watery grave in the late eighteenth century to bolster his antislavery argument, submitting a document to the British House of Lords titled "The Petition of the Sharks of Africa." Written tongue in cheek from the sharks' perspective, the petition recounted how they had prospered at the expense of the slaves they picked off during these transatlantic crossings, which gave them "large quantities of their most favourite food—human flesh." These "sharks" wrote they were confident the British lords shared sufficient "wisdom and fellow feeling" to ensure that this supply of food would continue for years to come.[35]

At times, sailors boasted about their narrow escapes from such sea monsters. Julius L. Esping, a sailor who struggled with drink and women early in his life before becoming an ardent Christian missionary, wrote in his memoir that he skirted death on a trip from Brazil to New York City:

> On our return passage I went into the sea to bathe, and while swimming near the ship, the captain, who was walking on deck, noticed a large shark approaching the vessel, and enquired of one of the crew if any of the men were in the water. On receiving an affirmative reply he ran to the stern of the ship and told me of the shark, barely in time for me to make my escape. Being informed of my danger, I looked around and saw the monster coming with lightning speed directly toward me. With a desperate effort I made for the martingale, and just cleared the water to save myself. All who witnessed the operation concluded that if the shark had closed its jaws on my body, "the New York harpies would have been heavy losers."[36]

In certain instances, sailors on whaling ships came into conflict with sharks because they were competing for the same prey. Once sailors managed to harpoon a whale, they still faced the task of hauling their prey up on board, often in the midst of the shark feeding frenzy that would inevitably ensue from such an attack. One of the best accounts of this sort of contest comes from George Barker's 1916 self-published memoir, _Thrilling Adventures of the Whaler Alcyone: Killing Man-Eating Sharks in the Indian Ocean, Hunting Kangaroos in Australia._ Barker, a Boston native who headed to sea on a whaler as a sixteen-year-old, describes how safety precautions for carving up whales in the water were nonexistent:

> The mate tied a rope under his arms and he jumped into the sea and slipped down between the whale and the side of the schooner and worked his way along until he came to the head. Fastening the rope securely, he shouted to the boys on deck to haul him up.
>
> When near the deck of the vessel he noticed that one of the crew was standing on a staging with a long lance in his hand, while another held a lantern, and all wore a scared look on their faces. Upon landing on the deck he asked the meaning of this, and was told that the water around the whale's body was filled with sharks and that several times the lances were thrown close to him to ward off these man-eating monsters.
>
> He then looked over the side of the schooner and by the aid of the lantern could see several sharks swimming about. He was then convinced that the officers of a whaler cared but little for a man's or a boy's life. Nothing further was done that night.[37]

While Esping and Barker were little-known American seamen whose brushes with sharks went largely unnoticed, the Englishman Brook Watson made sure to immortalize the 1749 attack that cost him his right leg just below the knee. At the time Watson was a fourteen-year-old orphan traveling on a trading ship in the harbor of Havana, Cuba: he went on to become a successful London merchant and eventually mayor of London and a baronet. John Singleton Copley's iconic 1778 painting depicts Watson, in a state of shock, while three of his shipmates try to pull him from the water and another prepares to harpoon a vicious shark, its jaws agape. The painting ranks as one of the most famous shark attack scenes of all time: the animal is a hulking menace, with a glowing yellowish eye and serrated teeth.

But the painting, which Watson presumably commissioned himself after meeting Copley in London four years before, was not enough for the survivor. When he was crowned a baronet more than half a century later, Watson asked for a coat of arms alluding to his attack. The design includes the Latin motto *Scuto Divino* ("Under God's Protection") and features Neptune, the god of the sea, using a trident to repel an attacking shark. The upper-left corner of the shield even shows the part of his right leg he lost as a teenager. The coat of arms' message is clear: Watson faced down the sea monster and, with divine protection, bested the animal.

These attacks on sailors began to permeate the public mind-set. No longer were sharks seen as complex creatures that could provide sustenance as well as mete out justice as part of some higher order. They were perfect, unrepentant killers, enemies in the sea.

Still, even though sailors had recounted horrifying tales of the predators they faced at sea, average Americans had been largely shielded from sharks until the summer of 1916. For one terrifying week a shark—or multiple sharks, it remains unclear—attacked and killed four people off the New Jersey shore. This deadly episode, which helped inspire the movie *Jaws,* was captured brilliantly in Michael Capuzzo's nonfiction account, *Close to Shore: A True Story of Terror in an Age of Innocence.* From that moment on, beachgoers in America had a reason to fear entering the water.

The attacks of 1916 tell us as much about changes in U.S. society as they do about shark behavior. For years ordinary Americans kept their distance from the sea, but this shifted during the late nineteenth century. It became fashionable to seek respite from the summer heat by heading for the ocean, and for the most part the victims of the Jersey shore attacks were adults and children enjoying the new popular pastime of spending time at the beach. When a great white started attacking swimmers near the New Jersey beach towns of Beach Haven and Spring Lake as well as in Matawan, more than a dozen miles from the ocean, it marked a turning point in Americans'—and by extension the industrialized world's—relationship with sharks.

On July 1, 1916, Charles Epting Vansant, a young textile salesman and recent University of Pennsylvania graduate, was vacationing in Beach Haven with his family when he entered the water for an early evening dip. He was joined by a dog—whose erratic paddling may inadvertently have attracted the shark's attention. The shark struck when he was in just three and a half feet of water, chomping his left leg below the knee. Onlookers managed to drag Vansant onshore, and his own father, a Philadelphia physician, tended to him back at their hotel. But Eugene Vansant could not save his son, who died that night.[38]

What followed was a terrifying round of shark strikes. Charles Bruder, a bell captain at Spring Lake's Essex and Sussex Hotel, was torn apart on July 6 during a solo swim around dusk. On July 11 a group of boys took a dip in Matawan Creek—five miles from the nearest bay—and fourteen-year-old Rensselaer Cartan Jr. felt something bump against him, leaving bloody scrapes across his chest. While the boy and a retired sea captain, Thomas V. Cottrell, tried to warn residents of Spring Lake that a shark lurked in the water, few paid attention. A day later the same shark killed both Lester Stilwell, an epileptic teenager, and the town's tailor, W. Stanley Fisher, who fought to recover Stilwell's body. That same day, July 12, the shark ripped off the left leg of twelve-year-old Joseph Dunn, before Dunn's older brother and a man passing through on a boat managed to pull him from the creek.[39] The debate over whether a single great white was responsible for the attacks or whether it was a combination of animals—bull sharks are well-known for entering creeks, since they can survive in both salt water and freshwater—has raged for nearly a century. But the public reaction to the spate of attacks was unanimous: people were scared. An urban population that had just begun to venture out to sea now saw the ocean as harboring a deadly threat.

Ironically, just before that series of shark attacks, prominent U.S. scientists and publications had downplayed the threat these fish posed. On August 2, 1915, *The New York Times* published an editorial titled "Let Us Do Justice to Sharks," which declared, "That sharks can properly be called dangerous, in this part of the world, is apparently untrue." The head of the American Museum of Natural History at the time, Frederic Augustus Lucas, did his best to dispel the idea of man-eating sharks in a letter to the editor in the *Times:* there was, he wrote, "practically no danger of an attack . . . about our coasts."[40]

At the same time that Lucas and others were assuring the American public that sharks could do no harm, Captain William E. Young was doing his best to convince his compatriots that they were brutal killers. Young, a native Californian who began his itinerant seagoing career in Hawaii, quickly developed a reputation in Oahu as a skilled "shark killer," or *kane mano*. (He preferred this moniker to the first nickname he picked up in Hawaii: Sharky Bill.) The Californian stumbled on his quirky career by accident while he and his brother were hauling trash from Honolulu offshore. One day they dumped several horse carcasses in the Pacific and sparked a shark feeding frenzy: from that moment on, Young was hooked on the idea of killing sharks for fun and profit. From the outset he saw the animals' fearsome reputation as a key element of their marketability, as when he collected $1,500 by charging local onlookers ten cents each to gaze at a tiger shark pregnant with forty-two babies that he had hauled in and refrigerated.

> To attract attention I rang a dinner bell. The curious, the novelty-seekers, the idlers, the good-natured and the gullible began to collect. Without any ballyhoo outside, my first gate proved extremely rewarding. People gathered around the refrigerated fish with gaping jaws, and oohed and aahed to their (and my) complete satisfaction. Women, holding their noses, came forward cautiously; then they forgot to hold their noses and became absorbed in the spectacle.[41]

Young realized he could make a career out of fishing sharks, and he became a hunter for hire.

In 1934, Young published a memoir titled *Shark! Shark!* that recounts his globe-trotting search for the biggest, scariest fish he could find. Throughout it he repeatedly emphasizes sharks' viciousness, invoking every possible cliché to describe their appearance and character:

> When one sees or hears the word "shark" a powerful mental image is generated of a cold-blooded rover of the deep, its huge mouth filled with razor-sharp teeth, swimming ceaselessly night and day in search of

anything that might fall into the cavernous maw and stay the gnawing hunger which drives the rapacious fish relentlessly on his way; a terrible creature, in short, afraid of nothing and particularly fond of tasty human flesh. There is something particularly sinister in a shark's appearance. The sight of his ugly triangular fin lazily cutting zigzags in the surface of the sea, and then submerging to become a hidden menace, suggests a malevolent spirit. His ogling, chinless face, his scimitar-like mouth with its rows of gleaming teeth, the relentless and savage fury with which he attacks, the rage of his thrashing when caught, his brutal insensitivity to injury and pain, well merit the name of Afriet, symbol of all that is terrible and monstrous in Arabian superstition.[42]

Apparently, American readers at this point still needed to be convinced that these animals posed a threat. As Young travels the world finding different ways to make money from sharks, he repeatedly tells people he meets that these fish can actually kill humans. In one instance Young spears a shark whose stomach contained the remnants of a blue serge jacket and human bones, the remains of a wealthy man whose plane had crashed in the ocean. Young tells the tale of the man and his jacket frequently during his travels, sometimes offending his listeners in the process.

Young's effort to stoke the public fear of sharks dovetailed with a new literary trend, where a group of contemporary writers were constructing an entire body of literature around hunting and fishing. As writers including Zane Grey and Ernest Hemingway penned books about this American subculture, they did their best to portray sharks as brutes. Both Grey's and Hemingway's writing glorifies men for taking on these animals in physical contests. A few species, like the mako, earn their respect, but most are like the shovel-nosed sharks Hemingway derides in *The Old Man and the Sea,* "hateful sharks, bad smelling, scavengers as well as killers."[43]

Just as Hemingway describes hand-to-hand combat in graphic detail, Grey revels in the battle he faces with a fish weighing more than a thousand pounds. In his book *An American Angler in Australia,* Grey recounts how he fought a tiger shark off Sydney as a group of onlookers watched from a nearby ship. He recognizes the fish's beauty—"Pearl gray in color, with dark tiger stripes, a huge rounded head and wide flat back, this fish looked incredibly beautiful. I had expected a hideous beast"—but he takes pains to ascribe the worst possible motives to the animal he had lured to its death.

> I had one good long look at this tiger shark while the men were erecting the tripod; and I accorded him more appalling beauty and horrible significance than all the great fish I had ever caught.
>   "Well, Mr. Man-eater, you will never kill any boy or girl!" I flung at him.
>   That was the deep and powerful emotion I felt—the justification of my act—the worthiness of it, and the pride in what it took.[44]

From Grey's perspective, he had done a public service by killing an animal that could have conceivably hurt some innocent swimmer. But Grey, Hemingway, and others wrote of deliberately battling fish with the skills they had honed over a lifetime; they were not amateurs venturing into the water.

Still, it was nearly three decades after the attacks of 1916 before the United States as a whole focused once again on a massive shark strike. While both world wars featured horrific attacks on ships that exposed sailors to these ocean predators, the single worst incident stemmed from the sinking of the USS *Indianapolis* on July 30, 1945. That incident—in which 880 of the nearly 1,200-man crew died in the water, many of them devoured by sharks during the four days it took for a rescue mission to mobilize into action—ranks as the single worst loss of life at sea in the U.S. Navy's history.

While the exact number of shark attacks during this episode is still not known, it's clear from both survivors' accounts and autopsies that these ocean predators played a major role in boosting the death toll: 88 of the recovered bodies had been bitten by sharks, and many of the survivors suffered damage from shark attacks as well.[45] The commanding officer of the USS *Helm,* the vessel that eventually rescued the remaining 316 survivors, wrote a report that not only described the carnage the animals had caused but also documented how they continued to feed on sailors even as their colleagues sought to save them.

At that point, sharks largely receded from public view for another three decades. But when the writer Peter Benchley reminded a worldwide audience why they had reason to fear going into the water, he unwittingly did more to instill the intense fear and hatred of sharks than anyone else in the twentieth century.

Peter Benchley's home lies just a few blocks away from the main drag in Princeton, New Jersey, a precious university town where even fast-food and coffee outfits must post their names in faux-British wrought-iron lettering above their doors. A beautiful gray manse with white columns, the late writer's house most closely resembles the eating clubs in town where F. Scott Fitzgerald and other Princeton luminaries used to socialize.

The third floor of the house truly captures the reach of Benchley's work. Pasted to the walls are a series of letters—some handwritten, some typed—from Benchley's fans. The paper has yellowed, and cracked in some places, and some of the ink has faded. But the intensity of the missives—along with that of the black-and-white and color photographs of nubile young women who wrote the author of *Jaws* in the hopes of scoring a date—remains unchanged. One woman writes that she's heard Benchley has a "freaky fetish" for not wearing anything below the belt during his television appearances, adding she and her girlfriends think it would be "really groovy" if they could all meet up sometime. Another admirer simply asks, "What is God's last name?" (Wendy Benchley explains drily, "That's from one of the schizophrenics.") Even the movie star Burt Reynolds gets into the act, writing to Benchley on demure gray stationery with a New York City letterhead, "Now that I'm unemployed and have lots of time, why don't we get together for some drinks."

Benchley didn't start his writing career with the intention of producing a terrifying cult 1970s classic. The son of the author Nathaniel Benchley and the grandson of the humorist Robert Benchley, one of the founders of the Algonquin Round Table, Peter struck a deal with his father during his teenage years that he could write during the summers and collect the same salary he would have if he had done more mundane chores such as mowing grass or working in a restaurant. He didn't need to show anyone what he produced, but he had to write.

When he started writing his first book, Benchley decided to draw upon the time he had spent in Nantucket—he had gone fishing there with his father, and had met Wendy there while sitting in a restaurant puffing on a Lucky Strike cigarette—to provide an eerie and compelling look at how small-town life is transformed when a man-eating shark starts preying on summer beachgoers. Nowadays the word "jaws" immediately brings to mind the ominous yet catchy John Williams musical score that accompanied the 1975 movie (DA-duh-DA-duh, DA-duh-DA-duh), but Benchley's book is more cerebral than that. Benchley described the shark in its most primordial state, with a scientific accuracy that holds up more than thirty years later.

Published in 1974, *Jaws* was an instant success. It rocketed up the best-seller lists, where it stayed for nearly a year. It didn't just sell on America's East and West coasts: it sold in landlocked countries like Tibet. Fidel Castro read it and raved about it, saying it offered a compelling critique of U.S. capitalism. The New York publisher sent giant packets of fan letters to the Benchleys' New Jersey home; eventually the couple tired of reading them and simply asked the publisher to stop.

Hoping to capitalize on this phenomenon, a young Hollywood director, Steven Spielberg, decided to make a movie based on the book, and when Benchley's agent called to say it would make it onto the big screen, the author was elated. Wendy Benchley, however, felt differently: "He was thrilled and I cried, and I figured my life was ruined."

The film didn't ruin the Benchleys' lives, but it did change their everyday existence. Released in the summer, a traditionally dead time for theater releases, it became the first movie to gross $100 million at the box office. (Ultimately, it grossed $450 million worldwide.) It created what Americans now think of as the inevitable annual summer blockbuster, before *Star Wars* or *Raiders of the Lost Ark* made it to the screen. It made the cover of *Time* magazine, spawned three movie sequels, a video game, and two unofficial musicals. (A producer has approached Wendy Benchley about creating a Broadway musical based on *Jaws,* but she seems even more skeptical about that than she did about her husband's initial book idea.)

Everyone involved in *Jaws* knew that it would come to define them. Benchley joked before his 2006 death that no matter what else he did in life, "When I die, the music that will be played at my funeral will be 'DA-duh-DA-duh, DA-duh-DA-duh.' " (He was right: it played at the start of his New York City memorial service.) Roy Scheider, who portrayed the police chief Martin Brody in the movie, felt exactly the same way: one of his obituaries noted that he once confessed before his February 10, 2008, death that he feared the role "will be on my tombstone."[46]

Benchley's book is both more sophisticated—it explores the sharp class divisions that help define summer vacation towns—and less frightening than the movie that stemmed from it. The film's terrifying nature stems, in part, from what amounted to a technical glitch in the course of making the movie: mechanical problems with the movie's fake shark (nicknamed Bruce) prevented the filmmakers from showing it too often.[47] As Wendy Benchley recalls, "They had all these days where the shark didn't work, weeks, months. They had to fill in." But that made *Jaws* all the more terrifying. It's the unseen, rather than the seen, that scares us the most.

For all its nuance, the book still includes a heavy dose of vengeance. At one point Brody and Matt Hooper, a scientist from the Woods Hole Oceanographic Institution, get in an argument about whether it's rational to, in Hooper's words, "get out a contract on him," and it becomes clear that the shark's demise is inextricably linked with the town's survival.

Brody was growing angry—an anger born out of frustration and humiliation. He knew Hooper was right, but he felt that right and wrong were irrelevant to the situation. The fish was an enemy. It had come upon the community and killed two men, a woman, and a child. The people of Amity would demand the death of the fish. They would need to see it dead before they could feel secure enough to resume their normal lives. Most of all, Brody needed it dead, for the death of the fish would be a catharsis for him.[48]

One of the striking things about the shark in *Jaws* is that, like the one that launched the 1916 attacks off the Jersey shore, it kills several people within a matter of days. By definition, this makes the fish a mass murderer and suggests a sort of conscious strategy on the shark's part that doesn't exist in real life.

Jaws highlighted the obvious: anytime a person enters the ocean, he or she is vulnerable to a shark bite. The fact that these attacks were rare did nothing to calm the public's nerves; it was their unpredictable nature that mattered. People were scared, and there was little scientists or statisticians could do to ease their fears.

The film does point out that sharks don't intentionally hunt people, though it also portrays great whites as lethal predators. Richard Dreyfuss, playing Hooper, manages to both pay tribute to sharks and freak viewers out as he explains how they operate. In an argument with the mayor over whether to close the beach in light of the recent attacks, Hooper explains, "What we are dealing with here is a perfect engine, an eating machine. It's really a miracle of evolution. All this machine does is swim, and eat, and make little sharks."

The film also exaggerates the size of great whites swimming off the New England coast, saying the shark is twenty-five feet long. When the gigantic shark emerges from the water for the first time, Brody turns to Quint, the boat's captain, and deadpans, "You're gonna need a bigger boat."

In writing *Jaws,* Benchley tapped into humans' natural terror of sharks. In their essay, "When Humans and Sharks Meet," Erich Ritter, Kai Lutz, and Marie Levine argue there are a number of reasons we are inclined to be afraid of sharks, something they characterize as "the ubiquitous selachophobia" that permeates modern society. Even though the number of strikes against humans is relatively small in comparison to sharks' abundance, they are still visibly threatening predators. Just as important, the authors argue, they play into humans' fear of the dark. All of this taps into our "biologically prepared fear acquisition," triggering a less-than-rational reaction.[49]

Every new report of a shark attack—the random, vicious strike from below, out of nowhere—reinforces this fear.

But by making the attack as vivid as it did—and bringing this message to such a broad audience—Benchley's work had a disproportionate effect on the public psyche. It was as if by bringing a nightmare to life, Benchley gave it a credibility, a sense of concreteness, it had never had before. As a result, we became convinced that sharks were a far graver threat to us than they actually are.

One of the oddest things about our view of sharks is that we're convinced they are everywhere. Several years ago Representative Earl Blumenauer of Oregon, a Democrat, was having lunch in the Members' Dining Room when the talk turned to sharks. Nowadays, lobbyists who have served in Congress are prohibited from snacking in this exclusive establishment, but for years it was a huge draw, which is why Blumenauer found himself sitting with South Carolina's Robert "Robin" Tallon, a former House Democrat turned lobbyist. After discussing news of a shark attack, Tallon speculated that sharks must cover the seas, outnumbering humans. Blumenauer—an environmentally minded lawmaker who represents Portland and founded not just the Congressional Bike Caucus but the Livable Communities Task Force to boot—would have none of it. The ocean's food chain couldn't sustain that many top predators, he reasoned.

"This fellow thought I was crazy," the congressman recalls, sitting in his office. "You know how banter can escalate, even without alcohol." The two bet $100 on the question. ("I wanted to up the ante, I was so confident," Blumenauer says now.)

It seemed like a simple question at the time of the bet, but Blumenauer soon discovered it was almost impossible to pin down. For years, the long-standing wager amounted to an unofficial research project for Blumenauer's office. Summer interns would make inquiries; sometimes even full-time staffers delved into the question. No one could find the answer. One night, at a Washington dinner party, I learned about the bet. The next day, I endeavored to figure it out.

I called the Dalhousie University marine biologist Boris Worm, who has spent his career seeking to quantify how many fish are in the sea, in Halifax. "Well," he offered, "there are nearly seven billion people on earth now, right? There are five hundred species of sharks, so in order to have more sharks than people, you'd have to have ten to twenty million per population. That seems like a lot. My guess would be there are more people than sharks in the world, but it's hard to say because there are some shark populations we don't know anything about, like deepwater sharks.

"Humans are now the most abundant large vertebrate on earth, by far," he continued. "Once you take out cattle and sheep, which come in roughly second and third, since we raise them, the next most abundant large vertebrate may be the crabeater seal in the Antarctic, which numbers somewhere between ten and fifty million. The worldwide wolf population, to put it in context, numbers only about 150,000. Brown bears are maybe half that."

A decent answer, but not definitive enough. So I e-mailed Sarah Fowler, who co-chairs the International Union for Conservation of Nature's Shark Specialist Group, in England. She responded with a more precise guesstimate, along the following lines. About half of the known shark species live in one bioregion of the world, such as tropical Africa and Indo-Malaysia. A significant proportion of them live in restricted areas, so Fowler posited that of these 150 species, they wouldn't number more than 150 million total. "However, the most fecund and abundant small coastal and shelf shark species that are more widely distributed in a single ocean or region (e.g., regional species of smooth hounds and cat sharks) could number in the tens of millions," she wrote. "Let's say about 7 million each on average for ~250 species that are moderately widely distributed. That brings the running total up to 2 billion individuals of ~400 species. Five billion individuals and 100 species to go."

Many of those remaining species, she explained, have a more global distribution, while others are rare. She assumed that about thirty are relatively rare or patchily distributed, boasting between 5 and 10 million individuals. Another fifty more common species might have about 40 million individuals, adding 2.2 billion to the total.

The last twenty species on the list are widespread and abundant.

Fowler decided to give these species an average of 100 million each, adding another 2 billion. And then she noted the UN Food and Agriculture Organization estimates the spiny dogfish, despite its substantial depletion through fishing, has a global population of 1 billion.

"OK, I cheated quite a bit to get to a figure very close to 7 billion," she wrote. "Total is highly dependent upon a few of the most abundant species, regardless of quality of estimates for the rarities and endemics."

In other words, there is no precise way at this moment to calculate whether sharks outnumber humans, or vice versa. It will take research for years to come.

But details like that don't bother Blumenauer, who considers Fowler's answer a "stamp of approval" for his position: "I think there is a super shark specialist who acknowledges reality, and I'm running with it." Sharks are the subjects of such intense myth, he reasons, it only makes sense that we've inflated their numbers out of proportion.

While it might not provide much comfort, sharks almost always attack humans by accident, rather than on purpose. The classic shark attack follows a pattern of "bite and spit": the fish will take a bite out of a person to determine if it's suitable prey, and more often than not it will then spit it out after the shark realizes human flesh is not its snack of choice. What bite it takes is critical, since sometimes a shark can deliver a devastating blow by severing an artery, while other times it may inflict a manageable flesh wound. When Deborah Franzman was swimming in the midst of sea lions off central California's Avila Beach Pier in 2003, a shark bit into her leg and severed the femoral artery: while it released her after pulling her briefly below the water's surface, she had bled to death by the time lifeguards reached her minutes later.

As any shark expert will tell you, seals and sea lions make far more attractive shark bait. The fat that seals contain in their outer coat accounts for half their body weight and has twice as many calories as muscle. Peter Klimley, who has studied sharks for three decades, says there's a reason great whites bite into humans and abandon them.

"Sharks don't eat humans. Humans are not nutritious enough.

They are not worth the effort," explains the UC Davis researcher. "Seals and sea lions, not people, are the Power Bars for the white shark."[50] In fact, great whites engage in a visible form of communication if two of them are targeting the same marine mammal, which Klimley has dubbed "the tail slap." In the late 1980s and early 1990s, Klimley and his colleagues examined a series of predatory attacks off the Farallon Islands near San Francisco, which boast large numbers of juvenile elephant seals vulnerable to attack between September and November. In more than two dozen cases, one white shark lifted its caudal fin out of the water and then slammed it down, splashing water in the direction of another white: in most cases, the shark with the most aggressive tail slap ended up consuming the elephant seal. While some of Klimley's peers mocked him at a 1993 scientific conference for offering this "tail slap" account of whites' feeding behavior (some even made a drawing of two white sharks high-fiving each other), his hypothesis offers the best explanation for how great whites compete for food when they home in on the same object.[51]

Three species of shark are responsible for nearly two-thirds of shark attacks worldwide: bull, great white, and tiger sharks. Several factors help explain this: bull sharks have the highest level of testosterone of any animal on earth, and white sharks seek out marine mammals, prey that can be confused with a human on a surfboard when seen from underwater. While great whites only need to eat occasionally, they tend to do their hunting during the day because their retinas have a higher proportion of cone receptors, which are used for daytime vision, than rod segments, which are used at night.[52] All three species seek out larger rather than smaller prey.

There are other factors that seem to heighten a swimmer's chances of luring a shark, according to the International Shark Attack File compiled by George Burgess, who directs the Florida Program for Shark Research at the Florida Museum of Natural History: the vast majority of attacks involve people wearing black or blue swimwear, even though many divers refer to yellow fins as "yum-yum yellow" for their tendency to attract sharks. Swimming with dogs may also lure sharks to the scene, since the rapid beating of a dog's heart, coupled with its quick movements, can mimic the signals of a fish in distress.

Certain parts of the world pose a greater risk of shark attacks than others, giving swimmers ample incentive to avoid them. While surfers tend to flock to Volusia County, Florida, for the great waves off New Smyrna Beach, they do so at their own peril, since the county has ranked number one in the world in shark bites for years. While the precise number varies from year to year, the sheer number of incidents—seventeen in 2007, and twenty-two in 2008—drives the overall trend in shark strikes worldwide. But since many of these amount to minor scrapes—blacktip and spinner sharks congregate in the area, and usually leave their victims with lacerations rather than major wounds—the surfers remain undeterred. "It's far from being the most dangerous place in the water," Burgess insists. For that you need white sharks congregating, whether it's off California, South Africa, or Australia. Historically, half of all reported attacks take place in U.S. waters, with Australia and South Africa jockeying for second place.

As more people head to the beach and spend more time in the water, the total number of unprovoked shark attacks has increased. The 1990s were the worst decade in the twentieth century for such strikes, according to records, with a total of 470 attacks and 61 fatalities worldwide, and the first decade of the twenty-first century broke that record with 646 incidents and 47 fatalities. While the annual number of attacks dipped after reaching an all-time high of 79 in 2000, the sheer fact that the global population continued to increase and more people flocked to the water helped sustain an overall rise in clashes between humans and sharks. Still, fatal shark attacks worldwide dipped to their lowest level in twenty years in 2007, when just one swimmer in the South Pacific died from a heart attack. By contrast, four people died worldwide from shark bites in both 2005 and 2006, and seven suffered the same fate in 2004.

While *Time* magazine declared the "Summer of the Shark" in 2001, its pronouncement stemmed more from the shocking nature of the attacks than their actual human death toll. On July 6 that year an eight-year-old named Jessie Arbogast had his right arm and part of his right leg torn off by a bull shark while wading the shallow waters of Florida's Gulf Islands National Seashore, prompting a flurry of media coverage. During Labor Day weekend two Americans lost their lives to sharks—Sergei Zaloukaev, who was attacked along with his companion Natalia Slobodskaya off Avon, North Carolina, and ten-year-old David Peltier, who was killed off Virginia Beach, Virginia. But the number of unprovoked shark attacks worldwide actually declined that year compared with the year before.

Put in a broader context, shark attacks fail to represent a serious threat to humans. Of all known shark species, only 6 percent are known to attack humans.[53] According to Burgess, sharks kill between four and five people a year worldwide. To put that in context, you are more likely to die from lightning, a bee sting, or an elephant attack than from a shark's bite. On average, more than forty times as many Americans seek hospital treatment for accidents involving Christmas tree ornaments than incidents involving sharks. Moreover, with recent medical advances, the chances of surviving an attack have risen dramatically, to 90 percent.

By contrast, the growing demand for shark fins—the most touted element in shark's fin soup—has driven such intense shark hunting that even some of the people who have suffered from shark strikes are now lobbying for heightened shark conservation measures. Researchers estimate 73 million sharks are being caught and killed worldwide each year to supply the fin trade, and the act of finning—cutting off a shark's fins and tossing the fish's mutilated body back into the water—has sparked opposition worldwide. For years the United States required sharks brought ashore from the Atlantic and the Gulf of Mexico—but not the Pacific—have their fins attached, deferring to regional fishery management councils. But environmentalists (including those who have experienced shark attacks firsthand) launched an intense lobbying campaign to change the law. As one of its final acts, the 111th Congress required all sharks landed in U.S. waters (with the exception of small dogfish, a concession to win one senator's vote) to have their fins attached.

Every shark attack survivor has a different story, though many of the details are the same: usually swimming around sunrise or sunset, they feel a sudden strike—frequently from below—and find themselves losing a tremendous amount of blood. Victims often don't experience much pain at first; that comes later.

In 1978, Mike deGruy was in his mid-twenties and working as a marine biologist in the Marshall Islands atoll of Enewetak when he and a friend decided to spend their Sunday diving. Fifty feet down, deGruy saw a gray reef shark engaged in what he now describes as "agonistic display": the shark was arching its back and raising its snout. Initially, the biologist backed up slowly and tried to be as still as possible so as not to provoke it, but when the shark did not move toward him, he couldn't resist snapping a picture.

"When the strobe fired, so did the shark," deGruy recounts, more than thirty years later. "It just came like a bullet." While deGruy tried to use his camera to block his attacker, the shark was undeterred, taking his elbow in its mouth and raking the back of his hand when deGruy put it out in self-defense.

While the shark sailed off, deGruy thought at that moment he was destined to die. Blood was pouring out in three distinct streams, he could see the bones in his hand, and he was well aware of how many sharks inhabited the water he was immersed in at that precise moment. "I thought, 'Christ, I'm in trouble,' " he recalls. "The sharks were there all over. They were everywhere. You toss a little blood in the water, and there are fifty sharks in five minutes." As he spent twenty-five minutes swimming to his boat anchored fifty yards away, deGruy thought of himself as "a living chum line."

DeGruy managed to make it to the twenty-one-foot Boston whaler, as did his diving buddy, who had also been struck. After hastily tying a tourniquet around his arm, deGruy radioed for assistance, help that took an hour to arrive; because the waves were strong, the military helicopter that came to the two men's aid had difficulty making out the white boat amid the frothy whitecaps.

In retrospect, deGruy thinks his fatalistic attitude after the attack saved his life. "If I thought there was any chance to make it, I wouldn't have. I would have panicked; I would have freaked out. I was 100 percent convinced I was going to die."

As deGruy is recounting his brush with death, he's sitting in the gleaming white offices of the Pew Environment Group in downtown Washington. Flush with money from the Pew Charitable Trusts, the group is both well financed and creative: its employees are constantly devising campaigns aimed at influencing both national and international ocean policy, along with a handful of other green issues. In July 2009 they came up with one of their boldest salvos, bringing roughly half a dozen shark attack survivors to Capitol Hill—deGruy among them—to lobby for the anti-finning bill.

DeGruy doesn't look, or act, like your typical lobbyist. Now a professional underwater filmmaker living in Santa Barbara, he's ebullient even when he's describing what it was like to feel the life draining from his body. He shows off his scarred arm, repaired after he underwent two skin grafts and eleven separate operations, without reservation. "It looks pretty good now," he declares with a bit of pride, looking at his lumpy but intact appendage.

And while he admits his attack made him more cautious about entering the sea, deGruy says it didn't shift his fundamental view of sharks. "My attitude before I was attacked is there isn't a creature in the ocean as adapted to the ocean and as beautiful as the shark," he says. "It is unchanged."

Wearing matching white T-shirts that bear a black fin jutting out of the water and the slogan "Shark Attack Survivors for Shark Conservation," deGruy and the other survivors made their way to the Senate for a brief handshake with Barbara Boxer and a longer conversation with her aides. By the end of the day, it was unclear how much headway they'd made in Congress, but they scored more press coverage than the Pew staff had ever imagined. Their story made the front page of *The Washington Post,* as well as featured segments on CNN, Fox News, and National Public Radio.

Mike Coots, a native of Hawaii who lost his leg to a tiger shark while surfing in October 1997, isn't surprised that he and the others managed to make news. "The media loves shark stories," he says matter-of-factly, relaxing at the end of the day in a Senate cafeteria, the American Grill. While most of those stories undermine the cause of conservation, Coots adds, this particular campaign has challenged the conventional wisdom.

"This is actually helping the sharks," he says, looking over at a reporter interviewing one of his fellow survivors. "The sharks are smiling today."

These survivors are effective, in part, because they make us face an unpleasant truth: sharks will always threaten us, in an unpredictable way. But if deGruy, Coots, and others can make their peace with that, why can't we?

From the moment *Jaws* became a hit, Peter Benchley made it clear he did not advocate killing sharks. Benchley spent years filming underwater adventure specials for a variety of production companies, highlighting the virtues of ocean exploration. But it wasn't until the mid-1990s that the best-selling author decided to become an environmental crusader.

In the immediate years after his book and movie came out, Benchley was fairly defensive when it came to the question of sharks: as reporters repeatedly called him for comment on incidents involving either human attacks on sharks or vice versa, the author became skilled at deflecting the idea that he started the war of man versus shark. "He had various ways of explaining to people why he shouldn't be responsible for everyone who was bitten by a shark, or afraid of sharks," Wendy Benchley recalls.

Toward the end of his life, Benchley became an environmental crusader, making short educational films for the New England Aquarium and conducting a speaking tour in Asia, and he started telling reporters he couldn't have written *Jaws* knowing what he now understood about sharks.

"He was looking for ways to get involved and use his reputation and his clout," says Greg Stone, chief oceans scientist for Conservation International and senior vice president for exploration and conservation at the New England Aquarium. "It's pretty much the way he spent the last ten years of his life."

Benchley died with this work unfinished. Even after a decade of advocacy, he had just begun to erase what seems like an indelible mark on the public consciousness. And even decades after the release of his book, plenty of people devote their careers to keeping the *Jaws* myth alive. As long as the myth persists, shark hunters will have many reasons to go about ridding the sea of them. How can you fault someone for wiping out a killer?

3

A DEMON FISH

In terms of the numbers of sharks we've killed, nobody comes close to us. We've caught just about everything there is left to catch. Sharks are fascinating, but we're trophy hunters. I get paid to kill fish. Some people don't like it, but too bad.

—Mark "the Shark" Quartiano,
Miami fishing tour boat operator

The massive scalloped hammerhead, swaying over the deck of *Striker-1*, brings Rosie O'Donnell to an abrupt halt in the middle of Biscayne Bay.

Driving a motorboat with a gaggle of female friends, the well-known comedian pulls up next to Mark Quartiano's fifty-foot Hatteras and begins peppering him with questions. Pointing to the now-lifeless body, she asks, "Is that for real?"

Mark "the Shark" Quartiano, who has operated a fishing charter here in Miami since 1976, is pleased with the attention. He works hard, seven days a week, and it's strangers' fascination with sharks that keeps his operation humming.

While the captain assures O'Donnell that the nearly nine-foot fish is genuine, one of the Texans who's spent the morning fishing with Quartiano has a question of his own. Dustin Self is a twenty-six-year-old roughneck who works on an oil rig for a living, but he's savvy enough to spot the celebrity who's just pulled up. "Are you Rosie O'Donnell?" he shouts.

She is, and it turns out O'Donnell's son, Blake, is a shark aficionado who has spied *Striker-1* before. The family has a vacation home on Star Island, the exclusive Miami enclave where the pop singer Gloria Estefan and the NBA star Shaquille O'Neal also own manses, and Blake O'Donnell has pointed out Quartiano's boat as it's cruised past their home on multiple occasions. In the past, O'Donnell told her son the vessel couldn't possibly hunt sharks, but she's happy to stand corrected. "My son's going to flip out!" she exclaims, before hurrying back to the island.

Within minutes, O'Donnell has returned on a gleaming dark red Jet Ski with Blake in tow. She is unabashed in her admiration of the hulking mass hanging by a rope, its black eyes on opposite ends of its rectangular head now glassy.

"We can't believe it!" she tells the Texas family, as she and Blake stroke the creature. "Oh my God. He feels like rubber."

O'Donnell wants to know who caught the shark—it is Self's girlfriend, Stephanie Perez, a recent Texas Woman's University graduate who's about to pursue her master's degree in speech therapy. This brings another flurry of praise from O'Donnell. "And you're the one who caught it," she marvels. "Girl power!"

Women are showing up more often on *Striker-1* nowadays. Shark fishing used to be an almost exclusively male sport, and Quartiano traditionally hosted bachelor's parties on his boat along with the usual businessmen's outing. Now he's booking bachelorettes as well, giving them equal billing on his Web site.

The captain—who has a deeply tanned, weathered face and the sort of blond-streaked hair that seems almost required for men and women alike in Miami—has no problem with this demographic shift. He is focused on maintaining as robust a clientele as possible, especially in the midst of a major economic downturn. "I'd rather have a woman than a man in the chair, because they listen to everything you say," he says, referring to the fishing chair off the stern where clients reel in their prize catches.

Quartiano can no longer count on Fortune 500 companies such as Coca-Cola, IBM, and Microsoft holding lavish conventions in Miami where gaggles of executives were anxious to head out for an afternoon of fishing. And on top of that, it's harder to find sharks. "I spend all day long trying to catch a shark, when twenty years ago, forget it. Ten minutes," he reminisces as he pilots the boat away from the Miami Marriott, where his ship departs. "It's a grind. It isn't easy."

"But you love it, right?" pipes up Perez's father.

"It's a lot of pressure, when you think about it," Quartiano muses, his eyes scanning the ocean's surface. "It's no fun fishing for somebody else. I've got to catch you a fish, and I've got two hours to catch it. Isn't that right?"

Perez's father has no rejoinder; the entire group is quiet. They've come out here expecting to see a big shark, and they'll go away disappointed if they don't.

Perez is a perfect example of the newer clients Quartiano's started serving: it was her idea to book a charter this morning, bringing along her parents, boyfriend, brother, and brother's friend for the ride. The men spend a while catching shark bait, including bonito, kingfish, and barracuda, but when it becomes clear a shark is on the line, she's the one who settles into the fishing chair for a half-hour tug-of-war.

Initially, Perez has trouble heeding Quartiano's advice. He tells her to try reeling in the shark only when it's not tugging at the line to avoid exhaustion, but the twenty-three-year-old has difficulty timing her efforts. ("I used to think girls could follow instructions," he says good-naturedly at one point, sotto voce.) But with her mother's encouragement—"Remember, honey, you just graduated from college; you can follow instructions"—Perez gets into the rhythm. As she toils away, her parents start debating whether she could ever mount a shark trophy in their house, located in the Houston suburbs.

"No animals in my house," her mother, Norma Perez, says, shaking her head side to side.

Quartiano is too superstitious to let the comment pass. "Let's catch him first, then you can talk about where you can put him."

Finally, the shark relents. Quartiano and his mate, Jeff Fasshauer, scramble to pull the hammerhead on board. Deeply tangled in the fishing line, with a huge hole in its side, the animal is essentially dead.

After all the debate on board, Perez isn't actually interested in making a wall mount out of her catch: "Probably pictures are enough for me." And she remains agnostic about whether shark fishing is good or bad. "I know this sounds harsh, but I guess it depends on how many sharks there are. If they're endangered, you shouldn't do it, but if they're bountiful . . ." Her voice trails off. "I'm really kind of indifferent on it, because I don't know enough to say anything."

Perez will walk away from the boat without her big fish—which is, in fact, classified as endangered by the International Union for Conservation of Nature—but it's enough to convince O'Donnell she should take her son Blake shark fishing aboard *Striker-1*. As the two of them zoom away on their Jet Ski, Quartiano notes with satisfaction, "I don't think she's Greenpeace, right? That's a future customer."

The shark has done the captain's advertising for him. "People ask me why I hang them up," he says. "That's why I hang them up. If you let them go, you don't have anything. You almost don't have a story."

If you're looking for a twenty-first-century incarnation of Captain Quint from *Jaws*, Quartiano comes pretty close. While he's a friendlier, more service-oriented version, the Florida charter-boat captain has built his entire professional reputation on his ability to slay the scariest sharks in the sea. The shift in public attitudes toward sharks, driven in large part by the success of *Jaws*, has helped propel an entire commercial industry in the United States that spans from the dock to the drugstore.

Quartiano used to hunt sharks for his own amusement off Miami Beach, but he's spent most of his career ensuring other anglers can tell their own big-fish stories. He started out working as a police officer and then became a firefighter, at which point he managed to work four days a week and fish the other three days. Once he cobbled together enough sponsors to support himself by fishing full-time, he made the switch, and at this point he's the only charter operator who still targets sharks. By his own estimate, he has killed at least 100,000 sharks over the course of his career: as he likes to joke, he's outlasted his competitors, as well as the scores of sharks he's hauled on board over the years.

Quartiano models himself in part after the shark hunters who used to fish off Long Island in the 1950s and 1960s—when there were still plenty of sharks around to catch—though he's quick to add that he manages to accomplish the same feats in a much less forgiving environment. After William E. Young toured the globe in the early twentieth century in search of sharks, men like the late Frank Mundus grabbed the spotlight. Mundus earned the nickname Monster Man for the sharks he caught off Montauk, and claimed he was the inspiration for Captain Quint, even though Benchley said he based the character on more than one person. Mundus caught two massive great whites in the course of his forty-year career, but embraced conservation after years of fishing, retired to Hawaii in 1991, and largely gave up shark hunting. Quartiano, however, has yet to temper his pursuit.

Quartiano prides himself on finding new species to kill in order to satisfy his customer, like the thresher sharks he's managed to cull from a nearby area where they gather to give birth to their young. He no longer is allowed to catch threshers under state law, which complicates this task. While he's careful to adhere to state and federal rules, he thinks people apply a double standard when it comes to shark fishing. "You get people who don't like to hurt animals but they're mostly hypocrites," Quartiano once told a local magazine. "They want to release everything, meanwhile they go home and eat big juicy steaks."

Quartiano cannot be called a hypocrite: he lets people know exactly where he stands. He parks his boat right outside one of Miami's big South Beach hotels, perched next to a black-and-white sandwich-board sign that extols the virtues of "Mark the Shark's Monster Fishing Charters." (These claims to fame apparently include "awarded #1 charter boat in the world" and "as seen on every major t.v. show," both of which seem like a slight stretch.) The tiny beachcomber shop he runs is yards away, and its walls are lined with at least a hundred shark jaws. "This is nothing, I've got a warehouse full of them," he explains as I marvel at the dry, jagged teeth looming above me.

Mark the Shark looks the part: he wears sunny yellow fishermen's overalls that are both practical and symbolic, evoking America's fish-

ing past, along with various items of clothing that tout his many
sponsors. For example, his T-shirt's slogan, "Just Stuff It," is a subtle
advertisement for Gray Taxidermy, which helps immortalize his clients' catches. Ironically, taxidermists don't even use the shark's carcass anymore to make a mount. An angler comes in, tells the shop the
species and size of the shark that's perished, and the staff takes down
a Plexiglas model that matches. It's cheaper and more efficient, though
it means losing some authenticity in the process. Some trophies still
feature a shark's actual jaws, but that's the only physical remnant of
the animal that has been dragged up from the ocean's depths. The
carcass is discarded; the shark has died for no ostensible purpose.

While Quartiano and I are discussing the fine details of taxidermy,
we're idling in his office waiting for customers to show up that were
expected shortly after dawn. A British stag party was slated to arrive
at 7:00 a.m. to start fishing; now it's more than two hours later and
they're still lounging, hungover, in their Ritz-Carlton hotel rooms.
We've been informed that they won't arrive until 11:30; there is no
choice but to accede to their wishes. Quartiano charges a party of six
$1,200 for a daylong ride, and so long as they've paid their money,
he does what they want. The charter captain wouldn't have minded
sleeping in as well, but that is not his call—he reports first thing in the
morning and shoves off only when his customers arrive.

Finally, shortly before noon, a collection of five amiable, pasty-faced
Brits arrives at the marina. Quartiano's focused on pleasing his customers, not giving them a guilt trip, so he's acting more like a camp
counselor than anything else. "We're going to do shark fishing, so
everyone who wants to catch a shark, come with me!" he announces
cheerily. Most boat tours that last more than a couple of hours offer
plenty of food to their customers, but Quartiano makes it clear that's
not an option today. "We only have liquids: beer, soda, water. No
food," he warns them. "That's fine," one of the Brits replies.

Quartiano is just as clear on who will be the focus of his attention this April afternoon: Michael Sandford, the bachelor boy. Just as
Stephanie Perez takes center stage when she's paying the bill, Michael
Sandford is the one who gets special treatment this time. "Michael's
the man," Quartiano declares. Being "the man" means catching a

shark, of course, so the two men running the boat arrange it so Sandford will be sitting at the gleaming white chair on the main deck, where he will be able to haul in the big fish on a black shiny rod with a golden reel. "Once you're in the chair, baby, it's hard to get out," Quartiano tells the group.

Sandford, who is getting married in less than a month, is fascinated by the possibility of catching a big fish. "How big can you go?" he asks Quartiano. "We've got a bunch of world records," the tour operator answers, with his usual braggadocio. "Any shark that swims, I can kill."

This sort of talk is a big hit with Sandford and his friends, all of whom are stock traders and real estate developers in their late thirties and early forties. Their Miami trip is a way to escape overcast English skies and their work responsibilities for a long weekend. Much of their trip has consisted of golfing and drinking, but Sandford likes going fishing, so they figure a trip with Mark the Shark can't hurt. Of course, Sandford adds, fishing on his side of the Atlantic has gotten a lot harder in recent years. "They're getting pretty scarce at home, fish," he says.

As they pull out of the marina, the boat's sound system blasts a song Quartiano saves for groups like this: Dick Pickle's "South Beach, the Official Anthem." Singing to the tune of *The Sound of Music*'s "My Favorite Things," Pickle croons about everything from silicone implants to celebrities:

> *Jews in Mercedes and nipples with rings*
> *South Beach has all of my favorite things.*

Several of the Brits chuckle. Quartiano knows his clientele well. His average customer, he says, is "a guy all pumped up, a big-game guy, kind of macho . . . I don't have too many Greenpeace folks coming on my boat. Usually, it's guys wanting to kill something."

Tim O'Hare, Quartiano's mate on this particular day, focuses on baiting the hooks rather than on the chatter that swirls around him on the boat as the Brits get comfortable. If Quartiano is the entertainer, O'Hare is the workhorse: he just wants to make sure these novices catch a shark, so they can declare victory and head for shore. But he relishes the struggle it takes to haul one of them into the boat. "These sharks are more exciting than any other fish. They're harder to catch," he says, as he handles the squid that will theoretically lure one of them to the boat. "It's the fight, and then just the nature of the animal."

O'Hare is well aware of monster fishing's detractors: like Quartiano, he sees these critics—especially those who call upon fishermen to "catch and release" their prey—as two-faced. "People call us slaughterers, murderers. We're just not hypocrites. Most of these fish, if you catch and release them, they're going to die." O'Hare has a point—many sport fish hauled up to the surface after a struggle end up dying anyway, depending on the duration of the battle, the given biology of a specific species, the wounds inflicted on the animal, and other factors. But most sharks can survive being dragged to the surface if they're let go quickly enough. Since they lack swim bladders, sharks are not vulnerable to pressure changes like other fish. And fishermen can use gear that increases the shark's chance of survival, including circle hooks that will lodge in its jaw rather than its gut, non-stainless-steel hooks that will rust out quickly rather than stay embedded for long periods of time, and a sufficiently strong line so that the person catching the shark doesn't have to wage an extended battle to deliberately tire it out.

While O'Hare and Quartiano do everything possible to spoon-feed their clients, preparing the fishing rods, handling the sharks once they land on the boat, they also see some risks as inevitable. "There are a lot of close calls," Quartiano confides. "You're dealing with live sharks. These things are going to happen, but nothing like we need a tourniquet."

Mark the Shark's clients expend little effort pondering what it takes to catch a shark, but that's because Quartiano and O'Hare have done the thinking for them. The boat is cruising along what Quartiano calls "the middle of a highway": it is a two-hundred-yard transect most of the fish follow as they move along the Gulf Stream, where they are easy prey. The two fishermen put the bait on lines of varying depth, at times dropping down as far as fifteen hundred or two thousand feet in order to lure six-gill sharks, which have six gills on each side rather than five and prefer deeper water. By covering the entire water column, they increase the chances that high-paying clients such as Sandford will manage to hook something while sitting in the comfort of the captain's chair, Budweiser in hand.

Which is what happens, by the end of the day. Sandford gets his hammerhead, and they catch one more for good measure. That's another satisfied client who can return to London and his future bride with full bragging rights about his monster-fishing adventure in America.

Mark the Shark has to work harder now to please his customers than he did in the past, and he blames commercial fishermen who set longlines for his predicament. These fishing lines with baited hooks frequently end up tangling and killing sharks, and there's no question that the sharks caught unintentionally from such activities, known as bycatch, far outnumber the targeted fish, be it tuna or swordfish.

"They've definitely gone down because of long-liners, not because of me," he says of sharks. "We never touch a population. Those long-liners do more damage in a night than we do in a year." And Quartiano simply does not believe that species such as bigeye thresher sharks are endangered, because he still hauls them in on his rod and reel. "I've caught more than anyone else on the planet. There's no way they're endangered."

Data collected by the National Oceanic and Atmospheric Administration's Fisheries Service tell a different story: federal officials estimate that recreational landings of large coastal sharks outpaced commercial catches for fifteen out of twenty-one years between 1981 and 2001, with U.S. recreational anglers catching 12 million sharks, skates, and rays in 2004 alone.[1] These numbers appear to be on the rise: the absolute number of sharks U.S. anglers caught increased by roughly a third between 2006 and 2007, according to NOAA.[2] Apparently, all those bachelor and bachelorette parties add up.

It's a classic case of tunnel vision: humans fail to comprehend the massive impact of our collective activities on the planet because we think of ourselves as lone actors. In 2007, for example, twelve million anglers made nearly 87 million fishing trips on the Atlantic, Pacific, and gulf coasts, catching roughly 468 million fish.[3] That's more than one fish for every man, woman, and child in the United States, and then some. Boris Worm, the marine biologist at Canada's Dalhousie University, puts it another way: "Say you have only one in a thousand Americans catch a shark each year. That's 300,000 sharks a year, just like that. I don't think we understand how many of us there are." We dwarf every other large animal on earth in terms of numbers, and that has consequences.

On a certain level, Quartiano acknowledges that he might be contributing to the fish's demise, though he still sees long-liners as the enemy. "In terms of the numbers of sharks we've killed, nobody comes close to us. We've caught just about everything there is left to catch. Sharks are fascinating, but we're trophy hunters. I get paid to kill fish. Some people don't like it, but too bad." If environmentalists have such a big problem with his activities, he reasons, they should pay him to park his boat. In an era of government bailouts, Quartiano jokes, he's happy to take his place in line at the federal trough. "Basically, my ultimate goal is to get subsidized by the government. They pay farmers not to farm, right? I want to get paid not to fish."

Despite his bravado, Quartiano has been feeling a little uneasy lately about his activities. He wants sharks to stick around long enough for his son Maverick—whom he describes as "fearless"—to kill them. So he's been bringing some of his catches back to local scientists, which he says more than justifies his business. "How else are you going to get data on some species of sharks unless [*sic*] we don't bring them to the scientists?" he asks, adding that it's no use throwing sharks back into the sea if they've died by the time they're hauled into the boat. "This is how they're going to get them. They may not like it. They're specimens. Like it or not, we're going to catch 'em. If we catch an endangered species, why should we let it sink to the bottom?"

In the end, he can only hazard a guess as to whether sharks will survive over the long term. "Sharks are cool," he says, shortly before I head out to catch my water taxi back to shore. "Hopefully, they'll be here after we're gone."

Circumstances belie his wish. The kind of recreational fishing Quartiano promotes is helping ensure the reverse outcome, since these activities take a serious toll on the shark populations that once thrived off the Florida coast. On one level, what these men are doing is nothing new: fishermen have been battling with sharks for centuries, and in the eighteenth century bored sailors often entertained themselves by hooking sharks. The explorer George Vancouver gave an account of these games from Cocos Island in the eastern Pacific during this time, saying:

> The general warfare that exists between sea-faring persons and these voracious animals afforded at first a species of amusement for our people, by hooking, or otherwise taking one for the others to feast upon, but as this was attended with the ill consequence of drawing immense numbers round the ship, and as the boatswain and one of the young gentlemen had both nearly fallen a sacrifice to this diversion, by narrowly escaping from being drawn out of the boat by an immensely large shark, which they had hooked, into the midst of at least a score of these voracious animals, I thought proper to prohibit all further indulgence in this species of entertainment.[4]

The difference is when Vancouver's men were dangling sharks off their boat, there were plenty of sharks congregating below, so the impact of one animal's death did not weigh as much. In addition, few people were hunting them at the time. Now the loss of a single shark exacts a far higher price on the population to which it belongs.

Quartiano's entire business is fueled by testosterone, but he has drawn two opponents who are nearly as brash as he is. While some scientists have earned their deservedly geeky reputations, neither Demian Chapman nor Neil Hammerschlag fits the stereotype. Chapman is a bold New Zealander in his mid-thirties, so exuberant that he started a food fight with his wife at their wedding (before becoming sick from drinking). Nicknamed Pointer—the name for great white sharks Down Under, since the species is mainly gray with white on the tip of its nose—by some of his fellow marine biologists, Chapman spent several years researching sharks in southern Florida before moving to the Institute for Conservation Science at Stony Brook University. He first earned his Ph.D. at Nova Southeastern University and then worked at the Pew Institute for Ocean Science, based in Miami, allowing him to observe the work of Mark the Shark and other fishing operations at close range. One of Chapman's strengths is that his hail-fellow-well-met demeanor allows him to bond with unlikely allies, which in turn lets him infiltrate enemy territory. Much of Quartiano's bread and butter comes from killing pregnant hammerhead sharks, since they tend to be large and make for some of the most impressive trophies. The fishing operator frequently fires off e-mails that include pictures of these sharks, strung up and bloody, towering well above his head, to show off his catches.

In 2002, Chapman befriended a taxidermist in South Beach who let him know when a haul of hammerheads was coming in. In April alone Chapman counted more than forty litters that had been killed through recreational fishing: some carried as many as twenty pups each. The toll such fishing takes on a population, he says, cannot be overestimated. "By killing forty pregnant females, you're killing eight hundred animals or more. It doesn't take a genius to figure out it's unsustainable to kill pregnant females of a selected species," he says, the scorn audible in his voice. "Think if aliens started hunting humans by killing off pregnant females. It wouldn't take long to wipe us out."

Chapman isn't the only young marine biologist who has Quartiano in his sights. Neil Hammerschlag, a research assistant professor and director of the R. J. Dunlap Marine Conservation Program at the University of Miami's Rosenstiel School of Marine and Atmospheric Science, is relentless in the attacks he has launched on Mark the Shark. Hammerschlag uses every forum he can to question the activities of recreational fishermen like Quartiano, debating him in a sportfishing magazine or crusading against him on his Web site, www.neilhammer.com. The elaborate Web site features not only a section on how recreational shark fishing is taking its toll (including a photograph of Quartiano displaying two massive dead sharks) but details about conservation efforts and Hammerschlag's own research.

Hammerschlag has mulled the idea of mobilizing activists to set up a picketing operation near the Marriott to lobby the weekend warriors who patronize Quartiano's business to eschew his fishing tours, but he's wary of giving Mark the Shark additional media exposure. "He's trying to live up to the legend he's trying to create for himself," he says. "He kind of likes attention."

Catching sharks as a hobby is, by definition, about getting attention. As Quartiano points out, you barely have a story if you don't have a big hulking shark dangling beside you at the end of the day. Nothing embodies this phenomenon more than shark-fishing tournaments, which are thriving up and down America's East Coast. They have become annual summer rituals, another way beach towns can lure tourist dollars to their area.

There's nothing subtle about these contests: each one of them plays up the danger of sharks and the manliness of those who catch them. There's the "Swim at Your Own Risk Mega Shark Tournament" in Pensacola, Florida; the South Florida Shark Club's "Big Hammer Challenge," with contestants such as "Team Vile" and "Reel Boyz"; and the "Newport Monster Shark & Tuna Tournament" in Rhode Island. Only brave and flamboyant contestants need apply, and their willingness to flout political correctness has begun to stir controversy.

Jack Donlon spent years organizing fishing tournaments for grouper, tarpon, and other species before he hit the jackpot with his "Are You Man Enough? Shark Challenge" in 2007. He remembers how he and his business partners fretted over attracting attention for their previous ventures: "The problem we always had was, how do you make fishing for grouper exciting? How do you make fishing for tarpon exciting? When you talk about sharks, it's exciting, then and there."

From Donlon's perspective, the explanation is obvious. While *Jaws* helped glamorize shark fishing by making the fish a public target, it's the perceived risks involved that make the sport popular. "It's something that can eat you. There's danger there. It's different from going out deer hunting. One misstep, and it can eat you."

Before Hammerschlag and his allies started making a fuss, Donlon's Fort Myers competition was thriving undisturbed. He looked down on nearby catch-and-release tournaments, where none of the sharks were taken back to shore, as boring. "They die of loneliness," he explains. The "Are You Man Enough? Shark Challenge" had significant backing from local businesses and had expanded to encompass a street fair, boat show, and kid fishing derby by the summer of 2009. Donlon took pains to describe the contest's "eco-outlook" on its Web site, writing, "There are laws on the books for recreational and commercial fisheries. We responsibly abide by these laws and we respect the legal decisions of anglers to keep or release their quarry in accordance with those laws . . . We are proud that after several years and hundreds of anglers, the tournament has had only 7 shark [*sic*] harvested."

But the contest required its participants to land their sharks if they wanted to vie for the winning title, and that drew the ire of conservationists. These large sharks were inevitably the pregnant females that had come into the area each year to give birth, just like the ones Quartiano finds in Biscayne Bay. The Shark Safe project, a group Hammerschlag helps direct, threatened to hold a rally two weeks before the June 6 and 7 contest. The unwelcome publicity prompted some local businesses to have second thoughts: for a region that's economically dependent on tourism, highlighting the fact that sharks swim close to the shore is not a selling point.

Then the Lee County commissioner Ray Judah weighed in, decrying the tournament's shark-killing policy. Judah first heard about the contest from a friend who has devoted her career to saving sea turtles, and then got an irate e-mail from a marketing agent the county had hired to promote the area to German vacationers. "I got an e-mail from Vera [Sommer] saying, 'What the hell are you thinking? Here we are trying to market our beaches for tourists, and here you are showing pictures of battered and bloody sharks!' " Judah mobilized his fellow commissioners, who voted unanimously to stop the tournament. While the move had no legal standing, it sent a message. At the last minute Donlon changed course and adopted a catch-and-release policy for much of the contest, awarding just $1,000 for the retrieval of one shark. He had little choice, faced with opponents he refers to as "e-mail jihadists."

Donlon is blunt about why he switched gears: he is no environmentalist. "The real decision came because of pressure. Not because of conservation," he says now.

The following year two entertainment promoters, Sean and Brooks Paxton, decided to retool the tournament. Rather than fighting with scientists and activists, they enlisted the aid of Robert Hueter, who directs Mote Marine Laboratory's Center for Shark Research, and the Guy Harvey Ocean Foundation. They opted for a more upscale, high-tech catch-and-release tournament, "The Guy Harvey Ultimate Shark Challenge," which has won the unprecedented blessing of the U.S. Humane Society. The contest allows only fifteen teams to compete at the outset: the first weekend narrows the field to five finalists, and in the finals streaming video allows fans to watch the fishing dockside in real time. Since the public can watch the sharks hauled on board and then thrown in the water, it compensates for the fact that they won't be able to stare at the shark carcasses that typically hang at marinas at the finale of any fishing competition. After all, shark fishing still has to be a spectator sport if it's going to turn a profit—the question is how to make it a bloodless spectator sport. In its first year 1,660 people showed up to watch the nonlethal contest, proving sharks still have allure even if they are allowed to escape at the end of the day.

These activists have succeeded, in part, because they sought to preserve something that helps sustain the local economy, rather than abolish it outright. "At the end of the day, the community didn't want people going out and slaughtering sharks off their beaches, and pulling up catches and hanging up sharks," Hammerschlag says. The community needed a little prodding, and Hammerschlag was willing to provide it. In many ways he and Chapman represent the new breed of marine biologists, who are researcher-activists. Faced with the dramatic decline of the fish they have set out to study, they have little interest in staying on the sidelines when it comes to policy debates. And while both remain focused on publishing academic work, they have consciously crafted research projects that aim to show the importance of keeping sharks around.

For years, activists and scientists have enjoyed a sort of symbiotic relationship, in which environmental advocates took the research academics had done and used it as ammunition to lobby for policy changes. But even as this went on, many researchers took great pains to distance themselves from the activist community, because they feared it would undermine how other academics viewed their work and could jeopardize their chances for promotion. "The word 'activist' is kind of taboo within the scientific community," Hammerschlag says, adding that when it comes to many of his colleagues, "They're kind of scared to use that word. It's a shame . . . Everything's agenda-driven anyway." Within the last decade or two the line between these two camps has blurred, with many scientists deciding they cannot afford to stay neutral on policy questions that affect the future course of the planet.

It's also not limited to the United States. Even as a Ph.D. student at the University of Cape Town, Alison Kock made the news many times for her work on the great whites that swim not far from her university. Kock believes that sometimes she has a duty to publicize her data even before she's submitted it to a peer-reviewed journal, a radical notion for a scientist who's hoping to ascend to academic heights. "There's a huge generational gap," she says, pausing for a moment. "*Huge.* Huge." Kock has studied under and collaborated with more senior scientists who feel differently, but she has become comfortable with the idea of bucking convention. "Given what's happening in the marine environment, if you have information and you just put it in a scientific paper years from now, from my perspective, it's not responsible."

This radicalization among conservation biologists is beginning to redefine scientific research. Not only are researchers such as Chapman, Hammerschlag, and Kock pursuing studies aimed at producing a specific policy outcome—an end to shark fishing—they are actively working to shift popular sentiment, through either the media or public protest. As federal dollars for nonmedical scientific research have shrunk, some nonprofits with a conservation agenda have stepped in to fund this sort of work. The Pew Environment Group, headquartered in Washington, D.C., not only pays for academics to research the overfishing of sharks but also publishes attractive, easy-to-read brochures summarizing the scientists' findings and pitches these results to reporters in order to generate favorable press coverage. While these groups are invested in promoting scientific inquiry, they view it as a means to achieve a policy end. And they can find several willing partners within academia, because these researchers have seen firsthand what's happened to their case studies. In the same way that many climate scientists have decided they have no choice but to push for limits on greenhouse gases in order to avert drastic global warming, shark researchers argue they cannot afford to remain silent while shark populations decline.

Dalhousie University's Boris Worm, a German who has helped drive international media coverage of ocean issues and befriended journalists across the globe, has published a number of studies that suggest sharks and other top ocean predators have declined much faster than others have thought. The evidence has been out there, he argues, but scientists were not looking for it: they were paying attention to whales, sea turtles, and other compelling marine animals.

"Sharks have been largely under the radar, even ten years ago. Our attention was more on things that were commercially valuable, or things that were pretty and cute," he says. "I have more concern about sharks than anything else, because we've been aware of these other things for a long time. With sharks, we're only now getting on top of the problem, let alone thinking of the solutions."

While academic scientific research can take years or even decades to complete, shark researchers are now rushing to gauge the extent of these animals' decline. They are scrambling to track how many sharks, and which kinds, humans extract from the sea each year. Without providing a precise body count, they stand little chance of arresting sharks' march toward extinction.

4

DRIED SEAFOOD STREET

It can be a very popular, and a very noble, food.
—Yip Chiu Sung, vice chairman of Hong Kong's
Sharkfin and Marine Products Association,
speaking of shark's fin soup

Probably the best thing that could happen to sharks is that people
lose their taste for shark's fin soup.
—David Balton, deputy assistant secretary of state
for oceans and fisheries under Presidents
George W. Bush and Barack Obama

Each kind of auctioneer has a style. There's the robust cattle auctioneer, who spits out numbers in a bold, singsong voice that determines where animals go to be bred or slaughtered; the elegant estate auctioneer, whose rich, mellifluous tone entices art and furniture collectors to fork over their savings; and then there's Charlie Lim.

A spectacled, wiry man in his early fifties, Lim sports a short-sleeved, button-down shirt and a modified bowl cut that lets his straight black bangs fall neatly across his forehead. Standing in front of the sort of shiny whiteboards that appear in classrooms and corporate conference rooms across the globe, he doesn't talk much as he auctions off his wares; instead, he shakes an abacus in short, regular bursts. Much of the time, the clicking of the beads is the loudest sound in the room.

Lim is a shark fin trader. More precisely, he's the secretary of Hong Kong's Sharkfin and Marine Products Association. And at the moment he's standing in a nondescript auction house whose spare white decor evokes a Chelsea art gallery. But when the auction begins, the buyers crowd around Lim in a semicircle, jostling for a look at the gray triangular fins splayed across the floor. A shark fin auction is as fast as it is secretive. By the time Lim takes his position at the front of the room, one of his assistants has already marked on the board behind him—in a bright red felt-tipped pin—which sorts of fins are being auctioned in any given lot. As soon as men dump the contents of a burlap bag on the floor, the bidding begins: any interested buyer must approach Lim and punch his suggested price into a single device that only the auctioneer and his assistant can see. The bidders must make a calculated guess about what price will prevail, rather than compete with each other openly for a given bag of fins. Within two minutes the lot is sold, and the winning price per kilo is duly noted on the board. Lim's assistants sweep the pile back into its bag, using a dustpan to gather any errant fins that might have escaped to the side. Another bag—containing the first dorsal, pectorals, and lower lobe of the caudal fins that are most valuable—is dumped on the floor, and the cycle begins again.

The group of men gathered here—and it's all men—are experienced traders who hear about these auctions through word of mouth. There is no downtime, no chitchat; in fact, there aren't even chairs for them to sit on during the auction. Given the quick pace of shark fin sales, they must be prepared to bid without hesitation. The bidders show no emotion during the entire process: this isn't fine art they plan to furnish their homes with, or livestock they will devote months to raising. It is a heap of desiccated objects they will seek to transfer to someone else as soon as they acquire it.

Lim does make a few remarks in Cantonese about the fins before his feet, but it's not the sort of chatter most auctioneers use to boost the price of a given lot. He's not saying, "Take a look at these gray beauties!" or anything to that effect. Sometimes he indicates the species that's collected in a given bag: blacktip, hammerhead, or blue shark. But a shark fin auction is not really about salesmanship. It's about moving product.

Some rare metals and stones have carried a high market price for centuries. Basic foodstuffs, including several fish species, have also held a quantifiable commercial value over time. The shark trade, however, is a more recent arrival to the world scene. Unlike many other fish, such as salmon or red snapper, for example, shark does not derive its value from its taste or nutritional worth. In fact, there's ample evidence that the high levels of toxins sharks accumulate in their bodies pose a potential threat to humans, just as tuna does. While many consumers—especially in China—view shark meat and fins as nutritious, sharks are likely to contain high levels of mercury because they are large, slow-growing fish that consume other fish as their prey, which allows mercury to build up in their muscle tissues. WildAid, an environmental group that crusades against shark fin trafficking, commissioned a study by the Thailand Institute of Scientific and Technological Research in 2001 that found shark fins in Bangkok's markets contain mercury concentrations up to forty-two times above the safe limit for human health.[1]

The market for sharks is based more on the animals' mystique than anything else. In the same way that De Beers has convinced young men across the globe that women will be more likely to accept their marriage proposal if it comes with a diamond ring, men like Lim have managed to persuade Asian consumers that the very presence of stringy shark fin cartilage in their soup speaks to their own social status. Other marketers have different pitches, bottling sharks' mysterious promise in a range of salves. One U.S. entrepreneur has made a decent amount of money peddling the line that sharks cure cancer, while other companies are in the business of advertising shark oil's anti-aging properties. None of these appeals are based on science, but they tap into our long-held beliefs about the power of an animal that can consume us. And nowhere do they resonate more strongly than in Asia, where an ever-expanding group of consumers is seeking new ways to demonstrate its upwardly mobile status.

While the shark fin trade has evolved into a global enterprise, spanning multiple oceans and continents, at one point or another it almost always stops here, in a warren of narrow Hong Kong streets that make up two neighborhoods, Sai Ying Poon and Sheung Wan. It's hard not to be impressed with the sheer variety of parched delicacies on display: seaweed, scallops, and oysters, all spilling out into the street. Auction houses have glass doors that keep their commodities out of the reach of ordinary customers, but these stores don't have the same rarefied rules. A nutty, slightly cloying scent pervades the entire neighborhood: the smell of the sea, withered up and left to die.

Roughly half of the world's shark fins move through Hong Kong, which serves as a gateway for both the mainland Chinese market and other Asian countries that consume shark's fin soup. Tracking the shark fin trade in recent years has become increasingly complicated as mainland China has started playing a bigger role in directly receiving fin imports from overseas, rather than using Hong Kong as an intermediary. In 2000, the five major markets for shark fins—Hong Kong, mainland China, Taiwan, Japan, and Singapore—reported importing 11,600 metric tons of fins, of which Hong Kong accounted for 47 percent. The numbers keep rising: in 2008, Hong Kong alone imported 10,002 metric tons of fins.[2] But as China's role as an importer of raw shark fins has grown, it's become harder to track the overall trade because Chinese government figures are so unreliable.

For example, the shark fin trade increased at a steady clip of 5 percent a year during the late 1990s and early twenty-first century (with the exception of 1998, when the Asian financial crisis depressed sales). But in recent years Hong Kong imports have dipped slightly, clocking in at 5,337 metric tons in 2006. This is due in part to the fin trade shifting to other cities in China, but it's hard to gauge what's happening there. Shelley Clarke, a biology professor at Imperial College London who knows the shark fin trade better than most people on earth, says China underestimates its fin imports by anywhere from 24 to 49 percent.[3]

Clarke has made a career of studying shark fin trading. While she doesn't blend in with the crowd in Sai Ying Poon—she is British, with fair skin and strawberry blond hair—Clarke has lived in Asia for more than a dozen years, and is fluent in both Mandarin and Japanese. As a graduate student, she made it her mission to infiltrate shark trade auctions, to get a sense of which types of sharks ended up on the chopping block, since traders use names that are not strict translations and often correlate to, but are not identical with, certain species. (Basking shark falls into the "Nuo Wei Tian Jiu" fin category, for example, but it's not the Mandarin term for that species.) To ferret out these distinctions, Clarke—working with Mahmood Shivji, a Nova Southeastern University professor, and Ellen Pikitch, executive director of Stony Brook University's Institute for Ocean Conservation Science—used DNA analysis to figure out which species were being traded and then used mathematical formulas to get a sense of how many sharks are killed overall and sold each year for their fins.

Their conclusion: 73 million sharks are being caught and killed worldwide each year to supply the fin trade. And regardless of modest market shifts, Hong Kong remains the center of the global shark fin trade. The majority of shark fins come in by boat, though a small portion come in by plane: in 2006 a grand total of eighty-four countries shipped fins here, and by 2008 the number of nations had risen to eighty-seven. While the order shifts from time to time, the list of countries bringing fins to Hong Kong remains pretty much the same, with Spain, Singapore, Taiwan, Indonesia, and the United Arab Emirates topping the list. The United States used to rank relatively high until President Bill Clinton, facing little political resistance, established a shark-finning ban off America's coasts at the end of his term in office.

The shark fin trade encompasses anywhere from thirty to forty different kinds of sharks at any given time, though the Hong Kong market tends to focus on about fourteen species, ranging from blue shark to scalloped hammerhead. Still, it's size rather than species that matters when it comes to price. Shark fins can sell for $880 per pound or more on the Hong Kong market, and a single fin from a basking shark—the second-largest fish in the world—sold in Singapore in 2003 for $57,000 (all values throughout are in U.S. dollars).

While several species, like the great white, whale, and basking sharks, are prized for their immensity, it's the fish nicknamed "the rabbit of the sea" that keeps the fin market humming. Blue sharks are the workhorses, the ones that reproduce regularly and aren't about to chew the fishermen who catch them into little bits. They make up at least 17 percent of the international shark fin trade, according to Clarke and Shivji, which means at least 10.7 million blue sharks—which fishermen from Mexico to Indonesia pull ashore—are killed annually. When you match those numbers with the stock assessments fishery experts have done of blue shark populations in the Atlantic and north Pacific, it comes close to those stocks' "maximum sustainable yield." And the fact that we're taking as many blue sharks out of the sea each year as it can afford to give up worries Clarke, since, in her words, "any catch that approaches or exceeds this level is of concern."

Fins arrive in Hong Kong because the place epitomizes trading. More than a decade after the United Kingdom relinquished its 155-year-old hold on Hong Kong and handed it to China as a "special administrative region," this 426-square-mile territory of roughly seven million people still excels at buying and selling goods. (Ten years after the handover, it had a higher per capita gross domestic product than Europe's four biggest economies, as well as Japan's.) At times the major islands that make up Hong Kong resemble different versions of the same mall, with air-conditioning blasting from shops into the streets and brightly colored neon signs touting different products with unbridled enthusiasm.

Decades ago, when Hong Kongers were more focused on producing goods rather than just passing them along, they used to hunt sharks. As far back as 1940, one Hong Kong resident named S. Y. Lin reported, "Sharks are plentiful, sharks are everywhere," and by the 1960s a specific fishery aimed at catching sharks had started booming here. Shark slaying was never a prestigious occupation: most fishermen belonged to a social caste called the Hokklos, hailing from China's Guangdong and Fujian provinces. Treated like social outsiders, Hokklos remain segregated today in Hong Kong society and can occasionally be spotted walking the streets in hobo-like clothing.

As overfishing depleted Hong Kong's local shark populations, its fishery went bust in the 1980s. But that only marked the beginning of the ascent of Hong Kong's shark fin market. The island's unique status in China made it the perfect place to traffic in shark fins. Under "one country, two systems," which governs China's relationship with Hong Kong, the former British colony is allowed to continue its particular brand of capitalism: bringing things in and shipping them out without imposing heavy tariffs.

If anyone is in charge of the shark fins coming into and out of Hong Kong, it's Cheung Chi-sun, who serves as senior endangered species protection officer for Hong Kong's Agriculture, Fisheries, and Conservation Department. Cheung is an elegant, kindly bureaucrat who has worked in the department for more than two decades. He attends international conferences like the Convention on International Trade in Endangered Species of Wild Fauna and Flora, which is held every three years, and he compiles plenty of statistics about the comings and goings of shark fins in his corner of the world. But he doesn't do much about it: his agency simply charges an administrative fee that amounts to about eighty cents per shipment of fins.

"In general, there's no control," Cheung explains to me as we sit in his cramped government office. "It all depends on how you see these kinds of things. Some people will say all things should be protected, and the government should regulate these things. On the other side, there is the argument for free trade."

Cheung and the Hong Kong government side with the free traders. "Fisheries in Hong Kong is not an important business," he continues. "Hong Kong is basically a very commercial, or financial, city." And when it comes to preserving sharks, he adds, "it's not a single country's responsibility; it's a global responsibility."

All the same, Cheung sees the identical numbers that Shelley Clarke does, and as he nears retirement, he's beginning to wonder if the boxes of fins moving through Hong Kong indicate a problem. Cheung envisions a world of "sustainable trade," where the sharks that fishermen take out of the sea each year are replaced through natural births. Whether that's happening, he says, "we really don't know. I must admit the volume of trade is really alarming . . . For thousands of years people are using natural resources for human benefit. The problem is people are using too much, so there may not be enough for the next generation."

While Cheung and others envision a world in which a moderate, regulated shark trade could thrive, this is an illusion. With a handful of possible exceptions, sharks cannot be harvested sustainably because they cannot reproduce rapidly enough to offset these human-induced losses. A sustainable shark fishery is as unrealistic as reasonable bald eagle hunting.

Several decades ago the world made a decision it was no longer acceptable to hunt whales, and in 1986 the international whaling moratorium took effect. Three countries have defied the ban over the years—Japan, Norway, and Iceland—along with a handful of aboriginal groups who were exempted from the moratorium at the outset. In each case, these societies argue whaling represents such a strong cultural tradition they should not have to abandon it altogether. The same arguments can be applied to sharks, of course. But for the most part the international community has rejected this line of reasoning, concluding that there are some marine animal populations that humanity has depleted to such an extent that they need extraordinary new protections if they are to survive. It is hard to make these policy decisions when the answer involves absolutes and there is no obvious compromise. But in certain instances, science gives us no other alternatives.

On a hot, humid evening in July, my friend Candice To and I make our way down Hong Kong's Hennessy Road to grab a bite to eat. Candice and I are searching for seafood, and we find it in Tanyoto restaurant, an impressive-looking, multistoried establishment that overlooks the busy thoroughfare.

While different parts of sharks' bodies can serve different purposes, depending on cultures and regions of the world, shark fin has just one purpose: to make soup. Since so much of sharks' current predicament stems from the rising demand for shark's fin soup, I want to taste it for myself, and this seems like as good a place as any. The dining room is draped in sparkling white Christmas lights, and the wait-staff displays the kind of intense efficiency I've come to associate with Hong Kong. Our server sports a black suit and has an elaborate piece of technology firmly attached to his ear, reminiscent of what a Secret Service agent would wear.

While I had heard of shark's fin soup costing enormous sums—$100 or more for a bowl that serves four people—Tanyoto's version seems like a bargain, at just $10 for a single serving. Within minutes our waiter brings a small, covered ceramic bowl to our table and sets it down, barking into his earpiece the entire time. He removes the cover with great fanfare, for my inspection. This is the famed *yu chi,* or fish wing, soup, which started in southern China but has now spread to every Asian outpost in the world.

I stare down at the concoction, which resembles a traditional noodle soup with seafood thrown in: a golden broth suspending items ranging from small prawns to unidentified circular objects. It looks perfectly attractive, but not extraordinary.

Candice dips her chopsticks into the bowl, digging for some elusive target. "Here it is, no, here, here I've found it," she declares, capturing a tiny, gelatinous string that measures an inch at most.

"That's shark fin?" I ask, incredulous. "You're kidding me."

"No, no, that's it," Candice replies.

I have found one of the primary sources of our global fishing frenzy. It is a translucent, tasteless bit of noodle, known in scientific terms as ceratotrichia, that fans out to support the fin in any given shark. This is the moment that I come face-to-face with shark's fin soup's amazing secret: it is one of the greatest scams of all time, an emblem of status whose most essential ingredient adds nothing of material value to the end product.

There are plenty of tasty but morally objectionable food items on the market: foie gras, which requires farmers to force-feed geese repeatedly; veal, which entails raising baby calves in cramped conditions before killing them; and fatty bluefin tuna, whose populations have been devastated in recent years as fishermen have sought to satisfy the upscale sushi market's considerable demand. While critics can make a strong argument for why these practices should be abolished—cities like Chicago have even banned the sale of foie gras on the grounds that the process of making it is too cruel to be tolerated—even they would acknowledge this suffering yields a gastronomic payoff. This is not the case with shark fin, which could be replaced with a plain rice noodle at a moment's notice.

This is the most stunning aspect of the entire economic empire that has arisen around shark's fin soup: it is, to be blunt, a food product with no culinary value whatsoever. It is all symbol, no substance. Throughout my time in Hong Kong, I asked whether a noodle substitute, which could feature the same stringy texture and lack of taste, would succeed in the marketplace. No one, not even the most ardent environmental activists, seemed willing to entertain this idea. It would be deceptive, they reasoned, to coax consumers into eating a shark's fin soup devoid of its central ingredient. Millions of people who scarf down California sushi rolls with fake crabmeat do not seem to have a problem with seafood-product substitution, but for some reason restaurateurs and conservationists alike are worried about asking shark's fin soup eaters to make the same sort of swap. Since the central premise behind shark's fin soup rests on the act of killing the shark itself, rather than the pleasure in eating it, there's no way to save the animal and still preserve the value of its namesake dish.

The people who produce shark's fin soup don't pretend this ingredient adds anything substantive to their product. One afternoon I am lucky enough to get an exclusive crash course in the making of shark's fin soup, and I can testify that shark fins are the least important part of the recipe.

Norman Ho is director of the Coral Seafood Restaurant on Des Voeux Road, in the heart of Hong Kong's dried-seafood district. He's an interior decorator by trade, having run a restaurant for two years in the late 1970s before switching over to decorating eating establishments full-time. In 2004 he took over the Coral Seafood Restaurant, a multistoried edifice he had once decorated.

Part of Ho's business is shark's fin soup. The restaurant's mainstay is dim sum, which it serves every day. But the majority of the business's income comes from the seafood and fish it serves, and shark's fin soup alone makes up as much as 20 percent of the restaurant's total take. During our talk Ho did some quick calculations in his head and realized that he serves 2,820 bowls a month of the stuff: a large bowl runs just under $80, with a small bowl costing a little more than $25. Ho is not particularly eager to peddle shark's fin soup: it's a hassle to make, and he says it's not as big a profit maker as some might assume because it costs so much to prepare. "Being a seafood restaurant, we have to sell everything," he explains. "It's the customers' request. If they have a wedding banquet, they order it. We don't want to sell shark's fin, but it's the customers' request."

Ho's problem is not that he's worried about sharks—"You can take them for a long, long time," he says—it's the fact that making shark's fin soup is an elaborate, costly process. He starts with the dried triangular fin that likely came into Hong Kong but was transported by barge on the Pearl River delta to Guangdong, China, where labor is cheaper and there are looser water pollution and sewage laws. It takes two to three days to process the fins, which are immersed in hot water before workers use a knife to remove the fin scales manually, along with the main bone. In the old days these fins would dry in the sun for a few days; now they're shoved into an oven for a few hours. (Ho says he still prefers sun-dried fins: "I can tell whether a fin has been dried in an oven. It's softer; a fin dried in sunlight will not bend.") Some shark fins need to be plunged into hot water again for anywhere between three and eight hours after the oven treatment, while others do not. The cream-colored fins Ho imports resemble massive feathers or quills, with one very smooth side. They smell vaguely fishlike, but in a nonoffensive way, and the price they fetch varies based on what sort of fin they are. Pectoral fins produce the most membrane-like "needles," as they're called, while dorsal and triangular fins offer up a more modest yield, making them less valuable.

Once the fins arrive, Coral Seafood Restaurant workers put the fins in cold tap water for half a day to soften them and then transfer them to hot water with ginger and spring onions to boil them. At this point the shark fin and the needles will be tender, and kitchen workers will soak them in tap water for four more hours. The entire preparation amounts to a winnowing process, leaving an end product that is just 30 percent the weight of the original fin. At that point the fin and the needles can be boiled for six to eight hours with chicken stock and Chinese ham to produce shark's fin soup's base: cooks will throw in plenty of meat, ham, chicken, and pork to add flavor, because Ho knows the same thing I discovered during my shark's fin soup tasting. "There's no taste," he says flatly. "All the taste comes from the soup. You have to put the shark fin and the soup together . . . To serve the shark's fin soup is more or less status." The power of shark's fin soup to convey status on those who consume it is enormous, and it pervades Chinese society. A coterie of interests have helped cultivate the delicacy's elevated status, from popular restaurants to wedding planners. While serving shark's fin soup at nuptials has been a tradition for many years among elites, the Chinese bridal industry has turned it into an essential element of any middle-class wedding. As China's economy expands, this means more and more wedding parties are putting it on the menu. Priscilla Chang, who works at Moon Love Wedding Planner & Production, makes sure that every one of her clients adds it to the list for their wedding day. "For people who attend the wedding, their friends and relatives, to judge whether the banquet is good, they'll look at the fish and the shark fin," Chang explains.

Most Hong Kong couples—and many mainland Chinese ones—buy set wedding packages, and it's the quality of the shark's fin soup, and the fish, that determines the price of the package. The soup alone accounts for 20 percent of the package price, Chang estimates. The soup even plays a key role in the banquet ritual itself: once it comes out and the couple has finished eating it, they have received their cue to visit each table and toast their guests. Everyone seems to acknowledge this: when I ask, through a translator, whether a young bride and her mother ever quarreled in her presence over the question of whether to serve shark's fin soup, Chang seems surprised at the question. "Everybody wants fins," she responds.

In the end, even a glamorous Western icon like the Four Seasons Hotel is no different from Coral Seafood Restaurant. From its perch on Finance Street, the Four Seasons Hotel has one of Hong Kong's best views, with a massive glass front overlooking Victoria Harbor. The hotel offers two ballrooms and five private restaurant dining rooms for couples looking to get hitched, along with a secluded room in the destination spa so the bride can prepare for the big event.

Nicola Chilton-Matsukawa, the hotel's spokeswoman, estimates the Four Seasons Hotel Hong Kong averages two hundred weddings a year, and all of them feature shark's fin soup. She looks a little pained when discussing the subject of shark fins, but hastens to emphasize that it's simply part of doing business in town.

"Weddings are a big business for us. And shark fin is a traditional part of the Chinese wedding banquet," she says. "It's just part of their culture. You can't not have it."

While shark fin purveyors primarily rely on major celebratory events to move their product, they also try to offer a range of health reasons to boost sales on a more regular basis. Lim, the auctioneer, says it "increases the amount of collagen in your bones." The owner of Yuen Fat Seafood Trading, Leung Cheong, whose store boasts an enormous four-foot-high ivory-colored fin wrapped with a red ribbon and encased in glass, says the fins "have anti-cancer properties, are for the kidney and for balancing the body."

Cheung, the Hong Kong fisheries official, doesn't buy all of that. He just knows that if his son had a wedding banquet, his parents would lecture him about serving shark's fin soup in order to preserve his family's good reputation. "It's some sort of showing of respect for the guests, not because it's good for your health," he says. "This is a tradition for maybe several hundred years."

Giam Choo Hoo, a Singapore-based representative of the shark fin industry, can tell you exactly how far back the shark's fin soup sipping tradition dates. It came to be considered a delicacy during the Sung Dynasty, which lasted from 960 to 1279, and it became an integral part of formal banquets during the Ming Dynasty in the fifteenth century. During that time, he says, a Chinese admiral named Cheng Ho journeyed to Africa with his fleet, and after seeing villagers discard the fins in favor of the meat, they came back with sharks as part of their bounty. But since Chinese fishermen were mainly focused on the meat, Giam says, people faced a quandary. "They thought, how are we going to use all of that?" The answer, of course, was shark's fin soup. Six centuries ago the world dismissed fins as worthless and tossed them aside; now it's the shark's body fishermen throw overboard while preserving its fins to generate cash.

As Giam explains this to me, I am surrounded by the shark fin trade heavyweights of Hong Kong. Lim, the secretary of Hong Kong's Sharkfin and Marine Products Association, has convened a special meeting in his organization's conference room for my benefit, so he and his colleagues can explain what exactly they do for a living. Giam has come in from Singapore; C. P. Mak—an elderly, balding gentleman with enormous, bushy white eyebrows whom everyone refers to as "the godfather of shark fins"—has come over from the street stall he still operates. Yip Chiu Sung, the association's heavyset vice chairman who heads its shark fin and sea cucumber team, in addition to running his own business, is there, as is the group's chairman, Chiu Ching Cheung. In the middle of the conference table there's a small plastic shark with gigantic white teeth encased in plastic, which strikes me as sort of endearing.

With me are two local university students I've brought along to translate. They represent the small but fervent pro-shark lobby in Hong Kong. Allen To and Shadow Sin, along with Vivian Lam, another graduate student, have begun to advocate for sharks within both academia and their own social circles, a sort of emerging rebellion against this long-held tradition. Once we leave the meeting with the fin traders, they explain how they are trying to shift public attitudes toward sharks.

Lam is a bubbly, brilliant researcher who studies marine science at the University of Hong Kong. A native Hong Konger, she is as devoted to her family and her puppy as she is to environmental conservation. This sparks conflict at home on occasion, like when she questions whether her father—who imports lumber from Thailand—is supporting illegal logging. (Under her prodding, Lam's father now adheres to a set of sustainable forestry practices.) Few moments have been as tense, however, as when Lam tried to resist eating shark's fin soup at a cousin's wedding in June 1999. Sitting with her family in Hong Kong's Convention and Exhibition Centre, surrounded by hundreds of guests, Lam whispered to her grandmother once the waiters whisked off the silver domes covering the bowls and set them down on the table. "I don't want to eat shark's fin soup anymore," she confided. "Can you eat it for me?"

Her grandmother was unrelenting. "You silly girl," she lectured Lam. "This is such a good shark's fin soup we have. It's already made. People will think you're ungrateful."

Lam gave in that day. But now that she's in her twenties, she, along with several of her friends, no longer eats shark's fin soup. The most environmentally conscious students at the University of Hong Kong now manage to reserve one or two "green tables" at their weddings where shark's fin soup isn't served: in fact, the university itself has adopted an anti-shark's-fin-soup policy. Tsui Lap Chee, the university's vice-chancellor, no longer lets professors or administrative officials expense shark's fin soup on their business meals. (Some university employees still try to skirt the rules, despite the vice-chancellor's best efforts.)

The attempt to make shark's fin soup socially unacceptable has moved in fits and starts. In March 2008, Delta Air Lines served "braised shark's fin soup with cucumber and fish maw" at its welcoming dinner celebrating the carrier's inaugural nonstop flight between Atlanta and Shanghai.[4] Other U.S. companies, however, have reversed course when it comes to serving the dish. When Disneyland opened for business in Hong Kong in 2005, the company declared it would serve shark's fin soup to its customers. The Sea Shepherd Conservation Society launched an all-out PR offensive against Disney, distributing T-shirts that depicted Mickey Mouse and Donald Duck holding knives over sharks that had been finned. At first, Hong Kong Disney-

land defended the practice, saying the theme park was simply trying to respect Chinese cultural values and would not use fins from
the three internationally protected sharks—basking, whale, and great
white—in their soup. But ultimately Disneyland backed down and
took the dish off the menu. Irene Chan, Hong Kong Disneyland's vice
president for public affairs, declared in the summer of 2005, "After
careful consideration and a thorough review process, we were not
able to identify an environmentally sustainable fishing source, leaving
us no alternative except to remove shark's fin soup from our wedding
banquet menu." Another Hong Kong theme park has gone further,
turning its refusal to sell shark's fin soup into a marketing ploy. James
Fin H2o is one of the main theme characters at Ocean Park, which
provides both amusement rides and a marine conservation message
for its customers. And more than fifty companies and institutions
operating in Hong Kong have now signed the World Wildlife Fund's
pledge to neither buy nor sell the soup as part of their corporate activities, a coalition that includes Swiss Re and the University of Hong
Kong as well as Pure Yoga and Mandarin Orange clothing.

A parade of Chinese celebrities have decried shark's fin soup,
including Yao Ming, the NBA star who once played for the Shanghai
Sharks, and the pop music idol Liu Huan, who have pledged not to
eat it.[5] The Singapore Chefs Association took the dish off the menu
for its 2009 annual dinner, a major break with tradition.[6] And in
some Asian cultures the delicacy has come to symbolize the excesses
of the idle rich: Japan's Princess Masako, married to Crown Prince
Naruhito, came under fire after a series of lavish meals, including
"shark fin soup at a top Chinese restaurant."[7]

Hong Kong restaurateurs know local popular sentiment about
sharks is shifting, but they're not worried. While shark's fin soup consumption is waning in Hong Kong, Norman Ho explains, this decline
is more than outpaced by the surging demand from mainland China.
"China is at the beginning of the cycle," he explains. "In China the
market for shark fin is growing as they are getting more and more
rich."

There was a time when shark's fin soup was frowned upon in China:

when Mao Tse-tung held power, such status symbols were seen as conveying undesirable class distinctions. Now that's the entire point. Poon Kuen Fai, a third-generation dried-seafood importer, sees this as part of a generational and economic shift. Poon, who was educated abroad and goes by the name Richard, runs one of Hong Kong's most prestigious stores in Sheung Wan, On Kee Dry Seafood. The store boasts a dizzying number of Chinese delicacies, including abalone, sea cucumber, and fish swim bladders, and its shark section is equally impressive: frozen shark with cartilage, dried fins, and instant shark's fin soup with bamboo fungi or chicken, your choice. Hong Kong's older generation viewed making shark's fin soup as an integral part of family rituals, but this allure has faded over time, and customers are only comfortable purchasing premade versions at this point.

"For my grandfather's and father's generation, shark's fin soup was quite popular," Poon explains as we sit in his executive office, a small suite on the second floor of his building that is sheltered from the frenetic movement of employees running back and forth to serve the flood of customers. "The younger generation doesn't know how to make the soup."

As a result, Poon explains, in Hong Kong people only order or prepare shark's fin soup for weddings or to celebrate the Chinese New Year. Rather than confine themselves to that market, shark fin sellers are marketing their product to suit mainland Chinese consumers. Some are even thinking of how "to farm the shark," he adds, following the model of salmon and shrimp farms. "The importance is how to continue the business," Poon says.

While shark farming seems improbable, given that these fish don't naturally congregate, there's no question that Hong Kong street vendors see mainland China as their customer base. Ming Li Hang has spent forty-five years of his life selling shark fins: on the afternoon that I pass by, he is patiently trimming fins as he sits on the street in front of his store. Ming has no interest in speaking to me, since he is hard at work. But his sister-in-law, a chatty woman who goes by the Anglicized name of Betty Cheung, is more than happy to discuss the details of their trade. The Hong Kong market is almost irrelevant to the family business. As Cheung observes, "In Hong Kong, nobody cooks at home." Instead, she estimates, they sell 80 percent of their fins to China (ironically, this entails having the fins undergo the circuitous route of traveling from Hong Kong to mainland China, back to Hong Kong, and then back to mainland China, but no one seems bothered by this) and 20 percent to a single Chinese restaurant in Canada. Chinese hotel operators sometimes come directly to the store to buy fins, Cheung says, along with tourists "coming down from mainland China to buy fins because the people in China are rich now." Business has never been better.

"We're selling more; the price is higher than before," Cheung says, smiling. While there are fewer fins available now, Cheung and most of the other shark fin vendors don't see this as a problem. "If you've got less, it's more expensive. People will still buy it."

This is one of the sad ironies of fishing economics: scarcity only accelerates the animals' demise. As a species becomes overexploited, the price shoots up, and the most rational thing to do is to continue fishing it in order to collect it before someone else does. The race only ends when the species in question becomes so scarce it's no longer worth pursuing, and at that point it's doomed. This is especially true when it comes to sharks because they—by definition—connote status, so an elevated price is not a barrier to sales.

Lin Ying Jui, another friendly shark fin seller in Sai Ying Poon, calls the shark fins in her shop "a luxury product," just like the swift birds' nests she and her husband sell. "If you're rich enough, you can afford it, if not, so be it," Lin says, adding that if sharks disappear from the sea altogether, "There's nothing we can do about it. We have to accept it."

Shark fin dealers feel embattled nowadays, and they point fingers at an array of people they see as the most hypocritical players in the conservation debate: Europeans who eat shark as part of their fish-and-chips habit, self-righteous Americans, and whiny environmentalists. Lim points out that Mexicans like to eat shark meat, for example, but no one blames Mexicans for the worldwide decline of sharks. And on a certain level, the Europeans bear responsibility as shark consumers and shark hunters.

Europeans like eating shark both as an elegant entrée and as the more plebeian offering of fish and chips; while you might not see the words "spiny dogfish" on a menu, it might be there nonetheless. According to the environmental group TRAFFIC, it will just be labeled "rock salmon" in Britain, *saumonette* in France, or *Schillerlocke* and *Seeaal* in Germany instead.[8] As Europeans have sought out the nearby fish that could meet their demand, the northeast Atlantic spurdog population—a European name for spiny dogfish, or *Squalus acanthias*—has dropped by 95 percent. Quite simply, they took as many sharks as they could off their shores until there weren't any left to catch, and then they began to look elsewhere. At this point the German fishing fleet catches 750 tons of shark annually, but the country imports another 14,000 tons each year to satisfy domestic demand. The German Federal Ministry of Food, Agriculture, and Consumer Protection tested an array of shark meat in February 2008 and reported that more than a fourth of the samples contained concentrations of the neurotoxin methyl mercury that violated both European and American health guidelines, but this has not hurt sales there.

But these nuances are lost on the traders' critics, Giam says. From activists to young people who are unwilling to work, he chimes in, "the whole world has been blaming the shark fins."

Yip, a man in his late sixties who heads the Dry Marine Product Trading Company, talks about his industry the same way an American farmer or fisherman might, as if he's the last generation who's willing to stick it out for the sake of the family business.

"The business is going down," Yip complains. "Nowadays, young people are not willing to work in this industry. Especially for the younger generation, they don't want to become fishermen. They want a more comfortable job. The smart guys, the professional guys, they run away from the business. Many young people are going out to work, maybe in IT, and make more money."

"Nobody wants to teach their son to do this business," Lim chimes in. "Nobody wants to get up at 6:30 in the morning to do work."

Nonetheless, these men are enormously invested in seeing their line of business survive. In Yip's eyes, Westerners simply fail to grasp the role shark's fin soup plays in Chinese culture. At the start of the interview, Yip spoke only in Cantonese, but as he and the other shark fin traders begin to question my assistants' translation skills, Yip decides to switch into English. "It's a misunderstanding of a Hong Kong tradition," he says. "They are very eco, Americans. Sometimes there's self-exaggerating Americans. I don't like them, strictly to the point."

At the same time, Yip admits he doesn't often eat shark's fin soup because "it's complicated to cook. My wife says, 'Don't bring home shark fin for me. I don't want to make it for you.' "

Just as shark fin traders are encountering resistance in their own kitchens, they recognize their product no longer has the same public appeal in Hong Kong. When Hong Kong Disneyland decided to banish shark's fin soup from its menu, Lim says, it was "a popular move." But this sort of activism has tarred shark fin traders as undesirable, he adds: "We are not so bad people. We want people to know the truth . . . We don't want sharks to disappear in the world. That would be bad."

Lim and his colleagues are determined to get the word out that they oppose finning, the practice where fishermen slice off a shark's fins and throw its body overboard in order to maximize profit and minimize the amount of cargo they have to haul back to shore. Lim tries to conjure up an improbable image to make his argument.

"Put a shark on the table and try to get a fin while it is alive," he says, getting visibly animated. "It is very difficult to get a fin from a live animal. Try it at home."

Lim is right, of course: chopping off a live shark's fin would pose a challenge to even the most skilled sushi chef. But his assertion—that shark finning cannot happen because it would be nearly impossible to pull off—is false, since fishermen only fin sharks once the fish are no longer alive. By the time fishing vessels haul their catch on board, most of the sharks are dead, and if they're not dead, the crew proceeds to kill them.

For something that's worth a lot of money, shark fins don't have the elaborate pricing system of other commodities, such as coffee or diamonds. Every time I press shark fin dealers about how they value their product, they're fairly vague, and it's not that they're being deliberately evasive. Several dealers say they can't be entirely sure where the fins they sell come from; Lim says when it comes to setting a price, it depends on "how big or small, that's all," along with the question of supply and demand. "Many times we don't know where they come from. They can come from one country and be reexported to another country." In the free-flowing Hong Kong market, the origins of any single batch of fins quickly become murky.

The shark fin trade remains an old-school business for the most part, with few of the modern practices that have come to define other commercial ventures in Hong Kong. All of the men I'm sitting with at this conference table have devoted their entire lives to dried seafood. Mak—the one they call "the godfather"—started work at seventeen and borrowed money from his relatives to operate his own stall, a stall he still runs today. These are men who survived the economic downturn that followed the 1997 handover to China, and they want to keep going until they retire.

Maybe that's why Lim is so intense about defending the honor of what he calls "a 170-year-old industry. We are one of Hong Kong's small businesses. We don't want to spoil the name of Hong Kong." He has little patience for my questions about the rules governing the auctions he runs—when I ask why a buyer has sixty days to hand over the money he's bid on one of the shark fin lots, Lim replies, "I would have to ask about 170 years ago, why did you do this system? All this is a business game."

Lim says fin traders have an overarching goal at this point: "We are trying to find somebody to save the shark." While that seems improbable, given that their entire business is dependent on killing sharks, toward the end of our last conversation he points out that at the end of the day, the market for shark fins is a world market. "This is not the only place," he tells me. "The whole world would have to think about this."

Sarah Fowler is the kind of person who has to think about what Lim is saying. Co-chair of the Shark Specialist Group at the International Union for Conservation of Nature, Fowler is—more than most scientists—responsible for gauging whether sharks are in trouble. Each year the IUCN Shark Specialist Group tallies up how shark populations are doing and assigns them to categories that describe their particular predicament (critically endangered, endangered, vulnerable, and so on): right now, as many as one-third of all species are threatened with extinction. Like that of many international bureaucratic organizations, the Shark Specialist Group's membership boasts a sprawling mix of personalities from a range of different backgrounds, and it takes tremendous diplomatic skills to keep it functioning. That is why, in part, Fowler invited Lim to join her organization a few years ago.

A number of factors prompted the move. It's better to have your opponents inside the fold than outside, she reasons, and Lim and his colleagues can offer conservationists information they cannot obtain from anyone else.

"I don't believe we can truly understand what the fisheries are until we understand what the trade is," Fowler says. We're sitting in the lobby of a hotel in Morro Bay, California, during a break in an annual meeting of some of the world's most elite marine biologists, far away from the Hong Kong streets that we've both traversed in search of shark fin traders. When Lim and Giam told me that they had reached out to Fowler several years ago on the issue of shark finning, I wasn't quite sure whether to believe them. But they were telling the truth, and Fowler sees their collaboration as a way of deciphering the often impenetrable world of fin trading. "We have a huge amount to learn, which they can teach us."

Rather than shunning the Hong Kong traders, Fowler hopes to win them over with the argument that they, in the words of Lim, could be the "somebody to save the shark."

"I do not believe it's in their interest, any more than it's in the interest of conservationists, to have their supply dry up," she argues.

Fowler is trying to win fin traders over with a straightforward economic argument: if they scale back on fishing sharks, they could make shark's fin soup into a rare treat, and guarantee their business will not die when they do. But while shark's fin soup has symbolized wealth and influence for centuries, it appears to be on the verge of going down-market. According to a report by the conservation group WildAid, this legendary dish has become so commonplace that some Singapore restaurants offer all-you-can-eat shark fin buffets for $8.99, and Japanese stores are stocked with shark's fin cookies, bread, and cat food. It's become just another product, no different from the tiny cameras and sleek eyeglass frames that you can get for cut-rate prices at the stores lining Hong Kong's Times Square. That means it now poses an even greater threat to sharks, since it will take an increasingly large supply to meet this demand.

"If it was my family business," Fowler says drily, "I would be worried."

Lim and his colleagues have devised a short-term plan to address their business concerns: press as hard as possible to expand the shark fin market in mainland China. The elegant coastal city of Shanghai—with its gleaming high-rise buildings, booming financial market, and sizable group of nouveau riche—has become a key target for what residents call *yue cai,* or Hong Kong food. In June 2010 Lim made a pilgrimage there to make his sales pitch to Shanghai's Department of Wildlife Conservation officials and Xu Hongfa, who leads the TRAFFIC wildlife trade program based at WWF China. Touting the quality of Hong Kong's dried seafood, Lim sketched out a vision of Shanghai as the next big shark fin market. And Lim has some reason to hope he can make inroads here, since the number of small shops selling fins have started to proliferate in Shanghai, even on the edges of the university campus where Xu Hongfa teaches. "Demand is high," says Xu, who opposes the shark fin trade but adds the lack of international limits on shark fishing makes regulation nearly impossible in China.

Xing Ping, a seafood and dried goods market in Shanghai's wealthy Xu Hui district, offers a glimpse into the city's growing shark fin trade. Only a handful of shops explicitly display the product; for the most part potential buyers have to offer money first and describe what sort of fins they'd like to purchase before a shopkeeper will bring any out. But wedged in between offerings such as dried red pepper, black fungus, and an array of noodles, the shark fins are there, costing anywhere from the equivalent of $100 to $200 for half a kilo. Lin Mei Yu, whose family has run the market's largest shark fin market since the start of the twenty-first century, is the rare exception, displaying more than a dozen bags of shark fins in her glass-paneled shop. All of her fins come from Hong Kong, and the vast majority of them are headed for the city's hotels, where chefs will prepare them for their highest-paying customers. In Shanghai, the future of shark fin trading looks bright.

And this demand for shark fins, moreover, is actually fueling the demand for shark meat as far away as Africa. Mozambicans have not traditionally consumed sharks. But as they've begun finning off their southern coast over the past decade to satisfy Asian suppliers, a local business in shark meat has boomed. Alice Costa, marine program coordinator for the WWF Mozambique Country Office, says coastal residents in her country now see the flesh of everything from whale sharks to snaggletooth sharks as akin to beef. "Now the Mozambicans are changing their culture," Costa explains. "They're going for the shark meat instead of the fish." It becomes a feedback loop, where everyone along the supply chain is now invested in catching sharks.

But if Asian shark fin traders want a glimpse at the future, they might want to look at what has happened in the United States, where the demand for shark products has already peaked and crashed. Ironically, several Americans spent years trying to commodify an animal that was widely hated, only to see the entire business collapse.

It took years to convince Americans that sharks were worth anything at all. In 1928, O. W. Barrett, the agricultural director of the Department of Agriculture and Labor in San Juan, Puerto Rico, wrote a report titled "Shark Fishing in the West Indies." Aimed at the U.S. audience, it detailed an array of potential uses for the sharks swimming within reach of America's shores. Each product made from "that much hated denizen of the deep" had promise, Barrett argued. Sharkskin leather might hold the widest appeal—"Of beautiful leathers there is no end, but none better, it seems, than shagreen," he wrote—but dried shark fillets "are a great boon to the housewife who never, even under the most favorable circumstances, likes the work of 'dressing' a fish herself." Shark meat discards could serve as fertilizer, he enthused, while shark teeth had a place in the commercial market as well. "By the way, mounted on pieces of turtle shell, these shark teeth make excellent watch-fobs; their indescribable shape, brilliant white color, and serrate, curved edges make very attractive ornaments." Barrett's marketing plan had a hint of revenge as well, since his basic premise was that there was ample justification for killing them:

> We have been hating sharks on general principles for centuries, and in some ways they have deserved it; but now it is high time that they should pay up. There are no more interesting animals in the world, and the ways and means of turning them into cash constitute one of the most fascinating of our modern industries.[9]

Shortly after Barrett wrote his shark-killing manifesto, shark medicinal products began to take off. In the 1930s and 1940s, merchants began selling shark-liver oil as both a lubricant and a source of vitamin A. When Germany invaded Norway in 1940, the United States could no longer get access to cod-liver oil. That led to a spike in shark fishing off the Pacific coast, where fishermen targeted soupfin sharks. The price of soupfins rocketed up from $40 to $1,500 per ton, and the Borden Company even started a shark division to obtain the vitamin A it needed for its milk.[10] This fishing frenzy caused the soupfin shark population to collapse: only recently have scientists concluded the species has largely recovered. Manufacturers figured out a way to create a synthetic substitute for vitamin A, eliminating the need for shark-liver oil. Today merchants have found a different medicinal use for sharks: they use chondroitin, which comes from shark cartilage and usually takes a powdered form, to ease arthritis or help craft artificial skin for burn victims. But this market doesn't reach quite the same scale as the vitamin A boomlet in the mid-twentieth century.

In one of the most recent marketing ploys, beauty companies have touted the benefits of using shark products to preserve women's youthful appearance. In the summer of 2007 the Washington, D.C.–based advocacy group Oceana launched a public relations campaign aimed at halting the sale of shark squalene, an organic compound found in the animals' livers. It's an odd ingredient to be touting in the first place: squalene and squalane, a product derived from squalene, are found in high concentrations in the livers of deepwater sharks, which they use to regulate their buoyancy. Beauty companies advertise it as a natural, "oil-free" moisturizer that enhances everything from anti-aging creams to lip gloss.

Oceana's chief scientist, Michael Hirshfield, and his colleagues discovered the marketing of squalene by accident. A consumer sent them an e-mail asking about the product after receiving a pitch from a doctor based in West Virginia. After doing some digging, they found out a company—ironically, named Oceana—was selling it as a skin enhancer in the Vermont Country Store, a venerable and quirky institution better known for selling inexpensive dresses for old ladies and socks aimed at mitigating athlete's foot. The New England store was not alone: popular cosmetic brands such as Pond's and Dove also use the compound for their products.

While Pond's didn't exactly shout about its shark-liver oil, the Vermont Country Store touted its $29.95 bottle of the company's Bio-Marine Topical Deep Water Squalane with all the enthusiasm of 1950s admen. "Japanese women are admired the world around for their complexions as smooth as porcelain," the copy read, juxtaposed with an image of a clear two-ounce bottle with a smiling blue shark atop it. "What's their secret? 100 percent natural squalane, derived from the livers of deep-water sharks and used in some of the most elusive and effective beauty formulas for over 100 years. Because squalane also occurs naturally in humans, our skin can quickly and completely absorb this fragrance-free oil, making it extremely effective in reducing lines and moisturizing dry skin."

Oceana—the environmental group, not the shark-peddling firm—is the sort of organization that specializes in launching public advocacy campaigns with a specific policy goal: in one of their most successful campaigns, they embarrassed several major cruise lines into treating their sewage rather than dumping it, untreated, into the open ocean.

Their lobbying is aimed mainly at influencing the public's perception of a given company: in the case of squalene, they wrote a series of open letters suggesting that major cosmetic companies should be ashamed of using the product. "Although companies are selling deep-sea shark products as 'pure' and 'natural' and 'wild'—all great marketing words—what they're doing is the same as peddling endangered rhinoceros horn or elephant ivory," Hirshfield says, scoffing.

Within a matter of months, the companies backed down in the face of the activists' campaign and jettisoned squalene. It wasn't too hard a sell: botanical sources such as rice bran, wheat germ, amaranth seeds, and olives can also yield squalene, and the fact that deepwater sharks are considered among the most vulnerable sharks around made the practice particularly distasteful. By January 2008 the Vermont Country Store took BioMarine Topical Deep Water Squalane off its shelves, and Unilever, the London-based manufacturer that produces Pond's and Dove, announced it would use a plant-based version of squalene instead. And exactly a year later Dr. Susan Lark, a major supplier of squalene-based cosmetic products, agreed to stop using the ingredient after receiving complaints from fifteen thousand members of the environmental group Oceana.

In this age of corporate responsibility, after all, some beauty manufacturers don't want to be responsible for driving a species to the brink of extinction. "Unilever is committed to running its business on a sustainable basis and we have a policy of not using products from species that are either in danger or in decline," wrote Gavin Neath, Unilever's senior vice president for global corporate responsibility, to the executive director for Oceana Europe, Xavier Pastor, in a December 10, 2007, letter. "As such I can confirm we have identified, and started to take steps to remove from our products, any squalene with animal origins and will replace it with plant based versions (including the Pond's brand that you mention in your letter)." That allowed Oceana—the ocean advocacy group—to declare victory.

The PR battle over squalene represents just the latest debate over claims that shark products can stave off aging and disease. For years, health-food stores have touted shark cartilage as a way to halt cancer, selling it in the form of powder-containing pills. The theory behind the product is that shark cartilage contains a substance that inhibits the growth of blood vessels—angiogenesis—that help tumors expand: if the vessels stop developing, so will the tumors. These products actually stem from what had been legitimate scientific research in the 1970s, when Judah Folkman, chief of surgery at Children's Hospital Boston, conducted tests using animal cartilage to see if it had angiogenic properties. The initial research—on rabbits—was promising, and studies later conducted by a former student of Folkman's and a new collaborator raised the possibility of inhibiting tumors by implanting shark cartilage pellets. While some studies of angiogenesis continue to this day, scientists were unable to reproduce these results with humans, so credible researchers gave up on the idea of using shark cartilage to cure cancer.

Still, a biochemist named I. William Lane seized upon these findings and co-authored a book in 1992 titled *Sharks Don't Get Cancer: How Shark Cartilage Could Save Your Life*. Lane got a major shot of publicity in 1993 from a segment by the newsmagazine *60 Minutes;* in 1996 he received a patent to market shark cartilage pills and co-wrote a second book titled *Sharks Still Don't Get Cancer*. Later, he founded a company called LaneLabs USA, headed by his son Andrew, and started selling a product called BeneFin that he claimed would help fight cancer.

In September 1997 the Food and Drug Administration issued a warning letter to LaneLabs stating that BeneFin—along with two of the company's other products that claimed to treat skin cancer and AIDS—violated the law because LaneLabs was marketing it as a drug rather than as a dietary supplement. When the company ignored the letter, FDA officials sued in 1999 to halt the sale of BeneFin and the two other products altogether.

It took five years, but on July 13, 2004, William G. Bassler, a federal judge in New Jersey, ruled the products amounted to unapproved new drugs. He issued a permanent injunction against their sale and ordered LaneLabs to pay restitution to anyone who purchased BeneFin and the two other supposed cures since September 22, 1999. The FDA's acting commissioner at the time, Lester M. Crawford, welcomed the decision, saying it sent "a strong signal that the promotion and sale of unapproved drug products, especially for the treatment of cancer and other serious diseases, will not be tolerated."

Since that legal decision, most of the American medical establishment has done its best to debunk shark cartilage treatments as a cancer cure-all. The National Cancer Institute reviewed the findings from the experiment trial Lane and his colleagues conducted in Cuba and called them "incomplete and unimpressive." Gary Ostrander, a research dean at Johns Hopkins University, investigated the claim that sharks are immune to cancer by sifting through the National Cancer Institute's Registry of Tumors in Lower Animals and found forty instances where sharks and their closest relatives, skates and rays, experienced benign and malignant tumors.[11] Lane concedes this point in his second book, though he dismisses it as immaterial, writing, "While *ALMOST No Sharks Get Cancer* might have been a bit more accurate, it would have been a rotten title."

In the most telling rebuke, the Mayo Clinic oncologist Charles L. Loprinzi and scientists in the North Central Cancer Treatment Group designed and conducted a rigorous test of whether shark cartilage improves the health of patients with breast and colorectal cancer. The study—a randomized, placebo-controlled, double-blind trial—showed the patients taking shark cartilage enjoyed neither an improvement in their condition nor a significant boost in their quality of life. In some cases, the patients taking the pills saw their quality of life deteriorate. The authors wrote in the July 1, 2005, issue of *Cancer,* the American Cancer Society's peer-reviewed journal, "Shark cartilage did not demonstrate any efficacy in patients with advanced breast or colorectal cancers."

While sharks possess a range of fascinating properties, they cannot stave off human mortality or aging. To suggest otherwise merely perpetuates the sorts of myths that have surrounded this fish for centuries.

Some U.S. fishermen used to make careers out of satisfying Americans' demand for shark, but the market they used to cater to has virtually disappeared. No career better exemplifies this arc than that of Eric Sander, a Daytona Beach, Florida, fisherman who has been intrigued by sharks since he was a little boy. A graduate of the University of South Florida with a natural sciences degree, he started working as a mate on a charter boat out of Daytona in the early 1980s. During the wintertime the charter-boat operations switched to commercial fishing in order to make up for the lull in tourism. They usually focused on bringing in snapper, grouper, and king mackerel, the sorts of fish that commanded the highest market prices. The charter boats would unload their catches at the end of the day on a dock near a few local restaurants, and on the rare occasions when they had snagged a shark by mistake, Sander remembers, it would draw a crowd. "You could drop all the amberjack and mackerel you want; if you dropped a big shark on the dock, everybody came down to your boat." Still, it was just for show: nobody was interested in buying the sandbar or black-tip shark the charter-boat operators were plunking down upon their return.

In 1983, Sander and his brother decided to strike out on their own and start commercial fishing full-time. They bought their own thirty-two-foot boat, christened it *Jawsome,* and headed out to make a living. They began setting longlines for king mackerel and other species and, on occasion, found themselves pulling up sharks. At the same time, federal fisheries managers were trying to ease up the pressure on groupers, and they started putting out literature on how sharks could appeal to restaurants that were seeking to broaden their menu offerings. Sander and his brother went to work outfitting the *Jawsome* for the task.

"We kind of jerry-rigged a longline system, and, lo and behold, we could sell sharks," Sander recalls, adding they relied on a hand crank to pull up the line. "In 1984 we went full-time shark fishing. We had tremendous success."

In the first year, the two fishermen brought in fifty thousand pounds of shark. "Everybody was watching us," he says. And within a matter of months, other fishing operations started imitating them. A fleet blossomed in Daytona Beach, supplying a steady local market with meat and fins. While selling the meat covered the fishermen's operating costs, the fins represented pure profit.

"It wouldn't have been as attractive if that money for the fins wasn't there. That was bonus money, gravy money," Sander relates. The price of fins kept going up, from $4 a pound to $9, to $10 and $12, and beyond. The shark fin dealers would gather on the dock, and the fishermen would have their choice of buyers.

By the late 1990s, however, the shark catches began to dwindle, and Sander noticed. He thought it might be time to go "up the hill," or start working onshore. After a Florida marine patrol officer saw him sorting fins on the dock, enforcement officers hired Sander as a consultant to nab illegal shark traders. He now works full-time for the Florida Fish and Wildlife Conservation Commission as regional coordinator for its Marine Recreational Fisheries Statistical Survey, asking anglers dockside what they've been catching.

Sander knows many shark populations have been declining off the Atlantic coast: he's seen it himself, and he emphasizes, "They're not just another commodity. They serve an important function in the ocean." But even though he regularly helps enforcement officers spot illegally caught sharks, he doesn't see himself as someone on a mission to save the animal he once hunted. Sander still sees it as a fish that might as well be on the menu of Daytona Beach restaurants.

For Sander, working enforcement is just another job, not some sort of moral mission. "I'm not really concerned with it. I'm out of the industry; I have been since 1998," he offers. "I'm not looking to make things right and restore it back to the level that it's been before."

From a practical perspective, it would be nearly impossible to bring the American shark fishery back to pre-exploitation levels. At this point, shark products have become relegated to a niche market, which provides enough of a commercial incentive to keep a relatively low level of fishing active off U.S. shores. There are shark teeth in South Carolina road stop knickknack stores, mako shark on the list of regular menu offerings at Atlantic Seafood Company in an Atlanta strip mall. They remain a banal relic, an allusion to an ancient seafaring lifestyle that is rapidly disappearing. As the sharks disappear, so does our connection to the sea.

In Kesennuma City in Japan, one entrepreneur has spent the last half century seeking a middle way when it comes to the shark trade. Kesennuma is a relatively small port in a country that defines itself as a seafaring nation: fewer than seventy thousand people live there, and the city's fish market lands close to $30 million worth of fish a year. But its residents have taken full advantage of the region's fertile fishing grounds—Japanese call its jagged coastline the Rias Coast, referring to its sawtooth-like shape, and it straddles two separate bays—for centuries. And the Pacific coast's riches continue to define the city's identity and economy.

Three hundred years ago Kesennuma fishermen ventured out in small wooden boats to catch sharks, a time-consuming and dangerous process that helped sustain the local population. Now the city is a lively port where fishing and tourism rank as the biggest moneymakers. As fishing vessels became more mechanized and sophisticated, area fishermen started targeting more lucrative species, such as tuna and Pacific saury, rather than focusing on sharks. But using sharp hooks attached to long lines of rope, they caught plenty of sharks anyway. And that gave Kasumasa Murata a major business opportunity.

Kasumasa Murata grew up far from here in western Japan, on Kyushu Island. But more than fifty years ago he married his wife, Yoneko, a Kesennuma native, and moved to her hometown. At the time Murata came here, the Japanese government was happy to help finance small industrial ventures in the fishing sector, and he decided the other merchants in Kesennuma were missing a possible source of income when they merely sliced off the fins from the sharks piling up on the city's dock and threw the rest away. "Shark fin in Kesennuma has been world famous, but other parts of the body have not been utilized very well," he says, sipping cold buckwheat tea in his fish market office. While fishermen in other countries still hack off the fin and throw the shark's body overboard, he adds, "that's not our style. I don't think that's good for the natural resource. Once we catch a shark, we utilize every part of the body."

Murata is not exaggerating. Since 1959 he has built up a small but efficient processing operation, a few minutes' drive from the port where the sharks come in each morning. The aging entrepreneur purchases half of all the fish that arrive at the dock all day, including most of the sharks: blue, mako, and salmon are the ones that swim off the coast here. A handful of workers immediately slice off the sharks' fins, which are still worth close to ten times as much as the rest of their bodies, before the remaining flesh is carted off to Murata's processing plant. The long, tubular bodies are placed in a watery holding pond for roughly six hours, to leach out the ammonia that dominates a shark's body once it's been killed.

The tiny factory Murata runs resembles a sausage-making plant more than anything else, with a touch of the assembly-line feel of an automobile factory. Each of the sharks goes through the identical process. A couple of employees skin them and place these skins into thirty-three-pound containers to be frozen, so they can be shipped to a separate facility and made into leather. Then they take out their cartilage spines, tossing them into a large, rectangular plastic bucket that is destined for yet another plant, where its contents can be dried and turned into a medicinal powder. The remaining shark meat is fed through multiple conveyers so it can be washed, sliced, and turned into light pink tubular noodles destined for a massive mixing bowl. ("It's pure stainless steel," Murata notes with pride as he takes me on a tour of his plant, pointing to the array of gleaming machines. "It is the best in Japan.") As the shark meat swirls around in the mixer, Murata's employees add the specific seasonings that his customers request. Some want sugar, others salt, and a few want some of each. Finally, workers smooth the shark paste that has been formed through this process into twenty-two-pound metal trays that they cover in bright blue saran wrap. It's ready for freezing in one of the building's cold-storage units, where it will wait until the trucks come each morning to ship it to different customers across Japan.

There is no waste in this efficient enterprise. Even the least-desirable shark meat becomes feed for cows, and the other shark by-products fetch an attractive price. The factory's main office includes a glassed-in display of shark leather items such as card holders, belts, purses, and pumps, all of which sell in the hundreds of dollars. Murata, who

wears a black shark-leather belt himself, boasts that he has shipped
the leather (which goes under the name KSP, or Kesennuma Shark
Products) to as far away as Hermès in Paris. He emphasizes that by
maximizing what he gets out of each shark, he's supporting his community and avoiding an ecological disaster at the same time. "Without taking care of the natural resource, we cannot survive, and we
cannot make the town prosperous."

It's unclear how sustainable this sort of fishing is: while the central
government ordered the town to slash its eighty-boat fishing fleet by
25 percent in the spring of 2008, and Murata says the fishermen take
pains to avoid areas where they know juvenile sharks swim, that is
likely not enough to ensure the sharks here survive. Mako sharks are
already vulnerable to extinction, according to the International Union
for Conservation of Nature, and scientists believe it's important to
protect older, more fecund females that will produce more offspring
than younger females.

While there are other shark processors in town, Murata—who also
heads the Kesennuma fish market cooperative—is comfortable with
his position of influence here. He bustles around his plant with cheerful authority and speaks glowingly of the financial model that helped
propel Japan to global economic prominence in the 1970s and 1980s.
He is nearing retirement but has two sons working in the business,
and is optimistic about shark fishing's future here.

Though tuna brings in roughly 30 percent more revenue than shark
in Kesennuma, the animal continues to help define the city and its food
culture. The local shark museum, located right next to the fish market, includes examples of small, tame sharks visitors can pet as well as
a battered diving cage they can enter. The city's restaurants advertise
shark's fin sushi and shark sashimi on their menus as local delicacies,
something that's rarely seen in other cities. Kesennuma was the first
Japanese city to join the Slow Food movement, and the Miyagi Prefecture government has started touting shark as an integral part of the
global push to eat locally. Its promotional literature, complete with
the inevitable cartoon figures, highlights shark's nutritional virtues.
"Rich in collagen and 6 times as much DHA as tuna!" the pamphlet
shouts, referring to docosahexaenoic acid, an omega-3 fatty acid. The

handout provides examples of the many shark preparations visitors and residents alike can savor, including shark burgers and shark stew. But even with the local government's help, businessmen like Murata face a major challenge at the moment. The Japanese, proud members of a marine nation, are eating less fish.

Yutaka Aoki, director of the Ministry of Foreign Affairs' Fishery Division within its Economic Affairs Bureau, flips through the government document before him. His eyes scanning bar graph after bar graph, he finally finds what he wants to show me. "Here it is," he declares, pointing to a chart of how Japanese protein consumption has evolved over time. For hundreds of years fish has occupied a central place in the country's diet, but cheap meat imports have begun to change that. In 2007, for the first time since the government has begun keeping statistics about citizens' daily eating habits, people reported eating an equal amount of fish and meat. A year later meat had edged out fish, by a tenth of a pound on a daily basis.

"The fishery agency is a little concerned about the change in lifestyle," Aoki admits. "Small children prefer meat." The Japanese government sees this transition to a more meat-based diet as a challenge on several fronts. It represents an assault on traditional culture. It is helping fuel a weight gain among the nation's youth. And it threatens what Aoki calls the nation's "food security." Few nations rival Japan for its ability to take fish out of the sea, but when it comes to supplying beef, pork, and chicken, most of it comes from countries such as the United States and Australia. Miyagi Prefecture is not the only institution to launch a fish-related public relations campaign; the central government has launched a drive to convince people that fish eating is key. But it may not work fast enough to help the fish-paste industry that Kasumasa Murata supplies.

Just like shark fishing in Kesennuma, Japanese fish paste has a long and storied history. Back in A.D. 1115, a minister for the emperor who hailed from the Fujiwara clan built a large house and held a party to celebrate his new home. According to the menu, he served a steamed loaf of fish paste cut into slices. Since it was wrapped around a piece of bamboo and took on the shape of the ear of a bulrush, or *kama,* it became known as *kamaboko.*[12] With the minister's culinary act, fish paste joined the ranks of traditional Japanese cuisine. To this day, the Japanese emperor and empress serve red and white *kamaboko* at official banquets.

But globalization, along with the depletion of fish stocks, has transformed Japanese fish paste over the years. Years ago a dozen regions across the country had their own distinctive form of fish paste, featuring different forms and species of fish. The rural Aomori Prefecture made *chikuwa,* a tube of paste hollowed out in the center lying on a wooden board. They made it out of the small dogfish sharks they caught, but their catch plummeted in the mid-1950s (most likely because dogfish mature so late and have a long gestation period for their pups). At first, Aomori fishermen switched to catching dogfish sharks off Hokkaido, Japan's northernmost island. But that population dipped, and now they import many of the key ingredients from British Columbia.

A classic fish cake, *hanpen,* has also changed with time. It acquired its name not from its shape but from the chef who created it, Hanpei.[13] During the Edo period (which began in 1603), residents of what later became Tokyo caught spotted sharks in Edo Bay and made them into this pillowy white fish cake. No one fishes anymore in what is now called Tokyo Bay, and much of the fish in *hanpen* comes from pollack caught in Hokkaido or elsewhere.

Shigeo Sugie, who heads the fish-paste cooperative at Tokyo's Tsukiji Market, spends much of his time thinking about the future of fish paste. (Like Murata, he wears two hats: he is, according to his formal business card, president and "food meister" of Neo Foods Company, a fish-paste producer.) Sugie, with his jet-black hair and the ready smile of a door-to-door salesman, looks as if he would fit better into 1950s America than modern-day Japan. But he is firmly entrenched in one of the most impressive global-trading operations: his office abuts the world's largest wholesale fish and seafood market, a bustling expanse with twenty-five hundred mechanized trolleys zipping around 760 stalls. There are five wholesalers dealing with shark meat paste, though this pales in comparison with the three hundred tuna wholesalers who operate in Tsukiji every day. Still, these men, along with other fish-paste sellers, are Sugie's constituency, and he's doing his best to represent them.

The problem, according to Sugie, is the vast array of food choices Japanese consumers now have. Like Aoki, he has watched meat consumption rise in recent years. "Unfortunately, the demand for fish paste in the market has decreased these days," Sugie allows. "As we have a lot of different types of food available in Japan, fish paste has come to be picked up less." While Japan's royal families may still serve it at their dinner parties, most average Japanese families do not.

The loss of fish cake's regional character isn't helping, now that fish paste comes from just a handful of sources: frozen pollack supplies half the fish-cake market, while most of the rest comes from fish imported from Southeast Asia. A few stalls in Tsukiji Market still sell *hanpen* made from shark meat, and Sugie says the viscosity of cartilaginous fish makes all the difference. "It's like marshmallow," he murmurs appreciatively as we sample the fish cake at the Tskugon store's stall. It's an apt description, because the cake is light and fluffy and features the kind of give that a marshmallow has. Like every other shark dish, it's the texture that defines it, since the product itself is essentially tasteless. Only after I dip the *hanpen* into a seafood broth does it gain a noticeable flavor and become a tasty snack.

Sugie is still fighting to reassert the role of shark fish paste in the Japanese marketplace. He and his colleagues sponsored a stall at the annual international seafood show in Tokyo, even commissioning artworks made out of colored fish paste to bolster their cause. And just to be safe, they've started holding a memorial service for sharks in early September at a fisherman's shrine near Tsukiji Market. They sacrifice a spotted shark—the kind fishermen used to scoop out of Edo Bay—and show their gratitude to the Shinto spirits. And on the side, they hope for better sales. "We are not just devouring shark meat and utilizing them. We show our appreciation," Sugie says.

But in a society that doesn't see the shark as a major status symbol, the animal doesn't hold the same culinary appeal. Fish marshmallows, after all, only go so far. Perhaps this is the best hope for shark conservation: when the cultural myths surrounding sharks either fade away or are exploded, the value of shark products plummets. Without this added premium the market can move on to alternatives, whether it's a different kind of moisturizer, bland fish meat, or gelatinous noodle. This doesn't mean there's no societal cost: this sort of shift may cause economic dislocation, and it does mean abandoning traditions that have lasted for centuries in some cases. But it's important to view this in context: eliminating sharks as a widely traded commodity is not the same thing as eliminating their place in global society or in the world's economy. In fact, the most effective ways of managing this transition involve redirecting our obsession with sharks into a nonlethal form of commodification. Given current economic and political realities, it may represent the most effective method of ensuring enough sharks exist so our fetishizing them doesn't wipe them out completely.

5

THE SHARK SLEUTHS

If it's cool, and rare, and unusual, and nobody else has it, I want it. I don't care if it's illegal, I want it. I don't care what it does to the animal, I want it. I don't care if it's bad for the environment, I want it.
—Lisa Nichols, Fish and Wildlife special agent, describing the mentality of a wildlife collector

At the moment our shark obsession is alive and well, and it's created a conundrum: sharks are desirable because they are dangerous, but many people want to keep these fearsome animals as pets. Most people might think of aquariums as a hobby for young kids whose parents dutifully bring home an array of aquatic species (goldfish, turtles) only to see them expire within a matter of weeks—or even days—after suffering under inexpert care. But there are plenty of adults who devote a serious amount of time to buying and selling plants and animals that can be displayed in private homes or commercial establishments. An array of Web sites now serve this industry, where aquarium aficionados can log in, chat about their hobby, and order fish via the Internet. But if you are not immersed in this world, it's hard to break into these online communities, especially if you're looking for the seedier aspects of wildlife trafficking. Online chats generally take place in a code that is impenetrable to outsiders, and members interested in criminal activity send e-mails to users offline, so they can arrange for the transfer of goods undetected by the authorities.

We like seeing sharks, as long as they're contained. The British conceptual artist Damien Hirst made the link between sharks and humans' mortality when he put a freshly killed tiger shark in his piece *The Physical Impossibility of Death in the Mind of Someone Living* in 1991; a decade later the piece fetched $8 million at auction. (The shark had decayed over time because it was not floating in formaldehyde, and Hirst ordered a new shark killed to replace it.) The hedge fund billionaire Steven A. Cohen, who now owns the artwork and paid for its restoration, told *The New York Times* he "liked the whole fear factor" of the piece. "I grew up in the generation of 'Jaws.' I knew it was the piece of the 90's."[1] In September 2008, Hirst created a second piece with a dead tiger shark, titled *The Kingdom,* which sold at Sotheby's for more than $14 million, more than 30 percent above its asking price.[2]

Such exorbitant art sales are rare. But the preoccupation with sharks as pets is much more widespread and has provided a powerful financial incentive for plundering, a subterranean network that robs the natural world of some of its most prized residents. The international trade in wild animals, sharks among them, amounts to roughly $6 billion a year.[3] And while much of the time these acts go unpunished, sometimes the perpetrators get busted. Whether it's using old-fashioned undercover work or high-tech genetic analysis, government officials and academics have begun collaborating to track the illicit trade in sharks worldwide. In doing so, they have also discovered aspects of sharks' movements, lineage, and behavior that were unimaginable just a few decades ago.

At least one site, www.sharkwrangler.com, gives a decent glimpse into the world of online shark trading. Like other men who make their living off sharks, Ken Moran appeals to consumers by tapping into their fear and fascination, assuring them he can handle the creatures they could never envision approaching. "Ken Moran, the shark wrangler, hunts, collects and transports large predator sharks for use in the aquarium industry," his site states. "He was drawn to sharks as a child with the release of *Jaws.* Gripped by its ability to tap the primal public fear of sharks, he became fascinated with the ocean's apex predators. Instead of fearing these powerful animals, he works confidently and carefully with them." The site gives a long list of sharks he has "handled" (it does not specify which he has put in aquariums and which he has worked with in the wild), including nine-foot-long bull sharks, nine-foot-long sand tiger sharks, ten-foot-long hammerheads, and fifteen-foot-long tiger sharks. While he makes a point of saying he is "NO cowboy" when it comes to sharks, he also goes to great lengths to point out how risky his profession can be. In the case of a fifteen-foot tiger shark, the site notes in brackets, "This size animal is not a hold in your arms specimen!"

In reality, of course, Moran and other dealers make more of their living off smaller, bottom-dwelling sharks that can live in a glass tank. Leopard sharks, which are easily found off the coasts of California, Oregon, and Baja California, Mexico, are the sorts of sharks that most people see in aquariums—and are tempted to take home. Tan, with dark spots, the fish are physically striking and less demanding to maintain than other shark species. Rather than needing to constantly swim in order to breathe, like some species, they're fine spending much of their time resting at the bottom of the sea, or in a tank. Spanning just ten inches when they're born, they reach up to six or seven feet, and they can live as long as a quarter of a century. However, these sharks often die early in captivity.

While the illegal shark trade can be profitable, it poses risks both in and out of the water. For more than a decade Kevin Thompson—pastor of the Bay Area Family Church, a branch of the Reverend Sun Myung Moon's Unification Church, in San Leandro, California—managed to pull it off, peddling leopard sharks on California's central coast. That was before Roy Torres of the National Oceanic and Atmospheric Administration started looking for him.

Torres, the son of Mexican immigrants, grew up in Imperial Beach, California, the most southwesterly city in the United States. Imperial Beach once held the title of "eighth funkiest town in the U.S.," a fact Torres relates with pride as he's navigating San Francisco's streets in his blue Dodge truck. His career philosophy combines hard-nosed law enforcement with an emotional attachment to animals, especially those of the sea. "I believe what we're doing is so important, enforc-

ing the laws the people of the United States, through their representatives, have passed, to protect the places where they love, their fellow
creatures," he explains as he drives on a surveillance mission. "It's
kind of a deep thing with me."

In 2003, an NOAA smuggling expert in Miami spotted an online
ad for a baby leopard shark and started making inquiries, eventually
handing off the case to Torres. Torres and his colleagues had been
checking out sites in Las Vegas to see whether establishments such as
Mandalay Bay Resort and Casino—which now boasts a Shark Reef
exhibit that, according to its Web site, houses "over 2,000 animals in
1.6 million gallons of seawater"—were housing illegal leopard sharks.
The casinos were clean, but the agents found leopard sharks less than
thirty-six inches long—a violation of California law, since citizens
cannot possess, take, sell, or buy leopard sharks that small—being
sold in places as far away as Georgia. "There's not a leopard shark in
Georgia," Torres says, adding that finding the fish for sale so far away
from its natural habitat raised an automatic question within NOAA's
offices.

At the same time, other federal agents were becoming curious about
what was happening in their respective jurisdictions. A U.S. Fish and
Wildlife Service agent based in San Diego, Lisa Nichols, got a tip that
a group was taking leopard sharks at night from San Francisco Bay.
Then Nichols got a call from Dave Kirby, a Fish and Wildlife special
agent in Chicago who had noticed that small sharks were starting
to appear in pet stores in Illinois and in other parts of the Midwest.
While a small percentage of marine ornamental fish can be raised
from fish farming, more than 90 percent are caught in the wild. In the
case of sharks, all specimens come from the sea—so any aquarium's
gain is the ocean's loss.

Given the broad scope of any illegal animal-smuggling operation,
Torres worked by tapping into law-enforcement authorities across the
globe. Over the course of three years his team pulled in help from the
U.K.'s Department for Environment, Food, and Rural Affairs Fish
Health Inspectorate and the Dutch General Inspection Service, along
with Fish and Wildlife special agents from Georgia, Indiana, Iowa,

Michigan, New York, Texas, and Wisconsin. But when it comes to trading in marine ornamental fish in America, there are just three major commercial centers: Los Angeles, Miami, and Tampa. In the case of Kevin Thompson and the Unification Church, Miami was where their operation started to unravel.

Torres approached the probe with the same sort of strategy used to crack other criminal conspiracies: nab a low-level participant who is likely to turn on his or her superiors when exposed to legal scrutiny. Ricky Hindra, an aquarium dealer based in Miami, was the first to talk. Hindra suspected that his leopard shark supplier was two-timing him by peddling his animals to another dealer, and decided to engage in Dumpster diving to prove his suspicions were justified. During one of his trash raids he came up with a cardboard air bill from his Los Angeles supplier, showing a shipment from San Francisco to Miami on American Airlines. At the time Hindra didn't know the significance of his find, and shoved the document into his office files. But when Torres spotted it, he used it to track down the shipper through the airline: it was Kevin Thompson.

That one air bill, however, was not enough to bust the pastor and his disciples. State and federal agents began learning how Thompson worked, how he recruited young men with low self-esteem, housed and fed them free of charge, and encouraged them to join his flock. The recruits served as the pastor's fishing crew, while his top lieutenants handled the business side of the operation. Initially, Thompson and his adherents stuck to commercial fishing, but given the rough waters and declining fish stocks off the California coast, the business didn't exactly thrive. One day, an associate of Thompson's, John Newberry, spotted an ad for leopard sharks in a trade magazine and realized they could make money off something that they had already been catching by accident and tossing back into the water. At that point, in 1991, catching leopard sharks was legal, but just a few years later the state banned the practice and the group faced a choice: give up their cash cow, or go underground.

They chose the latter. They weren't exactly slick about it, openly touting their business in faxes. In an August 15, 2006, plea agreement, the pet trader Ira Gass recounted, "Newberry solicited me via facsimile to buy sharks. I told Newberry that he should not widely distribute his facsimile solicitations because it was illegal to sell the sharks and he could get into trouble for doing so."[4]

Thompson was also comfortable discussing his pet store supply ring with his congregation, inside the walls of his church. Moon denied knowledge of Thompson's activities once he and five associates were indicted, but the pastor told his flock that Moon—who calls himself King of the Ocean—was well aware of the illicit shark business. According to an audiotape of a 2003 sermon Thompson delivered titled "Lessons from the Sharks," which was first reported in the *East Bay Express,* the minister told his congregation their leader backed the plan. "When I had the chance to tell our founder Reverend Moon about it . . . he told me, you know, 'You need *twenty* boats out there fishing!' " he said. "He had this big plan drawn out, you know."

Thompson and his cohorts also liked to amuse themselves with the captured fish, as he playfully described in the same sermon. "We usually do diving competitions—throw them up by the tail and see if they land, you know, nose first into the water," he told the audience. "Usually they do belly flops."[5]

But one of the young men within the pastor's circle, Brandon Olivia, didn't embrace this illicit game plan. The entire enterprise disheartened Olivia, who decided to move across the country to a different Unification Church outpost in Gloucester, Massachusetts. Once Torres learned about Olivia and his disillusionment, he knew he could crack the case.

Olivia found work at True World Foods, the King of the Ocean's commercial seafood operation based in Gloucester, which helps ensure the church's place as one of the nation's largest sushi wholesalers. Torres knew he would have to conduct a cold interview: once Olivia had a hint of what was coming, he might take off instead of ratting out his former mentor. So the agent contacted the Massachusetts environmental police, who were able to track down Olivia's commercial fishing license. Local authorities made up a story about how there was a problem with Olivia's license, and one afternoon Torres and a state officer showed up at the True World Foods seafood processing plant. Olivia was on the floor, and the three men headed outside to the parking lot to talk fish. They perched on the hood of Torres's rental car as traffic whizzed by on a nearby road.

Torres started the conversation in a low-key way, inquiring politely about Thompson's fishing ventures. Olivia prattled on about the various legal fish they caught: halibut, salmon, and other species.

After listening for a while, Torres got to the heart of the matter. "Can you tell me about the leopard sharks?"

Olivia got quiet. "Oh, you know about that?" he asked tentatively.

"Yeah," the agent replied. "I need you to tell me the truth about the operation."

That was when Olivia began to cry. In the end he told the officers everything he knew: about how Thompson and his cohorts targeted pregnant female sharks, egged on by escalating profits, even though they knew they were breaking the law. He confided how the entire business made him question his faith in the church. After initially demanding that Torres turn off his tape recorder, he agreed to tell the whole story again while it was rolling. "That was the last nail," Torres says now.

Torres soon discovered Thompson took full advantage of the Unification Church's resources in carrying out his trade, though it's unclear whether Moon explicitly condoned the poaching. The fact that the church—formally known as the Holy Spirit Association for the Unification of World Christianity—has such a big seafood wholesale business made it even easier for the shark smugglers to operate. Thompson maintained three of the church's fishing boats on True World's lot and kept the juvenile sharks he and his allies had taken from the wild in tanks on the sushi distributor's property.

Newberry, the pastor's number two, told prosecutors and the court that Thompson used all the Unification tools at his disposal and funneled the profits back into his house of worship. "He directed me and other Church members to catch, store, ship and sell the sharks. We fished for the sharks using Church vessels and stored the sharks at a facility located in San Leandro, California, owned by a business associated with the Church," he declared in his August 2, 2006, plea agreement. "I understand that monies made from selling the sharks were used to maintain Church boats which were used by Church members for ministry related activities in the Church's 'Ocean Church.' The monies were also used to finance living expenses of members of the Ocean Church."[6]

Torres can no longer talk about what the Unification Church did, or didn't do, when it came to Thompson's illegal enterprise. The church entered into a nonprosecution agreement with the U.S. district attorney in Oakland in which it agreed to pay $500,000.

Thompson and all five of his co-defendants did not get off so easily. After being indicted, they all pleaded guilty under the Lacey Act, which prohibits the interstate sale of wildlife taken in violation of state laws. The pastor admitted that between 1992 and 2003, he had led other church members in a scheme to illegally catch and sell leopard sharks to aquarium dealers in the United States and Europe: in return he was sentenced to pay a $100,000 fine and serve a year and one day in prison. While they sold some of the leopard sharks locally, according to their guilty pleas, the poachers shipped most of them out of the Oakland and San Francisco airports, selling them for prices ranging between $9 and $75 each. In a pet store, leopard sharks can fetch as much as $240 for a single animal.

During the time the criminal ring was operating, authorities estimate, Thompson and his associates—all of them church members—took as many as 25,000 baby leopard sharks out of San Francisco Bay and sold them for profit. They sold the sharks far and wide: in their indictment federal authorities accused the ring of selling 465 juveniles to companies in Miami; Chicago; Houston; Romulus, Michigan; Milford, Connecticut; and overseas in Britain and Holland.

The successful prosecution ultimately yielded a payoff for the region's wildlife: authorities established a $1.5 million partnership between the federal government and private foundations in order to restore habitat for sharks and other animals living in San Francisco Bay. The shark smugglers' $410,000 in fines, combined with a $500,000 contribution by the Unification Church and $600,000 from an environmental group and three foundations, provided the money for the fund. While the money is still in the process of being spent, it will help to restore 630 acres of tidal habitat for endangered species and 230 acres of pond habitat in an area called Eden Landing Ponds. The money will also help create a seasonal loop trail, a raised walkway, and a kayak launch, so people can visit the area and view wildlife without damaging the habitat.

A few of the smugglers' sharks managed to make it out alive. Officials from the Monterey Bay Aquarium, Chicago's John G. Shedd Aquarium, and the Cabrillo Marine Aquarium in San Pedro, California, all helped care for the thirty-six baby leopard sharks state and federal agents had confiscated during the course of the investigation. While seven died because they were in such poor condition when they were recaptured, aquarium officials returned twenty-five of them to the ocean and kept four of them on exhibit at the Monterey Bay Aquarium. The ones kept on display have microchips implanted in them, a precautionary measure officials took in case they needed to bring them into court as evidence against the shark traffickers. Agents called the effort Operation Finding Leo.

While the sting ended in success, Fish and Wildlife's Lisa Nichols is still fuming over the minister's hypocrisy. During the search of Thompson's house, agents came across large amounts of religious education materials that promoted the importance of ethics, she recalls, and the disconnect between Thompson's preaching and his criminal activities rankled her.

"When someone's the pastor of a church, and they consistently preach about being moral and ethical, and you have literature in your house that says you're a good family man, you're ethical and moral, and then you think, 'We're going to sell this animal to make money,' it doesn't matter what you use that money for. It doesn't matter if you spend it on kids, and taking them to sea to learn about the ocean," she says. "That doesn't make sense to me."

On the other hand, Nichols has spent enough time dealing with wildlife traffickers to know why leopard sharks proved to be such a big seller before federal authorities cracked down on the trade. Nichols saw the creatures in California's fast-food restaurants and casinos, to say nothing of the pet shops that she would visit from time to time.

When it comes to the wildlife collector's mentality, Nichols explains, "if it's cool, and rare, and unusual, and nobody else has it, I want it. I don't care if it's illegal, I want it. I don't care what it does to the animal, I want it. I don't care if it's bad for the environment, I want it."

Globalization has only boosted wildlife trafficking, as electronic commerce has made it easier to connect buyers and sellers worldwide. It's taking sharks out of the sea, one transaction at a time.

While Torres catches his suspects by chasing their colleagues down across the country and tracking their activities through secretive documents, Mahmood Shivji nails his in the confines of his lab. Shivji is a calm man with a confident air, the kind of academic who revels in getting a bunch of shark fins or frozen fish from a restaurant thrown on his laboratory table and telling you exactly which species they represent and why it matters. An Indian raised in Kenya, Shivji now makes his home in Fort Lauderdale, Florida, where he directs the Guy Harvey Research Institute at Nova Southeastern University. Nova Southeastern is, in many ways, America's school of the future. Founded in 1964, it now ranks as the largest independent institution of higher learning not only in Florida but in the entire Southeast. The school took off in the 1980s when its leaders decided to seize upon emerging computer technology and make online and distance learning a central part of its mission. It now has more than twenty-six thousand students, many of whom spend much of their time learning online.

As part of the school's transformation, university officials decided in 2005 to jettison their traditional mascot, the Knight (as in shining armor), for the Shark. For a school that lacked a distinctive image for decades, adopting this marine mascot has given it a sense of place, as well as a connection to some of its academic pursuits. "It has been the greatest thing we've done," says Nova Southeastern's president, Ray Ferrero Jr. While that may sound like an overstatement, Ferrero is serious, given the school's historic lack of identity. The campus's university center has a 250-foot-high mural featuring seventeen different shark species, and students—who suggested the switch in the first place—have embraced the new standard-bearer with enthusiasm. The change suits the school, which boasts classroom outposts on the Atlantic.

While Nova Southeastern's main campus is right in the middle of Fort Lauderdale's suburban sprawl, Shivji's lab is by the sea. His workplace in Dania Beach is distinctly less glamorous than the university's newer grounds: some of his researchers work in what amounts to a converted trailer. But Shivji's students seems unfazed by these details.

A plant geneticist by training, Shivji hadn't planned to work on sharks at the outset of his career. Shortly after arriving at Nova Southeastern, he happened to read a story in a local newspaper that detailed how authorities had difficulty keeping track of how many quantities of different sharks were being landed in the U.S. fishery because the animals looked so similar. Imagine a pile of gray logs: that's what sharks look like once you've cut off their heads, tails, and fins. Since they're so difficult to distinguish by the time they land on the dock, government officials often have no way of determining which imperiled species might have been hooked in a given catch.

"I didn't know anything about sharks at the time," Shivji recalls. "I thought to myself, as a scientist, 'That's not a complex question if you look at the DNA.' " He called up Lisa Natanson, a National Oceanic and Atmospheric Administration scientist based in Narragansett at the time, and asked whether she'd be willing to share some of her shark samples with him. Natanson complied, and Shivji's career headed in an entirely different direction.

Shivji set about developing diagnostic, species-specific "primers": short single-strand pieces of DNA that will bond only with DNA from specific shark species when put through a machine that makes copies of DNA using a chemical process called a polymerase chain reaction, or PCR. Shivji describes it as "a diagnostic fingerprint." He now has species-specific primers for thirty-two different kinds of sharks, which he provides to others for free.

Shivji's work has produced scientific breakthroughs, defining new species and forcing researchers to rethink some of their basic preconceptions about sharks. Demian Chapman pursued his doctoral work under Shivji, and the two collaborated on the revolutionary paper that confirmed a virgin shark birth in the Omaha zoo. In 2002, Shivji collaborated with three other scientists to prove that skates and rays, which were long thought to have evolved from sharks, actually belong to an ancient sister lineage.

But Shivji does not devote the bulk of his time to publishing academic papers. He's a pragmatist who's invested in producing concrete policy outcomes, which is why he's spent his time developing so many easy-to-use DNA tests. When law-enforcement officials are sorting through a passel of sharks that have just been unloaded on a dock, they're hoping to get an instant answer about whether the boat has brought in illegal goods. To do that, they need a test that can deliver a verdict quickly. While he describes his original motivation for studying sharks as academic—"I was looking at this from a science perspective; we can likely solve this problem through genetics"—Shivji takes pleasure in the fact that his innovations have translated so readily to the practical. In one study, he traced scalloped hammerhead shark fins on the Hong Kong fin market all the way back to their geographic origin in the western Atlantic, where they're classified as endangered.[7]

"It's infrequent that academic research makes a practical impact as quickly as this has," he observes. After all, other researchers don't have federal agents showing up at their lab with, say, moldy suitcases a woman from Ecuador tried to smuggle in through Miami, asking them to take a look. It turned out the luggage was stuffed with dried shark fins, sea horses, and fish swim bladders. Shivji wonders what the smuggler was thinking at the time. "You look at these suitcases bulging, and they smell. How would anyone imagine they would get by customs?" he ponders. But shark fins are light, easy to pack, and not likely to break in transit, making them ideal for smuggling across borders.

Many scientists work under the assumption they have years to produce a final result, and can spend significant sums toward achieving that end, but Shivji recognizes that law-enforcement officers in the developing world face both budgetary and time pressures when they're trying to analyze illicit goods. "In most parts of the world, they don't have the resources to do DNA sequencing. It's not something a resource-poor country can have their fishery managers do."

Shivji's analysis has already spread to developing countries. South African law-enforcement officials have asked Shivji's lab to conduct an analysis of confiscated fins, as has a Palau-based conservation group. An intergovernmental group representing Southeast Asian countries, SEAFDEC, asked him to determine if a group of fins they nabbed included any from the three shark species protected under international law. While none of the fins they sent to the lab violated the law, the group was impressed enough to dispatch one of its experts to learn forensic techniques at Shivji's lab in the spring of 2008.

Even law-enforcement officers in richer countries see the advantages of using rapid genetic tests to identify shark species. Before Shivji developed his form of analysis, NOAA agents would have to ship samples of confiscated shark meat packed in dry ice to the NOAA lab in Charleston, South Carolina. Often, it would take as long as a month for scientists there to conduct a test of the fatty lipids contained in the meat and make a positive identification. Shivji requires just a small section of a fin—the amount equivalent to the graphite tip of a pencil—and he and his colleagues can deliver a verdict within four hours. During peak times of operation, the lab can analyze eighty to a hundred samples in a single workday.

In the process of his experimentation, Shivji has become a shark forensics specialist, working with law-enforcement authorities and researchers alike to analyze dead sharks. And that, in turn, has led to more shark busts.

Even shriveled shark samples can yield some significant results. In 2003, officials from NOAA and New York's Department of Environmental Conservation were touring a seafood warehouse in New York City's Navy Yard on a routine inspection concerning black sea bass caught in North Carolina. Jim Cassin, an NOAA special agent based in New York at the time, and his two colleagues noticed the warehouse had a large number of shark fins in storage, along with a fairly elaborate fin-drying operation. Then they spotted a massive fin from a basking shark—a species that is strictly controlled under international trade laws—stretching more than three feet high.

"It's giant, there's no denying it," Cassin recalls. "We saw it almost immediately, but we tried not to let on we had noticed." In addition, they saw a huge nylon sack of fins that said "porbeagle" on the outside, signaling the fins came from a legally fished shark species, with a label on the inside reading *blanco,* or white, in Spanish. That, the agents suspected, meant the fins came from great whites, another one of the three internationally protected shark species.

After raising the issue with the business's owner, Marc Agger, who downplayed the matter, the agents kept the conversation light and took off. A week later they were back, with a search warrant, which enabled them to confiscate the bag and bring it to Shivji's lab for testing. The lab determined that more than 230 pounds of the fins came from species that are prohibited from harvest, including basking and dusky sharks. The bag that first alerted authorities contained twenty-one sets of fins taken from great whites.

On August 1, 2006, the Brooklyn-based Agger Fish Corporation agreed to pay $750,000 to settle the case, a rare win in the realm of shark fin smuggling. The seafood dealer agreed not to contest that it bought shark meat and fins without a federal permit, failed to report most of those purchases to federal authorities, and possessed fins from seven shark species that are prohibited under federal law. In addition to the federal penalty, Agger Fish had to forfeit nearly a thousand pounds of dried shark fins, including the prohibited species catch worth roughly $80,000. To this day, Cassin isn't sure whether Agger was deliberately flouting the law or just too lazy to check which species of shark fins he had stored in his warehouse. But he adds, "He was in that industry. He should have been making the effort."

Paul Raymond, an NOAA special agent based in the Southeast who has worked with Shivji on nearly two dozen cases, calls the professor's DNA analysis "a great asset." Nearly a decade ago, when the United States imposed anti-shark-finning laws, Raymond went down to watch Victor Chang, a shark fin dealer in Daytona Beach, practice his trade. He brought along an ichthyologist to help him distinguish among the species that fishermen had hauled in and were offering up to Chang that day.

As Chang sorted the different fins according to their value, Raymond wondered why the dealer sitting before him seemed more capable of enforcing the law than he was. Chang knew how to distinguish among shark species because his livelihood depended on paying the right price for a given fish. Raymond, on the other hand, was suddenly saddled with the burden of making the same distinctions in order to determine if someone had violated the law—but he lacked the knowledge required to make such a judgment. Chang would deal them out like a deck of cards. "This is silky shark, this is dusky, sandbar, sandbar," Raymond remembers. "He'd just squat down and sort them out, and write up an invoice and pay the fishermen. And I thought to myself, 'He just did that, why can't I? Because I've got these regulations to enforce.'" Now Shivji's lab provides Raymond with the answers he needs.

Shivji's students are also using their genetics knowledge to prove that shark populations are more genetically diverse than people might have thought, a finding that has serious implications for officials in charge of ensuring that species don't go extinct. Jennifer Magnussen, for example, has developed a primer that in a single test will not only indicate if the shark in question is a sand tiger shark but also determine if that shark came from the northwest Atlantic—in which case it's prohibited to harvest it. Another student, Christine Testerman, has found that porbeagle sharks in the Northern Hemisphere, which are in danger of being fished to extinction, are genetically distinct from those in the Southern Hemisphere. The upshot: you can't just count on porbeagle sharks from the Southern Hemisphere repopulating the depleted sharks near the United States, because the two don't interbreed. In the end, DNA doesn't lie.

———

Just as law-enforcement authorities have become increasingly focused on tracking illegal shark dealing, so have more academics. The Stanford University marine biologist Stephen R. Palumbi is a more flamboyant character than Shivji—the small ponytail gathered at the back of his neck pegs him as a child of the 1960s, and he belongs to a rock band called Flagella, which performs songs about achieving conservation goals, fishing out the sea, and slime. But Palumbi, who directs Stanford University's Hopkins Marine Station in Monterey, California, is just as committed to cracking the genetic code that helps determine the path of the global shark fin trade. A few years ago, he doled out an assignment to a bunch of graduate and undergraduate students: after giving each of the students $25, he instructed them to make a day trip to San Francisco's Chinatown and buy dried shark fins in one of the many apothecary and grocery stores there. With most of the fins costing between $250 and $500 a pound, the students could afford a fin measuring between eight and ten inches. The stores, in many ways, mirror their Hong Kong and mainland China counterparts, as glass jars of grayish fins stacked next to one another on the floor compete for customers' attention with dried ginseng and mushrooms, while delicate white feathered shark fins selling for nearly twice the price occupy a place of prestige high up on the wall.

A baby boomer with an irreverent sense of humor, Palumbi combines a geeky passion for technology with keen understanding of pop culture. It's not enough to send his disciples out into the world to see sharks strung up to dry; he wants to film the expedition and post it on the Web, and to use their finds to help construct an elaborate DNA database. Palumbi's Web site features "Short Attention Span Science Theater"—short video clips that bring viewers along for the ride as he and his students investigate Chinese apothecaries or test whether "Pacific red snapper" is really a fish species. It isn't, and in fact is a made-up name that markets use to peddle an array of different, less desirable fish.

While Shivji, in Palumbi's words, is invested in creating "a set of tools that give you an instant answer," so to speak, Palumbi takes a little more of a long-term, ivory-tower view of things. Palumbi is working up a hundred different protocols for a hundred different species: "a discovery-based tool versus a positive test tool." In other words, Palumbi is trying to give academic researchers a way to identify every single shark fin with laser-like precision so they can chart their evolutionary path as well as whether they're being illegally traded; Shivji is pushing to ensure the cops can nab a wrongdoer on the spot.

Palumbi is looking to broaden the academy's understanding of how sharks have evolved, as well as construct a detailed and comprehensive chart of what makes each shark species distinct. He has pioneered similar genetic studies on whales and has used his findings to challenge the scientific assertions of pro-whaling forces. While he's appalled at the paucity of data concerning sharks worldwide—"We didn't have the global database that would say, 'This is what these fins are' "—he admits that what he's doing, at the moment, amounts to an academic exercise.

"Right now there isn't any money in it. Is anyone going to pay me to do this? I don't think so," he acknowledges, comfortably ensconced in his sunny office, a stone's throw away from the Monterey Bay Aquarium. "At this point the case for doing this is not quite obvious to everyone."

Sitting in front of his office computer, he plugs a specific genetic sequence into it: sure enough, 1,146 bases begin to stream across the screen. The computer program he's using takes sixty-three taxa and scans their family trees, to see where the shark in question fits into the evolutionary path. This sort of letter crunching can provide a lens into all sorts of groundbreaking scientific findings: what shark populations looked like before humans started hunting them in earnest, for example, and whether they're poised to adapt quickly to the earth's changing environment.

Palumbi is fairly confident of the answer: they're not, because sharks evolve so slowly. While they've survived for millions of years, he explains, they've done so by sticking to a similar genetic formula.

"They have relatively little ability to adapt evolutionarily," Palumbi says. Unlike some marine organisms that can change quickly in the face of intense environmental pressures, sharks have historically adapted "on 40- to 60-, or 100-million-year timescales."

The genetic codes make it clear: just because sharks have survived for hundreds of millions of years doesn't mean they're well positioned to weather the most recent challenge to their existence.

One group of scientists, who are drawing on both Shivji's and Palumbi's work, have a grand vision of DNA mapping that will ultimately capture the most significant species on earth: they call it the Consortium for the Barcode of Life. A few years ago, only a handful of researchers were trying to assemble the genetic sequences of animals large and small. Now hundreds of them work on the project: they have already collected at least 300,000 records for 30,000 different species.

David Schindel, the consortium's executive secretary, describes it as "a sort of telephone directory of well-identified specimens" that will allow scientists to quickly determine what species they're examining. To ensure that it's a universal genetic marker, they are constructing these codes from the same mitochondrial gene regardless of the species: cytochrome oxidase 1, also known as CO-1. Using this specific marker, which is located on the gene that serves as the powerhouse of the cell, allows researchers to distinguish among even closely related sharks with a high degree of precision: Robert D. Ward, a scientist at CSIRO Marine and Atmospheric Research in Hobart, Tasmania, along with two collaborators, examined 945 specimens from 210 Australian shark species and distinguished them with 99 percent accuracy.[8]

To assemble this barcode directory, researchers are—in some cases—lifting samples from plant and animal relics that have been lingering on dusty natural history museum shelves for decades. "It's pretty remarkable how durable the DNA in specimens is proving to be," Schindel says. "We're using insect legs that are fifty, sometimes a hundred years old."

Robert Hanner, a biology professor at Canada's University of Guelph, coordinates the Fish Barcode of Life campaign, a subset of the overall barcode campaign. While the prospect of cataloging all the fish in the sea seems daunting—there are thirty thousand known fish species, and the number continues to rise—Hanner appears confident he's up to the task. (And, as Schindel points out, they try to keep the project in perspective: "We're not trying to do all species in all places.") In order to do their work, Hanner asks for five specimens per species, across a shark's geographic range. When it comes to elasmobranchs, which include skates and rays as well as sharks, the group has analyzed 6,074 specimens from 573 species, which means they've created barcodes for a little more than half of all known elasmobranchs. Many sharks are particularly easy to differentiate genetically because they developed so long ago, allowing them plenty of time to accumulate genetic mutations that distinguish one species from another.

"These are the early days," Hanner cautions, adding that once it's complete, it will represent "the biggest communal database for the molecular diagnostics of fish in the world."

Assembling a global barcode for sharks and other fish, he suggests, will give researchers a quick fix on whether they've stumbled on something new. Ultimately, these scientists hope, researchers can venture out with a handheld DNA sequencer to assess what they're encountering in the wild. "The value of barcoding is it can tell you very clearly, is this a match with something in your database, or is it an unknown?" Hanner says.

No such DNA sequencer exists as yet: Hanner believes private companies will be happy to develop it once they're confident enough barcodes exist to make it financially worth their while. "It's not until we develop the Yellow Pages so every species has a lookup number that these big companies are going to get interested enough to throw investment dollars at it," he argues. "People will say, 'This is a market opportunity that needs to be looked at.'"

In the meantime, however, Hanner and his colleagues have a long stretch of letter crunching ahead of them.

DNA analysis isn't used just to solve criminal and taxonomic mysteries, however. Shivji and Demian Chapman—his talented former student—have employed it to explain one of the most puzzling shark appearances in years. How sharks mate and give birth is one of the biggest remaining mysteries about them; genetics provides one of the few solid clues to understanding shark reproduction.

On the afternoon of December 14, 2001, aquarium employees at Henry Doorly Zoo in Omaha, Nebraska, found themselves confronted with an inexplicable sight: a baby shark had suddenly materialized in their tank overnight. The day before the zoo had three bonnethead sharks: all of them were four-year-old females that had spent all but the first six months in captivity. These sharks had not reached sexual maturity, and there wasn't any male for them to mate with in the tank. So the zookeepers puzzled over how one of them could have produced an offspring. Was it a prank, even though there was no sign of entry? Could one of the sharks have stored sperm for more than three years, which would have been an unprecedented act since this sperm has traditionally lasted for just six months inside a shark's womb? Within twenty-four hours a stingray living in the tank had killed the baby female, severely rupturing its liver, so aquarium officials took the shark's body out to preserve it, and wrote off the incident.

Over the years, however, other zoos experienced mysterious births similar to Henry Doorly's. In Detroit's Belle Isle Aquarium, a baby shark had appeared out of nowhere, and researchers reported similar findings from other institutions. These scattered reports of virgin births intrigued Chapman, who at the time was pursuing his Ph.D. at Nova Southeastern University under Shivji's tutelage. Chapman wondered whether these unexplained appearances meant that sharks, like some birds and reptiles, were capable of parthenogenesis, or asexual reproduction. In 2006, Chapman called officials at Henry Doorly and asked them to send him small samples from the baby shark's fin and from the three female adults. Then, working with scientists at Queen's University in Belfast, where he was putting in a short stint, he conducted a blind test of the four sharks' genetic makeup. Chapman, an ebullient New Zealander by birth, engaged in a bit of good-natured wagering with his colleagues on the final outcome of his hypothesis.

"We were bidding pints of Guinness on what it was going to be," he recalls now.

Within a matter of weeks the doctoral candidate had his answer: the baby shark (nickname: Jesus, despite being female) had exactly half as much genetic variation as one of the captive female sharks, meaning the shark had inherited an exact replica of its mother's genes rather than getting half its genes from one parent and the other half from its father. The female shark had produced the baby on her own. After making the discovery, Chapman literally ran across the room in his lab to look at Irish scientific textbooks that detailed some of the instances where this has occurred in other species, such as rattlesnakes and the Komodo dragon. When an egg is formed in one of these creatures, the animal also creates three polar bodies, a form of waste material that is genetically identical to the egg. Most of the time, these polar bodies are eventually discarded. But in the case of parthenogenesis, one of the polar bodies fuses with the egg, forming an embryo with half the genetic variability of its mother.

Chapman, who is now an assistant professor at Stony Brook University working at the school's Institute for Ocean Conservation Science, collaborated with Shivji and a Henry Doorly scientist to confirm the bonnethead's virgin birth, and subsequently identified another such birth at a second aquarium with an entirely different species of shark. He sees this capacity for parthenogenesis as both an asset and a liability. On the one hand, it highlights how resilient sharks can be in the most unforgiving of environments, whether they are isolated in captivity or in the wild, if fishing has decimated their numbers to the point where few mating partners remain. "It just goes to show, life will find a way," says Chapman, who published his findings along with Shivji and another colleague in the British journal *Biology Letters*. On the other hand, genetic variability is essential to a species' survival, so sharks produced through a virgin birth don't add as much to a population as normal offspring; a shark with half the genetic diversity of its parent will be less prepared to compete.

"Biodiversity is based on genetic diversity," Chapman explains. "Genetic diversity is like lottery tickets: you don't know which one will win out in the future. The more diversity they have, the more chances they have to win, and the chance to survive for the next thousands and millions of years."

After Chapman and Shivji's paper came out, a rush of aquariums started reporting suspected virgin births in a wide range of shark species. The Belle Isle Aquarium in Detroit examined the babies that a white spotted bamboo shark appeared to produce on its own, and determined the two daughters were born to a mother that had never engaged in intercourse. European aquariums have reported that a zebra shark and a whitetip reef shark may have produced offspring single-handedly. In one case, a shark held in a tank within a Texas classroom seems to have engaged in parthenogenesis.

Chapman and other researchers have been able to confirm that this phenomenon has occurred in at least one other instance besides in Omaha and Detroit: a nine-year-old female blacktip shark that had lived in Virginia Aquarium's Norfolk Canyon Aquarium died during a physical exam while under sedation, and it turned out the shark had been carrying an embryo despite having been separated from male blacktip sharks for at least eight years. Chapman, Shivji, and the Virginia Aquarium and Marine Science Center scientist Beth Firchau found that the shark, named Tidbit, had just reached sexual maturity and was carrying an embryo with no paternal DNA at the time of its death.[9] This finding also challenged the scientific assumption that smaller sharks might be more inclined to engage in parthenogenesis because these species live in more isolated habitats and therefore may have trouble encountering males: the blacktip shark is a large species that migrates across the ocean.

At this point, Chapman thinks researchers should start out with the assumption that anytime a female shark produces offspring in the absence of a male, it's likely to be parthenogenesis: "This form of reproduction is more common and widespread than anybody realized." And it may not be as disturbing a discovery as Chapman first feared: the two Belle Island Aquarium virgin births were alive and thriving more than five years later, showing no signs that they were any less healthy than sharks produced by two parents.

The revelation also underscores another, broader point about sharks: nearly everything about their reproductive and parenting life is weird.

Male and female sharks don't intermingle frequently, according to scientific surveys. And researchers are beginning to learn that the nitty-gritty details surrounding when they do spend time with each other—to have sex—are harsh. These revelations highlight a central fact about sharks: they cannot be anthropomorphized the way some other creatures have been. They are vastly different from humans in how they behave, and won't ever warm the hearts of the public the way penguins can.

For centuries humans have recounted only the most fleeting observations of interactions between male and female sharks. While Aristotle might have composed the first written record of shark sex in the Western world, a fur seal observer with the New Zealand Department of Conservation evoked a similar theme thousands of years later. After witnessing an incident in 1991, A. Strachan wrote, "I have unwittingly been fortunate to witness a mating [between two white sharks]. I had thought at the beginning they were fighting as one animal appeared to be attempting to grasp the other with its great mouth, making great gouges in its side."[10]

Many scientists don't like to talk about shark sex, because they worry it will only reinforce the popular perception that these creatures are brutish and unrelenting. But one day I coax Chapman to give me a lecture on the subject, despite his reluctance. We are sitting in an idyllic setting—out on a dock in Belize looking at the Caribbean—and there are dozens of other things he'd obviously rather discuss. But I'm after the facts, and he obliges me.

Shark sex is, as Chapman puts it politely, "very rough." Some of this reflects simple mechanics: male sharks have a pair of reproductive organs called claspers, which they insert into a female shark's reproductive opening, or cloaca. (No matter how sharks gestate their young, they need to engage in internal fertilization in order to pro-

Several species of sharks congregate at Triangle Rocks off Bimini, where researchers from Sonny Gruber's Shark Lab observe them. *Photo by Grant Johnson*

The mechanical shark Bruce, shown here on the set of the movie *Jaws*, which terrified moviegoers across America in the 1970s. *Photo by Edith Blake*

A shark-fin dealer in Hong Kong's Sai Ying Poon neighborhood preparing dried fins to sell to restaurants. *Photo by Juliet Eilperin*

Mark "the Shark" Quartiano, shown here with a dead hammerhead he's caught, makes a living taking tourists and celebrities to fish sharks off Miami Beach.
Photo by Mark Quartiano

Selam Karasimbe ventures out in a canoe off Kavieng, hoping to attract and fight sharks that are becoming increasingly rare.
Photo by Juliet Eilperin

Gray reef sharks swim over a pristine coral reef on the fore reef of Malden Island, in the southern Line Islands. *Photo by Enric Sala*

Blacktip reef sharks use the pristine lagoon of Millennium Atoll in the southern Line Islands as a nursery. While the United States has afforded protection status to Palmyra and Kingman in the northern Line Islands, three others in that chain (Kiritimati, Tabuaeran, and Teraina) and the five southern Line Islands (Flint, Vostok, Millennium, Malden, and Starbuck) belong to the nation of Kiribati and do not enjoy such safeguards. *Photo by Enric Sala*

A male Raja Ampat epaulette shark, or *Hemiscyllium freycineti*, sucking on the tail of its female partner. *Photo by Dos Winkel*

A local villager out on community patrol near the island
of Batanta, Raja Ampat, guarding against cyanide and blast fishing.
Photo by Sterling Zumbrunn/Copyright © Conservation International

Wayag Lagoon, in Raja Ampat, is host to an array of fish species and hard corals.
After years of negotiations, Selpele and Salio villagers agreed to ban damaging
fishing practices in the area. *Photo by Sterling Zumbrunn/Copyright © Conservation International*

A whale shark swims on May 28, 2010, in waters off Sarasota, Florida, where it was satellite-tagged for research by scientists at Mote Marine Laboratory. Mote researchers are using satellite tagging to track the travels of whale sharks, whose migration patterns they still do not fully understand. *Photo by Kim Hull/Mote Marine Laboratory*

A great white pursues a seal—one of its favorite prey species— off the coast of South Africa. *Photo by Neil Hammerschlag*

Great whites are perhaps best known for their teeth, which grow in rows
to replace those that break or become worn.
Photo by Neil Hammerschlag

In less than a second, a great white launches its one-ton body in pursuit of a seal off Seal Island,
South Africa, a frequent phenomenon that attracts both tourists and researchers to the area.
Photo by Neil Hammerschlag

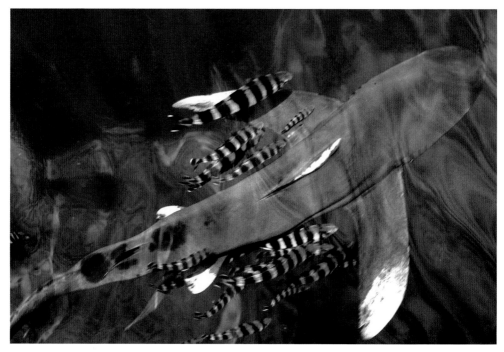

A rare oceanic white tip, accompanied by pilot fish, cuts through the open ocean in the Indian Ocean's Mozambique Channel. This species used to be common, but researchers have found it declined by 99 percent during the second half of the twentieth century. *Photo by Neil Hammerschlag*

A curious blue shark cruises in from the open seas off Rhode Island to investigate the scene. The species engages in such a rough mating ritual that female blue sharks have significantly thicker skin than their male counterparts. *Photo by Neil Hammerschlag*

duce their offspring.) These claspers, which harden as a male becomes sexually mature, have tiny hooks inside them, which allow them to hold the female alongside as they're mating. On top of that, during courting among larger sharks the male is usually biting the female to keep her around. This stems from the fact that, with a few exceptions, the female is almost always resisting the male's advances. Marine biologists have an easy time determining if a female has been mating in the recent past because her skin will be raw and possibly bleeding. Female sharks build up defenses, to the extent they can, to cope with such a brutal coupling. The skin of most mature female sharks is measurably thicker than that of their male counterparts, and the fact that females tend to be larger also helps them withstand the beating they take during sex. Smaller shark species often mate by intertwining their bodies rather than the male dominating the coupling, a slightly less violent form of courtship.

When mating season rolls around, female sharks—at least those that have been observed mating, a rare event in itself—tend to stay in shallow water. This is one of the few ways they can exercise any form of mate choice, since female sharks can resist being pinned down in shallow water. "If they stay in deep water, what's waiting for them is a roaming band of males," Chapman explains. "If she's in shallow water, it's difficult to roll her over; she will press her cloaca against the bottom. The key is to get her into deep water."

Once a female is cornered by a group of males in deeper water, they will take turns inserting their claspers in her. Often, a male shark will bite a female in order to grip her during mating. The end result? When a nurse shark gives birth to a litter of fifty pups, Chapman says, "what you'll see is there's anywhere from two to seven fathers." Lemon sharks exhibit the same phenomenon: a litter of twenty pups often boasts several male parents.

Of course, Chapman knows this, for the most part, from DNA analysis rather than from firsthand observation. Researchers rarely get to witness this mating—though nurse sharks are better observed than other species when it comes to intercourse—but advances in genetic testing have expanded our understanding of this ancient ritual. As Chapman notes, "You can actually use genetics to know what mating patterns they have."

One scientist has, most likely, viewed more shark sex than any other researcher in the world: Jeffrey Carrier, a marine biologist at Albion College in Michigan who conducts his research in the Dry Tortugas, a protected marine reserve that lies seventy-eight miles away from Key West. The animals his team has observed over the past two decades have demonstrated an amazing degree of fidelity to this site: the females return every two years, while the males come each year, during June. "We pretty much know who's dating whom," he explains. He's acquired this level of detail by watching more than a thousand shark mating attempts, a formidable record.

In 2000, Carrier co-authored a paper with the Mote Marine Laboratory scientist Harold L. "Wes" Pratt Jr. in the journal *Environmental Biology of Fishes* with the deceptively bland title "A Review of Elasmobranch Reproductive Behavior with a Case Study on the Nurse Shark, *Ginglymostoma cirratum*." It is the most definitive account of shark sex ever published, and it makes for fascinating reading.

Here are some of the facts Pratt and Carrier have to offer: among male sharks (as well as skates and rays) "biting or holding by some means appears to be universal." Female blue sharks—which produce young at a much higher rate than other sharks—seem to get the worst of it, since they "receive so much precopulatory biting that they often appear to be severely wounded while on the seasonal mating grounds."

One of the best sections in Pratt and Carrier's article is the chart they've constructed detailing the fish's "courtship and mating behaviors." When a nurse shark wants to demonstrate "acceptance," for example, "female arches body towards male, 'cups' pelvic fins." If it's "avoidance" she's after, then the shark opts for " 'lying on back' the female rests motionless and rigid." The sand tiger shark even engages in "stalking," according to the scientists, but at least it's not aimed at females. In this case, the sharks target other species within a captive environment, just to ensure that no other animal interferes with their chances of hooking up.

Carrier and his colleagues have studied their subjects' intimate dating patterns through a device called Crittercam, whose name sums up its function quite nicely: you attach the camera to the critter, and when you retrieve the footage, you can see what it's been doing. (Greg Marshall, the National Geographic scientist who invented Crittercam, actually did so after being inspired by watching a shark glide through the water in Belize with a small remora fish attached to its back. Remoras, which are sometimes nicknamed shark suckers, hitch rides on the large predators, and in exchange for getting some of a shark's leftover food, they pick off some of the parasites that attach themselves to their host. Sharks show no signs that they're even aware of the remoras' presence, which is why scientists have modeled their video observation system on the tiny fish.) The Crittercam footage has captured the gang-bang phenomenon nurse sharks engage in, a process Carrier describes as "a cooperative venture, where one male is successful and the other males keep the female from leaving." One of the most interesting aspects of this act is the fact that an implicit social order seems to determine who gets lucky.

"We think there's a social overlay, a social hierarchy, in a way that's startling," Carrier says. As in the world of humans, lions, and other animal societies, it's the dominant male nurse sharks that get the most play.

In the case of nurse sharks it's the big, dark ones that reign supreme, according to Carrier and Pratt, which explains why females may shift from shallow to deeper water depending on the suitor. "The 'refuging' female is observed to retreat repeatedly from smaller, lighter colored males which are perhaps younger, weaker or inexperienced. The arrival of one of the larger, darker dominant males often elicits a response in the female to remain in the lagoon's deeper water, or at least not to retreat when approached."[11]

There is a nice inverse of this among hammerhead sharks, which gather in large schools each year to mate. Among that species, the dominant females occupy a prominent place in the center of these schools, pushing more submissive females to the periphery. The UC Davis professor Peter Klimley, who has swum with hammerhead sharks and filmed them while they've schooled, describes it as sort of a mix between the old television series *Wild Kingdom* and a traditional 1950s social mixer where young women are waiting for their male suitors to make the first move. On the one hand, the scars on the upper portion of female hammerheads' bodies testify to the extent to which they fight each other over which sharks get to stay in the school's inner sphere. "This is what happens a lot in the animal kingdom," he says. "It takes one or two ritual combats to establish a hierarchy." On the other hand, the male hammerheads that manage to get near the school push themselves into its center, casting aside the females on the periphery.

Once they make it in, moreover, male hammerheads perform elaborate moves to copulate with one of the dominant females. After pushing their way into the inner sanctum, they rotate their claspers so that they're bent in half at a right angle and then throw their torso forward in what Klimley calls "a very sexual manner." Other times, the sharks will conduct a corkscrew somersault. This acrobatic maneuver gives off flashes of light, which help attract attention.

While researchers know what happens when some sharks mate, that's about where their understanding of shark sex ends. "That part's not in doubt," Carrier says of the mating attempts he's witnessed. "We just don't know what the hell's happening afterwards." After that point Carrier and his colleagues are no longer able to track the nurse sharks for months, until they return the following summer to repeat their courtship pattern once more.

But new technology now holds the promise of allowing scientists to move beyond what they've learned through Crittercam. Accelerometers—also known as acceleration data loggers—are the same motor-sensitive computer chips used in smart phones, iPods, and the Nintendo Wii, and they are providing unprecedented detail about how sharks move beneath the water. Accelerometer tags, which are a bit larger than AA batteries and are designed to fall off a shark's dorsal fin, can detect every flick of the animal's tail or tilt of its body. Nick Whitney, a postdoctoral scientist at Mote, worked with a team to fit four female nurse sharks with accelerometers in the Dry Tortugas and was able to document a range of mating behaviors, including thrashing, barrel rolls, and headstands. With any luck, Whitney and his colleagues will be able to attach the tags to more elusive species, such as hammerhead, sandbar, and bull sharks, in order to better grasp these animals' mating patterns.

One thing researchers already understand is that the brutal competition that defines mating among sharks does not stop there. Once the eggs are fertilized, shark fetuses sometimes eat each other in utero, acting out the harshest form of sibling rivalry imaginable. To some extent this is merely an extension of the sort of competition for paternity that usually takes place outside the womb: Chapman has determined through genetic testing that while a sand tiger shark is often fertilized by multiple partners, during gestation the offspring of a single father will consume its half siblings in order to emerge as the sole survivor.

There is another upside to this embryonic cannibalism, or ovophagy, which occurs in both sand tiger and white sharks: it helps prepare young sharks for the difficult conditions they will face once they exit the womb. In the case of sand tiger litters only two babies emerge each time, one from each of the mother's uteruses, since the surviving offspring has eaten everything from fertilized eggs to embryos inside the womb.

Chapman, who has examined sand tiger fetuses, describes them as having "big, wicked, nasty teeth" that help them devour their siblings while still in the womb. "They tear them to bits," he relates, in a dispassionate voice. "A female sand tiger gives birth to a baby that's already a meter long and an experienced killer."

In many ways genetic testing has provided us with the most brutal truths about sharks. It reveals which sharks are being killed by humans and which are being killed by each other. It can be a tool to mete out justice or, in some instances, a reminder that they have evolved over millennia to suit their surroundings. And it hints at one of the most promising aspects of this sort of academic research: when it comes to sharks, the golden age of scientific discovery has just begun.

6

SHARK TRACKERS

Right out there, it's the Serengeti. We just can't see it.
—Barbara Block, Stanford University marine biologist

It wasn't until a few decades ago that serious scientists began focusing on sharks at all. The renowned biologist E. O. Wilson became fascinated by them at age nine, just like many other young boys who imagine how they would fare against the wildest beasts on earth. "The great white and I go way back" is how he likes to phrase it. Seven decades later Wilson—who combines the courtliness of a southern gentleman with the patrician New England air of his longtime adopted home, Cambridge, Massachusetts—calls himself an expert in "selachology." That's a word he made up himself (though it takes its roots from the Greek word Aristotle favored, *selache,* or sea fish) and translates roughly into "the study of sharks." Wilson is a rumpled academic whose hearing gives him trouble at times, but having devoted his life to unlocking the mystery of the natural world, he is extraordinarily skilled in relating his findings to people who are less brainy than he is. Sharks are not just an obsession but a pedagogical tool that helps the professor explain a universe to which most people are oblivious.

Wilson has taught an introductory biology class to Harvard undergraduates for decades, and when he needs to convey the concept of "adaptive radiation"—how species evolve in different ways depending on the part of the world in which they live—he always uses sharks as his example because they boast such a wide array of physical forms across the globe. Their lifestyles vary too: Some move from deep water to breed in shallow water, lagoons, and estuaries; they can spawn between one and a few hundred offspring at a time. While they traditionally swim in salt water, some survive in freshwater. They live in the tropics and at the poles, in both warm and cold water. They began as what researchers at Dalhousie and Florida International universities, led by Francesco Ferretti, called "small coastal consumers" in one journal article, but over time evolutionary forces favored larger species that continued to grow and reached sexual maturity later, so they could "colonize deeper oceanic waters."[1] One group, known as sleeper sharks, live at incredible depths, like the Portuguese shark, which survives at twelve thousand feet below the sea's surface. These deepwater sharks are some of the longest-living sharks on earth: Greenland sharks live more than an entire century.

In this way, sharks serve as a lens into an array of worlds that have historically lain beyond our grasp. Researchers are still investigating why hammerhead sharks have such odd, flattened heads, but this form clearly gives them exceptional peripheral vision that helps them hunt. The fact that sharks' litter sizes vary so enormously reflects the wide range of habitats that the ocean offers: coastal sharks produce larger litters because their offspring enjoy more abundant resources yet at the same time face plenty of predators; open-ocean sharks produce a small number of babies that will have to work harder to find food but are less likely to be eaten. Coastal sharks can grow to be fearsome animals, but at their early stages of development they are prey to an array of species, such as rays and other carnivorous fish.

The range of shark litter sizes is enormous: the pelagic thresher and bigeye thresher tend to produce two offspring at a time, while the great hammerhead shark can produce several dozen young at once, and a tiger shark can produce more than a hundred.[2] Whale sharks are the most fecund sharks on earth, capable of producing three hundred young at a time. These sharks carry eggs at different stages of development, which could be, in the words of the Australian biologist Brad Norman, "a survival strategy" in which the mother births her pups when the external conditions are best, or it could just reflect how much space the shark has in its twin uteruses.

The variety of tails among shark species also testifies to their adaptability. Threshers boast the longest tail of any shark: its upper lobe alone is as long as its body, ranging between five and eight feet, and serves as a powerful hunting weapon. By contrast, nurse sharks, which stick close to the bottom and swim more slowly, have relatively weak tails. The fast-swimming sharks, including the great white and mako, have tails with upper and lower lobes that measure almost the same length. This particular design, called the thunniform fin, gives it more thrust per stroke. By using a larger surface area to push aside a greater amount of water with each tail movement, a great white or mako can turn forcefully or push itself forward, positioning itself better to attack its prey.[3] Tuna and other sharks in the family Lamnidae also boast this feature, allowing them to swim at high speeds and traverse long distances.

The fact that sharks have so many ways of existing in the world underscores how much they convey about the planet. Sharks have developed unique ways to eat, swim, and reproduce because they have survived such vastly different circumstances. Few other animals provide as clear a lens into the natural world as sharks, yet we are just beginning to crack this code. We would do well to learn from them, for the sake of our own survival.

Sharks—along with skates, rays, and the nearly extinct chimaeras—are all elasmobranchs. All of these fish have five to seven paired gill openings on the sides of their head. Some rays, like guitarfish and sawfish, look like sharks that have been flattened, which makes them an alluring fishing target because their large fins are ideal for shark's fin soup. However, they are not actually sharks. The fossil record boasts more than three thousand species of elasmobranchs, a hardened testimony to the diversity of sharks, skates, and rays that once roamed the seas. But this figure has narrowed over time. (Since their cartilaginous skeletons are seldom well preserved, it's sharks' spines and teeth, along with impressions of sharks in rocks, that constitute the species' fossil record.)

There are roughly five hundred known species of sharks, and this number is constantly inching higher: sometimes in tiny increments, other times in a massive leap. In any given year a scientist might find distinct species either through genetic analysis or by exploring remote waters. But in some instances the number can change on a larger scale, as when CSIRO Marine and Atmospheric Research's Peter Last, William White, and their team used DNA to identify a total of forty-six new sharks in the course of a year and a half. To put the current global shark count in perspective, it is more than twice as many species as scientists knew about in 1971 when the respected naturalist Peter Matthiessen published his book *Blue Meridian: The Search for the Great White Shark.* However, this does not mean sharks are doing better than they were several decades ago: it suggests some of these populations are more vulnerable, because they are smaller than previously thought. For example, the CSIRO team identified the northern river shark, which is unique to Australia, grows to be nearly six feet long, and ranks as one of the country's largest freshwater animals. Until recently, it was confused with another Australian freshwater species in an adjacent region, but now researchers understand it is distinct in its own right.

Great whites now rank as the world's most terrifying shark— E. O. Wilson calls them "one of the four or five last great predators of humanity." But these fish appear to be pikers compared with their ancestors, *Carcharodon megalodon,* which researchers estimate were double the size of great whites and boasted teeth twice the size of a human hand. Living between 50 and 4.5 million years ago, *Carcharodon megalodon* may have stretched as long as fifty feet and weighed twenty tons, equal to five elephants piled on top of one another.[4] Using three-dimensional computer modeling techniques, a group of researchers from Australia and California have calculated the bite force of both modern and ancient great whites: the largest great whites living today have a force of up to 1.8 metric tons of pressure, compared with the 18.2 tons a *Carcharodon megalodon* could exert. (For comparison, a large, modern African lion can produce roughly 560 kilograms of bite force and a *Tyrannosaurus rex* would have boasted a force of 3.1 metric tons—a sixth that of the ancient great white.[5]) In the history of the earth, virtually nothing has roamed the sea that is as scary as these animals.

Some living sharks are massive, of course: whale sharks are the largest fish in the world, stretching up to fifty feet long, and basking sharks grow up to forty feet long. But others are tiny—the spined pygmy shark, called *Squaliolus laticaudus,* is six inches long, and lantern sharks span twelve inches. Three feet represents the median length for sharks, with half of all species measuring less than that. Despite all the hype that surrounds sharks and their killing capacity, most of them aren't nearly as fearsome as their reputation suggests.

The sharks that swim in our waters today evolved about 100 million years ago, with a more powerful, mobile jaw that allowed them to target prey more effectively than their ancestors. All sharks have multiple rows of teeth on their upper and lower jaws, and as these teeth break or become worn, spare teeth lying just behind take their place in a sort of conveyor-belt fashion.

While sharks share a similar jaw structure across different species, modern sharks each take on their own bite sizes—and shapes. A shark's choppers depend both on the species and the age of the animal, since different types of teeth are effective for various types of prey. Saw-edged teeth, like the kind great whites have, come in handy when biting big chunks out of marine mammals. Baby great whites, by contrast, have pointed teeth that let them grab and swallow smaller prey. Fangs or spearlike teeth are better for gripping squid.

The cookie-cutter shark, *Isistius brasiliensis*—a dwarf shark that swims in schools and is bioluminescent, meaning it gives off a greenish glow in the water—extracts a perfectly circular chunk of flesh out of large fish for its meals, and for years researchers were at a loss as to how it managed to attack larger predatory fish such as tuna, swordfish, and even porpoises. In 1998, after making a series of close observations, the Harbor Branch Oceanographic Institute scientist Edith A. Widder figured out how they do it. The cookie-cutter shark derives its bioluminescence from thousands of very small photospheres around the edges of its scales. There is one part of the shark's body that lacks this phosphorescent gleam: a collar around its throat that is darkly pigmented. As the light streams into the water from above, this pattern provides a silhouette that acts as a lure to larger predators, which mistake the cookie-cutter shark for a small fish.

While many larger sharks travel as loners, these pygmy sharks congregate instead, which gives them an even greater advantage against their opponents. "Schooling may also explain how these very small sharks avoid a counterattack from the very large predators such as swordfish and porpoises on which their crater wounds are commonly found," Widder writes. "The damage these sharks inflict would make their company as appealing as a swarm of wasps."[6]

Other sharks adopt a more obvious line of attack: the thresher shark wreaks havoc within schools of fish by whacking them with its exceedingly long tail and then returning to consume the ones that have been the most immobilized.[7] Flattened sharks such as wobbegongs lie pressed against the ocean floor and then swallow fish as they swim by. A nurse shark has a set of feelers, or barbels, on its nose so it can ferret out small prey in the sand below it.

Sharks' jaws don't just tell us about their evolution: they reveal details about our own. For years scientists have studied vertebrates' transition from jawless animals such as lampreys to ones with jaws, because it was such a massive step forward in evolution. But they've been hampered by the inadequate fossil record dating from the Devonian period, which occurred sometime between 412 and 354 million years ago. For literally a hundred years, researchers focused on a 370-million-year-old shark named *Cladoselache,* because they had several good fossils to examine. But then a decade ago scientists found a shark relative from Bolivia called *Pucapampella* that predates *Cladoselache* by 30 million years.

John Maisey, a curator in the American Museum of Natural History's Division of Paleontology, determined that *Pucapampella* had a jaw that was attached to its braincase in a way that was more like a bony fish, or osteichthyan, than a chondrichthyan. The finding Maisey made along with Philippe Janvier at the National Museum of Natural History, Paris, has been bolstered by the unearthing of another early Devonian chondrichthyan fossil, *Doliodus problematicus,* discovered in New Brunswick, Canada.[8] The nearly 409-million-year-old *Doliodus* has sharklike jaws and rows of sharklike teeth, whereas *Pucapampella* has what Maisey calls "a very odd single row of teeth." Scientists are still puzzling over the fact that while the two specimens are very early chondrichthyans and date from roughly the same time, they are anatomically very different. They are also exploring additional clues—including osteichthyan fossils from the end of the preceding Silurian period, between 423 and 416 million years ago, and sharklike skin denticles from Silurian-period rocks—which indicate jawed vertebrates might have evolved earlier than previously thought.[9]

This research is significant because it suggests—for the first time—that modern shark jaws are a more advanced characteristic than the jaws of bony fish. It also indicates that an essential part of the human anatomy originated in fish. As Maisey said, "The psychology of evolution is interesting. People don't mind being called a primate or a mammal, but they don't like being called a fish."[10]

In his excellent book, *Your Inner Fish: A Journey into the 3.5-Billion-Year History of the Human Body,* Neil Shubin details the many evolutionary debts we owe to sharks. This includes not only the bones in our inner ear but also the lever system we use to bite. (The muscles and cranial nerves that enable us to swallow and talk are the same ones that move the gills of sharks.)[11] Not every aspect of our shark inheritance is a plus, at least if you're a man. Sharks' gonads are nestled near the heart. But in human males, gonads are positioned within the scrotum in order to keep sperm at the proper temperature. This has created a weak spot in the body wall, which in turn accounts for why men experience hernias. As Shubin writes, "Men's tendency to develop hernias is a trade-off between our fish ancestry and our mammal present."[12]

Our common ancestry with sharks extends to the genetic level as well. In December 2006 researchers revealed that the genome of the elephant shark, which is native to waters off New Zealand and southern Australia, features a large number of ancient DNA fragments held in the human genome. These fragments regulate genes that produce proteins integral to human development and physiology. The team from A*STAR's Institute of Molecular and Cell Biology in Singapore and the U.S.-based J. Craig Venter Institute described the discovery as a major development that could help scientists understand how our genes are regulated, and unlock the origin of several human diseases.[13]

Other aspects of shark biology, such as their electroreception, are totally alien to humans. Many shark species have a row of small holes that run from head to tail, which picks up weak vibrations. This network, along with tiny, fluid-filled sacs in their snouts and chins known as ampullae of Lorenzini, helps sharks find fish buried in the sand because they can detect the electromagnetic fields generated by a fish's beating heart or gills. Other fish have a lateral line to sense movement, but they do not have the gelatinous material that serves as a conductor for electric vibrations, radiating these signals out to a shark's nervous system.

This sensing ability, a critical asset in the wild, can prove a liability in captivity because the electrical signals emitted by an aquarium's lights, pumps, and metal can confuse the animals. But scientists across the United States are exploring whether they can capitalize on sharks' unique voltage-charged gel for more practical purposes. University of San Francisco physics professor Brandon R. Brown has extracted the material from dead sharks to gauge its thermal sensitivity, while Case Western Reserve University nanoengineering professor Alexis Abramson is leading an effort to develop a synthetic gel with similar thermoelectric properties that could be used to convert waste heat, from devices such as car engines, into usable electricity.

Sharks' extraordinary ability to hear low-pitched frequencies also helps them identify weakened fish: in the early 1960s, the University of Miami researcher Don Nelson theorized the spasms of a dying fish produce water movement sharks can detect through their lateral line and a staccato sound they can pick up through their inner ear.[14]

Sharks' ability to pick up vibrations also helps them migrate across ocean basins, because they can orient themselves within the earth's magnetic field. These magnetic particles, which became embedded in the basalt in the aftermath of volcanic eruptions, provide a path for sharks to follow. The UC Davis marine biologist Peter Klimley describes it as a series of underwater highways as elaborate as anything surrounding a major American city. "You end up having these magnetic roads," Klimley says. The seafloor boasts a pin-striped pattern of strong and weak magnetic fields, which only sharks know how to navigate. Periodically, the earth's magnetic field reverses, a shift that sharks can detect without a problem.

Klimley views sharks' multiple senses as their greatest asset. Having studied hammerheads swimming around Pacific seamounts, he's documented that each night as they forage for food, the sharks swim more than twelve miles in one direction and then return along the precise same path, in the dead of night.

When you add in sharks' sense of smell, which can detect a scent from miles away or help them find a mate, the species boasts a total of six senses, outpacing humans. Their acute sense of smell stems from a series of nasal flaps that lie in front of a shark's mouth. When seawater passes over these flaps, they guide it to delicate membranes that can detect small substances in the ocean. As they glide through the ocean, sharks can determine where the scent is coming from by comparing what they perceive from one nostril with the other. This question of timing is crucial: sensing small differences in when the scent hits each nostril helps sharks steer the most efficient path toward their prey, as they follow an odor plume to its source.[15] Some scientists estimate that more than a fourth of a shark's brain is dedicated to its sense of smell. Their eyesight isn't shabby either: while it's not as keen as humans', sharks have a reflective layer over their eyes, called tapetum lucidum, which makes it easier to see in the dark.[16] They can also see in color and have several mechanisms to protect their eyes when they attack prey: many species have a nictitating membrane that closes when they strike, and some roll their eyes back in their heads so their victims cannot scratch or poke their eyes out.[17] Every sense they possess works to their predatory advantage.

But it is the way sharks resemble humans—and differ from most fish—that helps account for why they are now in trouble. While most people think of fish as spawning millions of eggs, only a fraction of which will survive, sharks generally take the opposite approach. They take years to mature sexually—sometimes more than a decade—and only then do they produce a small number of young, which stand a good chance of making it to adulthood. This is why sharks are so vulnerable to human predation: while they are adept at devising different ways to produce their offspring, they simply don't generate enough young on a regular basis to withstand a sustained assault from fishing.

There's no single way sharks produce their offspring. Some species give birth to live pups; others lay eggs encased in yolk in leathery cases, which can sustain the embryo through its gestation. Others disperse eggs at the bottom of the sea. The number of young that sharks produce varies just as widely. While some sharks can carry dozens or even hundreds of eggs at a time, a spiny dogfish takes nearly two years to produce a single pup. The spiny dogfish's pregnancy ranks as one of the longest gestation periods recorded in the animal kingdom, rivaling that of the elephant, which leaves it particularly vulnerable to overfishing.

Of the roughly 40 percent of shark species that reproduce by laying eggs, known as oviparity, many do this shortly after fertilization. The mothers anchor these eggs, which have a tough protective layer covering them, in the seabed so they will hatch in the sharks' nursery grounds. Horn sharks produce a spiral-shaped egg case that can be wedged into rocks, while cat sharks anchor their egg cases to whatever is growing on the seabed. Over the course of their gestation these shark fetuses will receive sustenance by absorbing the yolk contained in the egg. Some species, however, choose to lay their eggs only a matter of weeks before they hatch in order to ensure that other ocean predators don't have a chance to eat their young.

Even the sharks that engage in live births do it in very different forms. Both whale and spiny dogfish sharks keep their eggs internally, allowing the young to consume the egg yolk and hatch inside of their mothers, before releasing them into the wild. Other species don't rely exclusively on the yolk sac, and instead produce infertile eggs they feed to their fetuses to keep them growing. This hybrid form of reproduction, called ovoviviparity, takes places in about a quarter of shark species.

Still other sharks engage in the more sophisticated form of reproduction, placental viviparity, in which they produce a placenta and engage in live births. This form of birth, which takes place in 10 percent of sharks, most closely resembles humans': the fertilized egg develops into a placenta, which is connected by a cord to the uterine wall so the mother can feed her pup. In the case of hammerheads, which can produce a few dozen young in a single litter, each pup is connected to its mother through an umbilical cord. The similarity between humans and sharks ends after labor, however, because once a shark gives birth, her kids are on their own. Right after birth lemon sharks will rest for a short period, still attached by an umbilical cord, before breaking it by swimming away. At that point the babies must depend on mangroves and other natural fortifications, rather than their parents, to protect them.[18]

In many ways, the mother shark is doing her offspring a favor: in the immediate aftermath of birthing, female sharks experience a rush of hormones that minimizes their natural instinct to attack their children. But after a period of time those hormones dissipate and the mother takes off, leaving her children—which are born fully independent—to fend for themselves.

I got to witness this phenomenon myself when I waded through Bimini's mangroves with Sonny Gruber and two other shark researchers, Ellen Pikitch and Elizabeth Babcock. After we trekked to one of the island's most reliable lemon shark nursery grounds and threw a bit of fish into the water, a parade of juveniles came flocking over. The whole experience amused me: Gruber has developed plenty of shark tricks over his years in the field, and one of them is that he can hypnotize a shark by flipping it over. It's an impressive yet comical feat: while the shark first struggles and flaps about as Gruber repositions it, within moments it lies harmless and still, in a trance. Soon I was holding my own small lemon shark, suspended upside down. I felt the rough, scratchy surface of its skin, and then, having put it right side up, I released it back into the wild to join its companions.

By this point the water was teeming with teenage sharks—not exactly in a school, but rather a disorganized pack, roaming together for a finite period before each one broke off to pursue its own target. There was something a little sad about it, this group that had no real bond. There are instances when sharks travel in schools out of self-interest, such as when female hammerheads are seeking mates or when smaller sharks need a form of defense against larger predators. Whitetip reef sharks gather together for a very specific purpose: to seek out and consume their prime targets, bony fish. These fish are out and about on the reef during the day, but they hide in the cracks and crannies of the reef once night falls. That's when the whitetips emerge, traveling in groups in order to more effectively sniff out the fish they plan to tear to pieces.

"They are the most vicious predators; they hunt in packs, like wolves," relates Elliott Norse, who heads the Marine Conservation Biology Institute in Bellevue, Washington. "They put their faces in every crack of the reef—they are social predators. I don't know of any animal who has that strategy in the ocean."

Most large shark species, like tiger sharks and the lemon sharks that circled before me, have little need to travel with their kind once they become adults, because other sharks represent potential competitors for food, rather than allies. As I looked at them, I reminded myself that sharks aren't about bonding or establishing elaborate social structures. They're about surviving and dominating everything that comes in their path.

Pikitch, who directs the Institute for Ocean Conservation Science at Stony Brook University, has devoted a significant portion of her career to tracking sharks in locales such as Glover's Reef, an atoll by Belize in the western Caribbean. I journeyed with her there to get a sense of the mechanics of how such tracking works, since no matter how high-tech the devices scientists use, attaching them to sharks can involve backbreaking work. Most of the time researchers employ traditional fishing methods, which may involve a baited line, spear, or lasso. Hovering over the water in Glover's Reef, I learn how addictive lassoing sharks can be.

To figure out what shark lassoing entails, I must hang over the side of a motorboat that Ellen Pikitch has commandeered for research. Pikitch started out as a mathematician in college but became drawn to studying fish during grad school, even though she pursued her doctorate in landlocked Indiana. She speaks in the often flat tones of a Brooklynite and approaches her work with clinical precision, hoping to discern the sorts of mathematical patterns she studied earlier in her career. But Pikitch is passionate about two fish in particular— sturgeons and sharks—and her insatiable curiosity has prompted her to spend more than a decade conducting the longest-running shark survey in the world. To survey sharks properly, Pikitch and her team must tag them. And in order to tag sharks methodically, lassoing is required.

Naturally, one must perform this rodeo maneuver with some degree of skill, to guarantee that the subject in question doesn't bite your hand off. There's a straightforward way to ensure this doesn't happen: first and foremost, make sure the shark has gotten hooked on a longline before you begin to lasso it. Many fishing vessels use lines that stretch for miles, but Pikitch and her colleagues rely on a line that measures a few dozen yards instead. They suspend fishing line baited with at least fifty hooks between two buoys, and then let it sit for a couple of hours to maximize the number of sharks that get caught in the line. Establishing a longline with baited hooks is the best way to catch sharks, as opposed to dragging a large net through the water that sharks could tear apart with their teeth. After the sharks are caught on the hooks, the lassoing can begin.

Once we've pulled up a line with a shark hooked on it, one of Pikitch's colleagues holds the fishing line near the shark's snout while the lassoer (me, in this case) grabs a rope that's been knotted to form a noose. At this point the shark is floating in the water, parallel to the boat, so the entire procedure can transpire with the least amount of damage to the fish. With my left hand, I grab the dorsal fin to steady the shark while slipping the noose around the shark's tail. Then I rapidly bring my left hand over to anchor the knot while pulling the rope tight, and, voilà, the shark has been properly lassoed.

This is anything but easy: during the entire procedure, the shark is focused on escaping my grasp. After taking over lasso duty on Pikitch's boat, I am faced with the undeniable fact that not only are sharks not as dumb as they've been historically portrayed but even the reassuringly named nurse shark is a fighter.

Shark wrangling gives you an acute sense of these animals' muscular bodies and the extent to which they can maneuver themselves in the water to elude any potential foe. On top of all that, grabbing a shark tail that's swaying back and forth and covered in denticles is akin to having a baseball bat covered in sandpaper rub up and down your hand.

There's a simple reason why we're lassoing sharks today: it's the easiest way to keep a shark pinned down if one is hoping to implant a radio transmitter in its body, which is what Pikitch and other researchers are planning to do. The fact that they need to resort to such elaborate tactics suggests how difficult it is to study sharks in the first place. They spend their lives underwater, where it's hard to spot them, and they move fast. If one gets close to them, they might attack. None of these attributes make them nearly as easy to examine as, say, lab rats.

Pikitch is the kind of woman who actually craves run-ins with sharks. She divides her time between the Upper East Side and Stony Brook, but spends much of her work life in habitats such as Glover's Reef, which she first began visiting in the mid-1990s. At the time, Pikitch was starting up the Wildlife Conservation Society's marine program, and she was investigating the idea of establishing a research station on an island on the atoll called Middle Key, which a British noblewoman named Claude Kinnoull had left to the nonprofit. One day she was hanging out on the dock, chatting with Archie "Chuck" Carr III, a fellow WCS scientist, when she spotted two baby lemon sharks darting in and out under the pier.

"You don't have baby sharks unless there's a nursery," Pikitch thought to herself. She soon set out to answer a basic question: What kinds of sharks, and how many, spend their days navigating the more than 750 patch reefs that make up Glover's Reef, and is this pattern changing over time? This straightforward query, unfortunately, can only be answered if you can deploy enough technological gizmos on fish with sharp teeth.

The methodology of tagging—which has been applied to both terrestrial and marine creatures in recent years—has dramatically expanded scientists' understanding of sharks. These devices can range from the mundane—plastic spaghetti strips with numbers, which simply let researchers know if they've recaptured an animal—to the high-tech, $3,500 satellite tags that can track where an animal has traveled, how deep it has gone diving, and how much energy it has expended in the process. Quite simply, these devices allow scientists to track marine life once it disappears below the surface, which amounts to a revolutionary advance.

This sort of information is so valuable in part because it gives scientists a sense of what parts of the ocean need to be sheltered more than others. Faced with the enormity of the sea, and the many different demands on it, conservationists are trying to identify the most ecologically valuable regions so they can establish marine protected areas. That way they can strike a deal with competing groups such as commercial and recreational fishing interests: leave these parts of the ocean alone, and you can exploit the rest.

Pikitch and her top assistants, Demian Chapman and Elizabeth Babcock, have been tracking their sharks with fairly straightforward, inexpensive monitoring equipment, spaghetti tags and radio transmitters, both of which can be applied to a shark once it's lassoed. The spaghetti tags help researchers identify individual animals once they're recaught, while the acoustic tags send radio signals that provide scientists with a sense of where a shark has traveled over time.

Once I've conducted the lasso operation with Chapman's assistance, the scientists first record some basic information about the shark we've secured to the side of the boat. Using a simple band of measuring tape, they record the shark's species and gender along with three separate lengths for the shark, because different researchers rely on different measurements. The first measurement captures the distance between a shark's snout and the upper part of its tail, the second goes from the snout to the fork in its tail, and the third reaches from the snout to the tail's end. Then it's time for a quick surgical operation.

While keeping the shark secured in the water, Chapman makes a surgical incision about an inch long, right next to the dorsal fin. This allows him to insert an acoustic tag that will send a unique signal every time the shark swims within 1,640 feet of the nearly two dozen radio transmitters the team has stationed throughout the reef. With a few swift motions Chapman stitches up the incision, and we prepare to release the shark, taking care to make sure it doesn't savage us in the process. I loosen the noose, he clips the hook with a pair of pliers, and I yank the rope back, sliding it easily over the shark's tail. Then it's off, thrashing furiously as it leaves behind the researchers who detained it from its usual cruising activity.

One of the oddest aspects of surveying sharks is that, in the end, it's still fishing: you never know what you'll wind up getting. In order to get a sizable variety of sharks, Pikitch and her team fish at night as well as during the day, since different species are active at particular times of day.

Because Glover's Reef is full of shallow patch reefs, negotiating the waters at night without wrecking the boat amounts to a feat in itself. Only one man seems equipped to do this: Norlan Lamb, a Belizean fisherman who has worked on Pikitch's project for nearly a decade. While Lamb uses GPS maps to get a general idea of how to negotiate the reefs, he relies mainly on instinct to avoid a shipwreck. He sometimes wears his sunglasses at night—it's sort of a Zen approach, from what I could glean from our conversations.

Once Lamb has zipped across the reef to the study site, the researchers begin to check the line they set earlier in the day for sharks. The first shark that appears is a pregnant sharpnose: when it makes it onto the deck, its babies are squirming visibly inside, their small bodies forming clear and shifting outlines on her stomach's surface.

The shark's eyes sparkle in the reflection of the assorted headlamps pointed in her direction; after Chapman and Babcock place a simple spaghetti tag on her, they let her go. Then they turn their attention to two male Caribbean reef sharks caught on the line; since both of them have been tagged in the past, they just jot down the tag numbers and identifying characteristics before releasing them. Still, even this basic summary requires the whole lasso routine, which at times doesn't go so smoothly.

Once the scientists manage to tag their random collection of sharks, it's up to the fish to let them know what's happening underwater. The twenty-two monitors sit at the bottom of the sea for six months at a time, and before long these relays begin to blend into their surroundings in the way that a shipwreck does. The team refers to one of its relays as a "lobster farm" because, in Chapman's words, "it's got little wee lobsters all over it." Another is so covered with algae it looks more like the outcropping of a reef than a piece of electronic equipment. But how they look is, ultimately, irrelevant. All the researchers care about is what signals they receive and transmit back to the research station.

After a decade of surveying Glover's Reef and acoustically tagging more than fifty sharks, Pikitch and her colleagues can draw some basic conclusions. The sharks they find here stay in the atoll year-round: unlike some pelagic species, which roam far and wide, these animals display a remarkable fidelity to these waters. But they defy expectations in some respects. As Chapman observes, "These sharks are thought of generally as shallow, coral reef sharks." But the acoustic tags testify to something different. One of the sharks they tracked dived down twelve hundred feet into water that was just thirty-nine degrees Fahrenheit. "You throw some technology at it, and find they live way down deep," he says, adding that technology has "almost completely rewritten our understanding of their life history and biology. If you read shark books from a decade ago, large tracts of them are incorrect."

Researchers used to think great white sharks were largely coastal dwellers; now they know these creatures are pelagic as well, capable of crossing vast stretches of ocean. They had believed sharks of all species could conceive only through copulation; Chapman has proved them wrong. And now that scientists are capable of attaching sensors to sharks that track their dives below the surface, researchers are beginning to understand how low the sharks go. A decade ago conventional wisdom held that Caribbean reef sharks live almost exclusively up on top of the reef, but tagging now proves they regularly dive anywhere from four hundred to a thousand feet below the surface.

The sharks in Bimini confounded the scientists' expectations in a number of ways: nurse sharks have the reputation of being "couch potatoes," in Pikitch's words—they're the sharks you're most apt to run into if you're snorkeling in a reef, since they often just rest at the ocean's bottom—but according to radio tracking they're fairly active. In July 2004 the team tagged a young female they describe as "Nurse Shark 3333": this shark circumnavigated the entire reef, which spans 116 square miles, several times within a 150-day period. Caribbean Shark 3348, an adult male tagged in May 2004, proved to be a little more adventurous. At times during his 150-day tracking period this shark left Glover's Reef entirely: at one point he swam nearly nineteen miles to Lighthouse Reef, where a separate set of researchers picked up his acoustic signal on their equipment. These results suggest that if Belizean authorities established stringent marine reserves in Glover's Reef that were off-limits to fishing, they would protect the sharks from harm, since the fish tend to remain in the same general area. More broadly, now that it's clear some pelagic sharks can cross ocean basins, international policy makers need to start thinking of ways to regulate fishing activities on the high seas.

Glover's Reef, one of just four coral atolls in the Western Hemisphere, already enjoys some shelter from exploitation as a UNESCO World Heritage site. At the moment 30 percent of the reef experiences no fishing at all, and authorities prohibit gillnetting and longlining—the more damaging fishing techniques—throughout the rest of the reef. Gill nets—massive mesh operations anchored by a lead line below and a float line on the sea's surface—catch anything and

everything that swims into their path, earning them the nickname
"wall of death." As a way of making peace with local fishing interests, the researchers have worked to construct a sort of shark park:
part of it is off-limits to fishing, while a "general use zone" allows
only artisanal fisheries, which generally inflict less damage than large,
industrial-scale fishing operations. When local authorities initially set
the rules, they were more focused on banning industrialized fleets than
protecting Pikitch's study subjects. "It just happens it's worked bloody
well for sharks," Chapman observes. But the scientists are now pushing for even more restrictions, and local government officials have
indicated they're willing to expand upon the current regime. In 2007,
the local fishery management council proposed banning shark fishing entirely in Glover's Reef. Rachel Graham, a Wildlife Conservation Society scientist who lives full-time in Belize and has surveyed a
broader range of sharks there, has spent years working with authorities there in an effort to ban shark finning nationwide.

"They still have a chance here in Belize," Pikitch insists, even
though she knows there's a limited amount of time for activists to
protect the reef. The top predatory shark populations within Glover's Reef have remained stable between 2000 and 2007, according
to her survey, which is no small achievement given the rise in shark
catches elsewhere in Belize. But other reefs don't enjoy the same level
of protection, and they're the ones that are coming under increasingly
intense fishing pressure.

When Pikitch first came to the country in the mid-1990s, she rarely
saw sharks at the market, which she regularly visits to buy bait. Beliz-
eans don't particularly crave shark: the fish only started showing up
for sale once the shark fin market began to boom in the late 1990s. In
2005, Pikitch was concerned to learn that a nurse shark—which has
relatively small fins, and therefore fetches just a modest price—was
for sale at the market. As the demand for fins has risen, fishermen
are going to any lengths possible to bring sharks to market to take
advantage of the high prices before they disappear.

"I just gasped, because that is really scary," she says, as we prepare
to head out on our fish shopping trip in Belize City. "The sharks are
starting to go."

While Pikitch and her team can handle most of the sharks in Glover's Reef with relative ease, not all sharks can be monitored by swinging a lasso around them and surgically implanting an acoustic tag. Given that whale sharks are roughly the same size as a school bus, it's not easy to haul one of those fish over the side of their boat and cut it open. This is where the slingshot comes in.

One of the best places in the world to spot whale sharks is off Isla Holbox, site of a former pirates' cove off the Yucatán, lying roughly ninety miles northwest of Cancún. At this point Isla Holbox, a sleepy tourist town whose only motorized vehicles are golf carts, has become a critical research location where American and Mexican scientists are seeking to determine the migration patterns of sharks that cross national borders regularly as they traverse the Mesoamerican reef.

Robert Hueter, from Mote Marine Laboratory, spotted his first whale shark in 1975, when he was a graduate student at the University of Miami and a whale shark managed to make its way up Florida Bay. The whale shark eventually disappeared, and a week later it was found dead. Hueter didn't spot another for a quarter century.

He started coming down to Isla Holbox back in 1994. At the time, he was researching blacktip sharks, which gave birth in one of the island's secluded lagoons. After nearly a decade some of the locals informed Hueter that in late May and early June—just after he would leave town to return to Florida—a posse of whale sharks would come into the region. Curious, he helped convene a group of fishermen, activists, and Mexican and American scientists to determine what was happening.

Like Pikitch, the survey Mote scientists have constructed with researchers from Proyecto Dominó, a Mexican-based conservation group, seeks what amounts to bare-bones information about the sharks that arrive at the start of each summer and depart by the time fall arrives. What does this animal population look like, why do they come here, and where do they go when they leave? Rafael de la Parra, who heads Proyecto Dominó (the locals coined the nickname *dominó* for whale sharks because of their many spots), says he and his colleagues can't expect to protect the sharks if they don't have a clue about how they operate. While shark researchers are using some of the most sophisticated scientific techniques that now exist for tracking their subjects' movements, they are starting from a base of knowledge that lags decades behind their terrestrial counterparts. All that, and in order to get any work done, they have to aim a fancy slingshot at a beast that could easily crush them.

At first glance, Rafael de la Parra doesn't look like much of a spear carrier. De la Parra—who generally goes by Rafi—is a somewhat portly, middle-aged Mexican in a black Speedo and snorkeling mask, holding a tagging spear. He boasts a beatific smile nearly all the time, except when a given tour operator pisses him off. Then he glowers.

But right now he is smiling, because we have spotted a congregation of whale sharks, and he's ready to dive in. He has a clear goal in mind: jump in the water and deploy the elastic band on his metal pole as soon as he gets within striking distance of the shark, which is about three feet away. At that moment, once he's angled it properly, he releases the elastic with his thumb so that the tag will shoot forward and attach itself to the side just below the fish's front dorsal fin. De la Parra can accomplish this feat in a matter of seconds, with the ease of an expert javelin thrower.

With little warning, de la Parra slips off the boat and heads toward the massive polka-dotted animal that's swimming alongside our vessel. I scramble in after him and manage to get close enough to see him fire the tag into the shark's body. De la Parra is within reach to determine the fish's sex: as he pops up on the surface, he shouts, "Macho!" before submerging once again.

De la Parra has done this dozens of times: at this point researchers have tagged more than seven hundred whale sharks in the region since they started studying them in earnest in 2003. In fact, tagging whale sharks is the least difficult part of their job: Hueter, who has personally tagged at least three thousand sharks over the past thirty years, says whale sharks are easy targets. "In a thirty-foot long shark, they don't even flinch." But once they've gotten an animal tagged—especially if they're using a satellite or acoustic tag—the challenge begins.

On this particular afternoon, for example, I've joined de la Parra, Hueter, and another Mote senior biologist, John Tyminski, as they track the path of the shark to which de la Parra has affixed an acoustic tag. Standing by the tracking equipment, Tyminski recaps what we've done today when it comes to placing the tag on the shark. "At 13:20, we put it in a mature male seven miles north of Cabo Catoche, ten nautical miles north of Cabo Catoche point." The biologist can also record water the shark started cruising in once it was tagged—it's 78.96 degrees Fahrenheit, composed of 14.4 percent dissolved oxygen. But where's the shark now?

Nowhere to be found. Apparently, something has gone wrong. We circle the water in broad loops for hours, hoping to pick up a signal from the tag, which conveys a high-frequency beep every second to a hydrophone the scientists are monitoring on the boat. If the animal is within thirty-seven miles of the tracking equipment, the researchers should be able to use the hydrophone to determine which direction the sound is coming from, and thereby keep track of the shark. But in this case, either the shark is an extremely fast swimmer or the equipment—a $650 acoustic tag with a depth sensor—has failed. We are practically, as Hueter explains, "looking for a needle in a haystack."

"Active tracking has never been one of my favorite things to do," he says, as the afternoon wears on and the sun continues to beat down on us. "Even when it works, it's very tedious." And, in this case, it's not working.

This is the fundamental problem with shark tracking: it's costly, complicated, and unreliable, even though it's essential to understanding these ocean predators. Rachel Graham of the Wildlife Conservation Society uses three different methods to monitor the whale sharks she tracks: photo identification (each whale shark has a unique spotted pattern), satellite tags, and acoustic tags. Back in 2000, Graham placed the first pop-up satellite archival tag on a whale shark. These instruments contain a miniature computer that measures pressure, light, and temperature. This combination of measurements gives scientists a precise sense of where the sharks are traveling, in terms of not just latitude and longitude but also depth. Researchers like Graham program the tags for a set period of time, and when they pop off the animal, they transmit streaming bytes of data to an earth-orbiting satellite, providing a snapshot of what the shark was doing at a given point in time.

These tags can provide a treasure trove of information. Once Graham, diving with her husband, Dan, spotted an archival tag she needed to recover. "Get that tag!" she screamed. (They were underwater, but he got the point.) The tag offered up 206 days of information on what a whale shark had been doing—including diving to unprecedented depths of nearly five thousand feet.

And while Hueter and his colleagues have lost tags on many occasions, the ones that have stayed on have provided promising clues to where whale sharks travel when no one can see them. For years, scientists have suspected the animals give birth in remote areas of the ocean, because no one has spotted their young off the Atlantic coast. In 2007 his team attached a satellite tag to a twenty-five-foot-long female with a rotund belly they nicknamed Rio Lady. Over the following 150-day period, the whale shark traveled nearly five thousand miles from the Yucatán Peninsula through the Caribbean Sea to south of the equator between Brazil and Africa. The area where she ended up, north of Ascension Island and south of St. Peter and St. Paul Rocks, is remote but full of marine life, including sea turtles, billfish, and other sharks. Hueter believes he's found one of the whale sharks' elusive pupping grounds, though it will take more research to verify whether that's true.

Whether it's satellite and radio tagging or genetic sampling, shark tracking has produced several of the most significant advances in how we understand sharks' movements and their evolution. It is how we have come to know that great white sharks off the coast of California hover much closer to us than we previously thought.

To discover this, however, researchers such as the Stanford University graduate student Chris Perle had to spend plenty of time at sea, trying to retrieve the very tags they attached to sharks in the first place. Perle was out on the water on a sunny mid-October afternoon in 2006, while I was interviewing his adviser, the Stanford University marine sciences professor Barbara Block.

Block, who works out of the Hopkins Marine Station in Monterey, is the unquestioned queen of shark tagging. She has worked with a group of collaborators to pioneer the Tagging of Pacific Predators program, which has tagged more 4,300 predators from twenty-three species since 1999. That includes great white, salmon, thresher, blue, and mako sharks, along with a wide assortment of seals, whales, seabirds, and tuna. Tagging a great white shark involves an elaborate procedure featuring a seal decoy, which researchers use to lure the shark close to their boat. As Block puts it, "It takes incredible man and woman hours to do that kind of work."

Even though she's been doing this work for several years, Block can't help marveling at how the high-tech tags help her keep track of elusive sea creatures. "You can, in real time, see where a shark is on the blue planet," she explains as she points out the tracks the great white and salmon sharks have made according to satellite data. "I wake up every day, get my cup of coffee, and see where my sharks are."

The promise of that modern marvel is what had Perle searching for a small, titanium-encased, seawater-resistant item awash in the Pacific Ocean. The day before the tag had popped off a female great white shark's fin, to which it had been attached for three hundred days. Despite having its rough coordinates and $7,000 worth of monitoring equipment in hand, Perle and his colleagues couldn't locate it. So he called Block for advice.

Block checked her computer, rattled off a few coordinates to Perle via cell phone, and then explained she and her researchers were "throwing everything we've got at this," even though it amounted to "a small thing in a big ocean." And, as she admits, most of the time the scientists are making it up as they go along. No one has ever tried to track animals, when they are not visible, on this global scale. Block describes it as "constructing mission control" for the sea.

Sometimes the researchers at Hopkins Marine Station get lucky, since if ordinary citizens stumble upon a tag they often return it in exchange for a $500 reward. One woman recovered one of Block's pop-up tags in Hawaii, while another time a five-year-old named Calvin Wisner discovered one while walking on the beach with his parents near San Francisco just after Christmas in 2005.

For Perle, no such luck. It turned out the radio signals from the tag were bouncing off local cliffs, making it impossible for him to pinpoint exactly where it was, and on top of that it drifted twenty-five miles down the California coast in the course of a week. Still, Perle persisted, walking along the cliffs himself in order to scan the shore and the sea.

He found the tag, but got such a serious case of poison oak from his beach walk—"the worst case of poison oak in my life"—that he landed in the emergency room, and it took him a month to recover.

Block has not only managed to tag dozens of great whites off the Pacific coast; she's helped establish an elaborate acoustic receiver system that lets her and other researchers know where the sharks are migrating along an aquatic corridor between California and Hawaii. This project has provided Block with one of her most astounding finds: white sharks stay much closer to U.S. shores for a longer period of time than anyone realized, and in greater numbers.

Block, working with researchers such as Stanford University's Salvador J. Jorgensen, used either satellite, acoustic, or mitochondrial DNA tags from a total of 179 white sharks over the course of eight years to prove these creatures were not wandering aimlessly in the open ocean. Deploying a decoy made out of carpet that resembled a seal's silhouette, they attracted great whites to their boat and inserted the tags with the aid of a 2.3-inch titanium dart and a lance. Many of these tags managed to track a shark's movements for an average of six and a half months; one did it for just over two years.

Since great whites are capable of traversing vast ocean basins, scientists had thought they would explore large swaths of the sea rather than stick to a single pattern. But to their surprise, they discovered that they migrated in the same sort of predictable, long-distance route year after year, like pronghorn antelope on land and purple martin songbirds in the air. Each winter the animals left the central coast of California and headed between 1,240 and 3,100 miles offshore, along the Hawaiian archipelago. By August, they had returned. While foraging off the California coast, the sharks tended to congregate around certain "hub spots," including the entrance to San Francisco Bay and off Carmel Point, a popular beach.[19]

These migrations are so regular, in fact, that the white sharks of the northeast Pacific have become genetically distinct from two sets of counterparts on the other side of the ocean, one close to Australia and New Zealand and another off South Africa's coast. There are no visible differences between the whites swimming off California's coasts and those on the opposite side of the Pacific: Carol A. Reeb, a research associate in Block's lab, was able to make the determination by examining differences in mitochondrial DNA, which mothers pass directly to their offspring through the egg. Reeb estimates that the great whites circling close to San Francisco likely descended from migrants that came from the other side of the Pacific during the late Pleistocene, between 150,000 and 200,000 years ago. And Mahmood Shivji, who works for the Save Our Seas Shark Centre in addition to the Guy Harvey Research Institute, has used DNA analysis to determine that almost all species with global distributions have distinct genetic populations within individual ocean basins.

Scientists do not yet understand why this happened, but it highlights an incongruous fact: the predator Americans have fixated on for years has been much closer to us than we have realized. And beyond the question of great whites' lineage and migration patterns, the work of these scientists suggests that sharks may not interbreed with their own kind across ocean basins, which means they may be more vulnerable than previously thought.

Block still doesn't know how the white sharks managed their travels with such exactness. "Are you born with this node in your head?" she wonders. "These sharks are coming back with such precision to these areas. They do it with whatever they have in their brains."

After making this discovery, Block and several of her colleagues have pushed their research even further by counting the number of individual white sharks that spend their time in the northeast Pacific. While these animals are notoriously elusive, the UC Davis marine biologist Taylor K. Chapple and six other researchers had two things working in their favor as they embarked on this daunting task of identification: The trailing edge of a white shark's dorsal fin, like a human fingerprint or a humpback whale's fluke pattern, has unique ridges and indentations that become worn over time and can be used as a form of identification. These white sharks spend a good amount of time at the surface investigating prey, allowing the researchers to photograph and identify them. By feeding this information into a sequential Bayesian mark-recapture algorithm, researchers have been able to estimate white shark abundance off central California.

The results are stunning: scientists identified 129 whites by taking 321 photos, and concluded there are roughly 217 individual great whites swimming off central California. It is, in the words of Chapple and his co-authors, "an order of magnitude smaller than populations of other large marine and terrestrial predators currently protected internationally."[20] Until scientists learned how to count great whites, they had no idea how their ranks had dwindled.

On one level, the new research suggests this population of white sharks may be more vulnerable than previously thought. On the other hand, the fact that more than two hundred top predators are thriving off the West Coast provides further proof of what Block had suspected for years, and shared with me as we sat in her office, looking out over the water: "Right out there, it's the Serengeti. We just can't see it."

Even less stunning areas than California's central coast boast a bevy of sharks. New York's waters, for example, serve as home to at least two dozen species. They range from some of the most fierce—great white, bull, and tiger sharks—to lesser-known ones, like finetooth, chain dogfish, and silky sharks.

It is hard to appreciate something invisible to the human eye. But if we could see the ocean for what it is—a vast expanse of wilderness, filled with even more extraordinary creatures than those roaming the African plains—we might begin to value it for its true worth.

7

LIVING WITH SHARKS

We see white sharks as an asset and a value.
—Gregg Oelofse, head of environmental policy
and strategy for Cape Town, South Africa

The more scientists understand about sharks—the modest threat they pose to us, and the grave threat we pose to them—the harder they have worked to carve out places in which these animals can survive unmolested. In many ways marine biology is at a pivotal moment, when we are discovering the richness of the ocean at the very time we are grasping how we've managed to deplete it over the last few centuries. Preserving what's left, as well as rebuilding parts of it to a semblance of what it used to be, requires us to relinquish some of the power we have exercised in the past. It requires living with sharks.

There are places across the globe where sharks still thrive. And these are the places where humans must negotiate a different path with them, to ensure these animals still have stretches of sea to dominate. The very act of finding them is just the beginning.

Amid the undulating wave of sea grass, a glittering eye suddenly appears, reflecting the glare of our flashlights. This three-foot-long specimen of *Hemiscyllium freycineti*—better known as the Raja Ampat walking shark—shimmies across the seabed, using its pectoral fins to propel itself forward. But then Mark Erdmann—senior adviser for Conservation International Indonesia—reaches for it, and the flash now comes from its teeth as it hisses and struggles to escape the scientist's unwelcome embrace.

Hemiscyllium freycineti has existed in this corner of the world for millennia, tucked away in a bay that's allowed it to evolve separately from other sharks a matter of miles away. The Bird's Head Seascape—an area on the northwest tip of the island of Papua named by Dutch cartographers in the nineteenth century for its distinctive shape—boasts a myriad of unusual creatures like this one, and it has recently become known as a sort of lost world, where most underwater trips regularly turn up species new to science. Within the Bird's Head Seascape sits Raja Ampat, a series of 672 islands whose name—Four Kings—pays homage to its four biggest ones, Waigeo, Batanta, Salawati, and Misool. It is, in Erdmann's words, "the crown jewel" of the region's biodiversity.

Since Conservation International launched an expedition here in 2001—the first major scientific survey of the area in decades—researchers have cataloged 1,350 fish species in the Bird's Head Seascape, along with 700 mollusks and more than 540 species of hard coral. (That's ten times as many species of coral as in the entire Caribbean and means that nearly 70 percent of all known coral species on earth reside here.) Gerald Allen, an ichthyologist and Conservation International consultant, identified 335 different marine species in a single dive, setting a world record, and in one six-week period in 2006 Erdmann's expedition discovered 50 new species.

Allen, who co-led the first CI expedition in 2001 after spending three years waging "a one-man campaign" to get conservation groups to pay attention to the area, describes that first trip as "everything that I dreamed of, and more. It was like stepping back in time two hundred years and being on one of the first expeditions to New Guinea."

The fact that this far eastern spot in Indonesia has just emerged this decade as a sort of marine biologist's Shangri-la is a function more of politics than of science. The Dutch colonized the region, along with the rest of Indonesia, in the eighteenth century, and European explorers began investigating it in earnest in the early nineteenth century. While scientists made a flurry of discoveries during the turn of the nineteenth century, these petered out as the Dutch tightened their hold over western New Guinea. When Indonesian authorities won back the area in 1962, they were just as reluctant to let foreigners in, which meant that exploration was at a standstill at the very time when the advent of scuba diving was allowing scientists to conduct studies at unprecedented depths. The sharks were here, but untouchable.

Across the globe, researchers are using new technologies to expand our knowledge of sharks in radical ways. Over the last decade these discoveries have changed our understanding of everything from how sharks feed, mate, and travel to what forms of them exist. And they have made once-remote places like Raja Ampat a living laboratory.

There are plenty of different kinds of fish in Raja Ampat, but that doesn't mean it's easy to figure out which ones are new to science. Some researchers, like Gerry Allen, have an incredible capacity to ferret out this sort of information. Before working for Conservation International, Allen served for two decades as the curator of the Western Australian Museum, and he's described more than four hundred species during his career. Many tourists to tropical isles have read his work without even knowing it: he's the lead author of the alluringly titled *Reef Fish Identification: Tropical Pacific,* the book that sits in the common room of most diving resorts. Using a slate with waterproof pages underwater, he usually gazes at the fish swimming around him and scribbles down their scientific names without looking at his writing tablet. While most divers rely on these tablets to communicate among themselves, Allen often uses them for note taking. In some instances, however, he even forgoes the tablet and relies on his memory instead.

"Gerry Allen," wonders Max Ammer, a Dutchman who runs a couple of eco-resorts in Raja Ampat. "He dives and then he takes a shower, sits down and then writes down every fish he has seen from his head. And he does this twice a day, and sometimes he can do that three times a day."

About five years after Ammer settled in Raja Ampat, he convinced

Allen to come and take a look at the region's riches: this, in turn, helped inspire Conservation International to launch its first expedition there in 2001, with Allen at the helm. Erdmann made it to the region for the second and several of the successive expeditions, helping Allen chronicle what was there. While the scientists came back from each journey with an array of new species to show for it, the grueling schedule took its toll. Most of the time they focused on looking for species when it was light: in February 2006, Erdmann, Allen, and their colleagues were diving in Cenderawasih Bay as many as six times a day, leaving them exhausted by nightfall. One evening, however, Erdmann decided to enter the water to record nocturnal species that tend to hide during the day.

"I found an epaulette shark, pretty much right away," Erdmann recalls as we traverse the Dampier Strait in his speedboat, surveying the Raja Ampat region. "It struck me as being quite different from the only known epaulette from the Bird's Head region, so I pinned it down and swam with it back to the ship. By the time I got back, Gerry [Allen] was asleep, but I woke him to examine my find. Clearly not amused at being awoken, he dismissed my shark as *Hemiscyllium freycineti,* the Raja Ampat epaulette shark described by explorers in 1824, and told me to throw it back. I decided to keep it overnight, alive in a large cooler full of water, so that he could examine it while in a better mood in the morning.

"The next morning, he agreed that the shark did have an unusual spotting pattern, and decided we should at least photograph the animal for a permanent record. We sedated the shark with clove oil, returned her to the seafloor, and took photographs of her from every possible angle. As she awoke from sedation, I scribbled on my slate to Gerry, 'Should we keep her?' He hesitated but wrote back, 'I think it's just a Raja Ampat shark. Let it go.' "

It was only after the two men emerged from the water and started comparing their photographs to images of epaulette sharks on Allen's computer that they realized the shark they had just set free belonged to a different species. "Basically, he made me release the only specimen we had," Erdmann recalls. "It was sort of a bummer."

Later that spring Erdmann and Allen returned to Raja Ampat for the fifth research expedition, this time to Triton Bay, another part of the region. One night during a dive Erdmann spotted another epaulette shark and went after the fish with a vengeance: "I went down and wrestled the damn thing out of the cave. This time we didn't let it go. I put it in the ship freezer. I took a syringe and pumped it full of formaldehyde."

Sure enough, the shark was a separate species from the Raja Ampat walking shark. But it also looked different from the shark Erdmann had captured and released a few months before. Now Erdmann had no choice but to return to Cenderawasih Bay.

With his wife, Arnaz—an experienced diver herself—in tow, Erdmann took a seven-hour boat ride to Cenderawasih Bay in the fall of 2006. They immediately found a couple of specimens and brought them back to Bali, where they live. The most reliable way to identify sharks is to count their vertebrae in an X-ray, so Erdmann schlepped the dead shark to a bunch of hospitals in town. Unsurprisingly, he was turned down. "They didn't want to x-ray my shark," he confides with amazement. Finally, he lucked out with a veterinary hospital, and they determined it was, in fact, distinct from either the Triton Bay shark or the one discovered more than a century ago. The fact that Cenderawasih Bay boasted an entirely different epaulette shark spoke to the region's topography as well as the animal's physical limitations: since it couldn't swim long distances, it didn't venture far out and interbreed with other sharks. Over time, it adapted to its narrow corner of the Bird's Head Seascape, with its own unique features.

Erdmann was pleased to have identified the new shark species, especially since it had eluded him months earlier, but he did not see his discovery of two new shark species as more remarkable than other expedition finds, such as a new lionfish, damselfish, and dottyback. By September 2006 he was helping Conservation International's press office come up with a press release and telling them about the different species they could tout in the media package. "I don't think anyone paid a lot of attention to the shark at the time," he recalls. "I told the press office about the video we had of the walking shark and they were like, '*Walking shark?*' " It was a fish made for marketing.

On September 26, 2006, the press office put out a release describing how the fourth and fifth modern expeditions to the Bird's Head Seascape had uncovered more than four dozen new species. There are other sharks in the world that can crawl, like a certain bullhead shark, but that didn't seem to matter. The next day, media outlets on every continent except Antarctica trumpeted the discovery of a small, sinuous creature that could propel itself forward on its fins: a walking shark. "I guess it just sort of captured people's imagination," Erdmann says now.

In a world of unrelenting bad press about the oceans—where commercial fish stocks may disappear altogether within a few decades, lovable whales find their blubber chock-full of PCBs, and colorful coral reefs are likely to find themselves bleached and acidified out of existence by the end of the century—the Bird's Head Seascape offers a reassuring alternative. There are still regions of the world that boast an almost unimaginable array of marine creatures, which testify to the ocean's fecundity and diversity. And unlike rich terrestrial ecosystems, which have been scrutinized and cataloged by humans for centuries, we still have only a rudimentary sense of these underwater worlds. These are the parts of the planet that still offer a chance for discovery.

Raja Ampat is not entirely pristine. Ammer, an avid diver whose Kri Island resort Erdmann uses as a launching pad for much of his work, remembers when he would go diving and the seas were teeming with all sorts of sharks, not just the endearing walking sharks and wobbegongs, slothful creatures that still lurk on the seafloor with their wide, flat heads and snaggletoothed mouths. Neither of these sharks boasts large fins, so they have little market value. Poachers have taken many of the other sharks that used to traverse these waters, such as most of the blacktip and whitetip sharks that drew European explorers here two hundred years ago.

But by and large, the region remains a corner of the world that has yet to be ruined. While shark finning is still legal in Indonesia, the local government in Raja Ampat is the one regency (a subdivision of the national government) that refuses to issue licenses for those interested in slicing off a shark's most valuable parts and dumping the rest in the ocean. Huge mantas still swim here unmolested, tiny pygmy sea horses dot Raja Ampat's sea fans, and many of its coral reefs appear to be resistant to the rising sea temperatures that are decimating reefs elsewhere.

So Erdmann and his colleagues have embarked on a second mission that involves less science and more politics: preserving the Bird's Head Seascape before it collapses under the pressure of poachers, mining entrepreneurs, and all the other outsiders who are encroaching on this remote paradise. It's a new way to market conservation, an approach with both opportunities and pitfalls.

Ammer has been practicing his own, somewhat authoritarian form of conservation in the region for years, in which he just tells other people what to do. Ammer sold Harley-Davidsons in Zwolle, Holland, before coming to Indonesia in 1990, initially to retrieve military vehicles, aircraft, and Coke bottles that were abandoned during World War II. After making a comfortable profit on these finds, he returned and settled in Raja Ampat in 1993, founding a succession of resorts. As one of the area's biggest employers, he holds considerable sway over many locals. He ran into trouble while operating his first resort on Wai Island, because Yarefi villagers came to view him as God. They believed he matched the description of a "man who had the power of life and death," in local legend. This mythical figure, according to folktales, originally had dark skin like other Papuans but then developed a disease that turned his skin white. According to the myth, this divine savior didn't eat pork and eventually moved to Holland after being treated badly by the locals. Ammer matched this description in certain ways—he's Dutch and light skinned, and as a Seventh-Day Adventist he doesn't eat pork. Some villagers started actually worshipping him, which made the local chief jealous, and the controversy ultimately forced him to abandon Wai for Kri Island. But it helped give Ammer a sense of the influence he can wield over many Papuans.

In 1993, Ammer decided to teach a local fisherman named Nikson a lesson about the importance of protecting sea turtles. "He had two turtles in his boat," Ammer remembers. "I said I'd buy them. As he was still counting his money, I grabbed the turtle and threw it out of the boat. Nikson went after the turtle, thinking it had slipped out of my hands. While he was doing that, I threw the other turtle out of the boat. He thought I was crazy. Now he works for me."

Ammer doesn't spend his time throwing turtles out of boats anymore, but he refuses to let anyone fish sharks in the waters under his control, and he urges locals to practice restraint out of self-interest. He understands the economic realities of the region—"In Raja Ampat there are very few ways to earn money. You can catch grouper, you can make salty fish, or you can catch shark"—but he also knows native tribes here don't embrace the cyanide and bomb fishermen who have come here to decimate the reefs. There are two particularly destructive ways to fish on a reef: set off an underwater bomb that destroys everything in its path, or squirt cyanide through a syringe at the fish, which immobilizes them and makes them easy to scoop up. Both of these techniques translate into lasting damage.

"They listen to what I say, and what I say makes sense," he says, adding that his tough-love lectures usually center on the fact that the most exploitative fishermen in Raja Ampat hail from faraway islands like Sulawesi. The fishermen from elsewhere operate like bandits, he argues, plundering one part of the ocean before moving on to their next target. Locals can't afford to practice the same approach, he adds, because they lack the financial resources that would allow them to go off and poach on others' turf, the way the men from Sulawesi can. "I tell them, 'You see that boat? It's not from here. Where they live, they've destroyed everything, and now that they've done that, they come here, and they're going to destroy what's here. When they do that, where are you going to go? You don't have a boat.'"

Erdmann echoes some of the same themes in his message to locals, telling them they need to adopt a long-term vision when extracting resources from the sea, but frames it a little more diplomatically. He and other Conservation International officials envision a network of marine reserves in the region, where local fishermen will be allowed to continue operating but all other fishing activities would be off-limits. Scientists and environmentalists are increasingly turning to marine reserves as a way to preserve the last, best places, on the grounds that protecting critical areas of the ocean from commercial exploitation will allow these ecosystems to recover.

When Erdmann lays out his plan for winning over local Raja Ampat villagers, he slips into a form of environmental bureaucratese, describing how he's trying to "create an enabling environment for conservation." But his road map is straightforward: he's aimed at winning over the people who live in eighty-eight remote villages throughout Raja Ampat. Conservation International is helping underwrite seven radio stations as part of a "community conservation radio network," and they've convinced Radio Republik Indonesia, a station based in the nearest big city, Sorong, to air a two-hour environmental talk show each Friday night. The show, which is called *Radio Gelar Senat Raja Ampat* and mixes in local Papua languages with Indonesian, consistently scores high ratings with local songs and folklore about marine protected areas. CI has launched the conservation education vessel *Kalabia* (which means "walking shark" in the local language), and it's financed a newspaper called *Tabloid Raja Ampat*. "It's soft-sell conservation," Erdmann offers.

On one level his plan seems quite doable: there are only 35,000 people living here, so the area is much less dense than other parts of Indonesia, with just 353 residents per acre. On the other hand, it took six years to convince the Indonesian minister of fisheries to announce the creation of seven marine protected areas spanning 3,475 square miles. Even with that accomplished, it took years for the government to put fishery management plans and effective patrols in place.

Initially, Erdmann explains as we head to meet with one of the local villagers who will help determine what happens to Raja Ampat, Conservation International and its allies were hoping the Indonesian government would offer sweeping protection to the region right after the first major expedition in 2001. But in the early stages the fanfare did not translate into new protections, so environmentalists decided they were better off building grassroots support for conservation efforts.

The future of marine protected areas here lies in the hands of men like Leonard Ayello. In his camouflage T-shirt, hooded sweatshirt, and Ginotti flip-flops, Ayello doesn't exactly look like a village elder. But as the son of the Selpele village's spiritual leader, he wields power.

Landownership in Raja Ampat is different from other places. The islands are owned by tribes (Ammer, for example, rents Kri Island from a local tribe), and by extension they own the reefs that extend from their land. Just because a tribe owns an island doesn't mean its members live there: the villages of Selpele and Salio own Waigeo, which is uninhabited.

Sitting in the northwest corner of Raja Ampat, Waigeo is a site of forbidding beauty. Made of karst limestone—uplifted coral reefs that over time and exposure to the air and rain have melted into undulating peaks of varying heights—the rock formations look like beehives, or haystacks, rising out of the water. With just narrow strips of sand to serve as beaches and unforgiving soil, the islands offer little opportunity for even subsistence farming. But the waters surrounding Waigeo provide refuge for an array of creatures, including blacktip sharks, sea turtles, and a vast number of fish.

American conservation groups see Waigeo as a key part of their plan to preserve Raja Ampat, but to make it into a reserve, they need to convince the residents of Selpele and Salio to give their blessing. And to do that, they have been courting people like Ayello and his father.

Ayello, like many Selpele and Salio villagers, has spent part of his life working for Atlas South Sea Pearl. Cultured pearl operations are one of the region's biggest sources of income; as the company's general manager in Raja Ampat at the time, Markus Pieper, tells me over tea one morning, "We're the only industry here." The company employs 220 workers in three different sites: most are locals, looking after the 700,000 oysters that are growing at any one time. Ayello is one of the few headed for college, but he decided to work for Pieper once more in the summer of 2007 to save up some money.

At first Ayello is reluctant to talk, but at Pieper's urging he explains why his village wants compensation for the sort of protection environmentalists are hoping to bestow on the region. The young man speaks quietly, but his tone is defiant. "The area is all owned by us," he says, speaking in Indonesian. "Why wouldn't we utilize it on a regular basis? It's still ours, and we want to receive benefits from it."

But Ayello also respects the logic of men like Ammer who suggest that locals are being ripped off. "We feel like the resources there are being used by outsiders, and we're not receiving the benefits," he says. From that perspective a deal with groups like Conservation International and the Nature Conservancy—which will presumably bring in patrol boats and with them jobs for locals as patrol boat officers—makes sense. Selpele leaders are "behind the idea," Ayello says. But it's not sewn up, he adds. "Some are still undecided and feel they need a fuller explanation."

While Pieper supports Erdmann's work and gets along well with village leaders like Ayello, he wonders privately if they will be able to show the restraint necessary to keep Raja Ampat as unpolluted and bountiful as it is today. Chinese companies constantly lobby to mine for nickel on Waigeo: such operations would suffocate nearby reefs by covering them in silt. But they're offering to share nearly a third of the profits with local tribes, and Pieper is unsure of whether the villagers will reject the prospect of such a payout.

"They take everything," he says, recalling how he watches his employees take mangoes from the trees before they're ripe. "It's a mentality of 'If we don't get it now, someone else will.' At the end of the day, they look at the profits and rupiah in front of them today."

But the seven local communities around Raja Ampat—including Ayello's village—have decided to place a long-term bet on creating marine reserves. While Chinese mining operations initially opened up in seven separate locations around Waigeo, the massive amounts of red earth that ran off from the mines into the sea smothered the reef and sparked an outbreak of skin rashes among village children. The governor of West Papua and the head of Indonesia's naval installation in nearby Sorong cracked down and halted all mining operations in the area. And Raja Ampat's villages opted to protect their waters from exploitation.

In December 2006, they made traditional declarations to set aside 2.22 million acres of the waters under their control in seven marine protected areas. Six months later the Raja Ampat government added its legal muscle, issuing a decree that connected the network of preserves. At this point, the area had a total of 2.23 million acres under protection. Then, after months of lobbying by the local communities around Waigeo, which welcomed the community patrols and efforts to crack down on bomb and cyanide fishing in the area, the Raja Ampat government signed a new law that dramatically expanded two of the seven reserves. As a result, 2.95 million acres of Raja Ampat's waters are now protected.

Ayello and his neighbors, the Selpele and Salio people, went even further than Erdmann had expected by declaring the entire reserve under their control off-limits to any sort of fin fishing whatsoever. They asked for just two things in exchange: the right to take three coveted invertebrate species from one-fifth of the reserve every two years, and the opportunity to serve as paid community patrols in the area. The first time they opened up the area again, in October 2009, their collective take of sea cucumbers, spiny lobsters, and top shell brought in nearly $15,000. And more than fifty men from the two villages, including Ayello, serve in the patrol force, a gig that provides them with not only a salary but food and lodging during each two-week posting at the protected area's field station. Saving sharks and their prey is paying dividends that Ayello couldn't even envision a few years ago.

Financing these conservation efforts—from the patrol boats to the meals laid out at Waigeo's marine protected area's field station—takes money. While the Selpele and Salio people may eventually be able to finance these initiatives themselves, Conservation International needs to foot the bill for the immediate future. And the vagaries of the global economy—a stock market crash in one country, the devaluation of another nation's currency—can have a huge impact on a nonprofit that depends on the largesse of others.

Raising money is central to Conservation International's mission: for its Bird's Head Seascape project alone, it has gotten financial commitments from the Packard Foundation, Gordon and Betty Moore, and the Walton family (of Walmart fame). These wealthy Americans view Raja Ampat as worthy of their personal attention: Rob Walton, one of Sam Walton's sons, has toured the area along with other major donors and CI's president, Peter Seligmann. But Seligmann and his colleagues have realized that they need to explore less traditional ways of raising money if they want to protect the area over the long term, and that's how they decided to sell the right to name one of Indonesian Papua's new species to the highest bidder.

Erdmann hatched the idea himself after he saw the enormous press coverage the two walking sharks generated in the fall of 2006. By convention, the people who write the first scientific paper describing a species get to name it, so he and Allen have the power to either dub the walking sharks with the name of their choice or put that right up for sale. As long as it complies with the rules set out by the International Commission on Zoological Nomenclature—that it's in Latin and includes the genus name in conjunction with the new species name—it can pass muster. To Erdmann, the act of naming the sharks is a sort of mathematical problem, where the challenge lies in turning "public excitement about the walking shark into conservation dollars."

The idea of auctioning off a species' scientific name is not without precedent. In late 2004 the Wildlife Conservation Society scientist Robert Wallace found a foot-tall brown and orange monkey weighing about two pounds in Bolivia's Madidi National Park. Locals had known about the monkey for years, but researchers suddenly happened upon it and sketched out a few details about its behavior. Wallace wanted the Madidi National Park to benefit from the Internet auction, so he and the other authors writing the academic paper describing the species gave the naming rights to Bolivia's SERNAP (National Protected Area Service) and FUNDESNAP (Fundación para el Desarrollo del Sistema Nacional de Áreas Protegidas), government and nonprofit groups committed to protecting the area.

The online auction, which took place between February 24 and

March 3, 2005, generated a significant degree of Hollywood buzz. The talk show host Ellen DeGeneres declared she wanted to get in on the bidding, urging the viewers of *The Ellen DeGeneres Show* to make nonrefundable donations to "Ellen's Monkey Naming Pool." Other celebrities, such as Orlando Bloom and the late Heath Ledger, also donated items for the auction.

In the end DeGeneres and her viewers didn't emerge victorious: it was GoldenPalace.com, an online casino, that plunked down $650,000 for the privilege of buying a small Latin American monkey as its mascot. In a press release following the auction, the Wildlife Conservation Society touted the fact it had raised $650,000 to help protect the park, which includes lowland forests and alpine glaciers in an area the size of New Jersey, but declined to name the winning bidder. Eventually, GoldenPalace.com trumpeted its purchase.

Wallace and his colleagues dutifully named the species *Callicebus aureipalatii—aureipalatii* means "golden palace" in Latin; to the casino's regret, the ".com" could not be Latinized—and the $650,000 park trust fund has added eight guards to deter poaching. The casino's CEO, Richard Rowe, rejoiced at his company's purchase, which far exceeded the $28,000 it had paid in 2004 for a ten-year-old, partially eaten cheese sandwich said to include an image of the Virgin Mary. "This species will bear our name for as long as it exists," he said in the statement. "Hundreds, even thousands of years from now, the GoldenPalace.com Monkey will live to carry our name through the ages." And just so people remember, the casino has set up an official Web site, www.goldenpalacemonkey.com, where curiosity seekers can listen to the monkey's cry as they learn about the species and buy GoldenPalace.com Monkey T-shirts, tracksuits, and thongs.

Erdmann sees the Wildlife Conservation Society auction as his role model. "Golden casino aside, $650,000 for conservation is a lot of money," he points out as we're scaling a ladder leading to the dock off Ammer's Kri Eco Resort. Then again, Erdmann doesn't want to name a walking shark after a casino. And some scientists and government officials are even more skeptical, declaring it yet another sign of how much merchandizing has encroached upon scholarly pursuits. In their view, it's one more assault on academic integrity, like Exxon Mobil's $100 million donation to help Stanford University study global warming. As environmental groups and individual scientists seek new ways of funding their work in an era of dwindling public resources, some ask whether they're ignoring the inevitable conflict-of-interest questions that arise from such arrangements. Does it bestow legitimacy on certain corporations, especially those with compromised environmental credentials, if they're allowed to endow conservation initiatives? Should rich people be allowed to name a species just because they have dollars to donate?

These practices have also raised some alarms among officials at the International Commission on Zoological Nomenclature, the venerable group that has arbitrated disputes over scientific names since 1895. The commission's former executive secretary, Andrew Polaszek, a chatty wasp specialist who has named more than a hundred species himself, started polling his organization's twenty-seven commissioners in 2007 to see what they thought of the new trend. Their opinions were all over the map, from praising the idea to decrying it as undermining taxonomy's scientific credibility, and the commission has yet to take an official position on the matter. For his part, Polaszek sees both sides of the argument.

"If new species start to acquire a commercial value that's pretty hefty, then there's suddenly an incentive for people to 'discover,' and I use that word in quotes, new species. And the ramifications of that are enormous," he explains.

On the other hand, Polaszek allowed, there could be advantages to auctioning off species' names—especially if these auctions were conducted under the auspices of the International Commission on Zoological Nomenclature. "It could be a good thing, depending on how it's controlled. And we're just control freaks," he adds, laughing.

But some scientists are less amused. During dinner one night, a prominent marine biologist and conservationist—after telling me he doesn't want to be identified—says Conservation International's strategy should be seen in the context of streetwalking.

"It's the distinction between a courtesan and a prostitute," he says.

"A courtesan gets a man to fall in love with her, and they enter into a mutually beneficial relationship that has financial benefits for her. A prostitute has a more straightforward 'rack rate,' if you will."

"And in this case, Conservation International is the courtesan?" I ask tentatively.

"In this case," the marine biologist replies grimly, "Conservation International is the prostitute."

That assessment is too harsh by any measure. It is the group's scientific research that drives its fund-raising, rather than the other way around. Moreover, the staff at Conservation International is too smart to be caught in an act of hypocrisy, providing green cover to some environmentally offensive corporation. Rather than placing the Raja Ampat species up for bidding on the Internet, the organization enlisted Prince Albert of Monaco to host the Blue Auction in his country's world-renowned Oceanographic Museum, with just two hundred invited guests attending the black-tie affair.

As Erdmann sees it, auctioning off a species' title for conservation purposes is not any different from the old system of patronyms, which dates back to when Linnaeus first invented the modern system of taxonomic classification in the eighteenth century. During the eighteenth and nineteenth centuries, explorers would frequently name the flora and fauna they found after whoever funded the trip—usually a king, duke, or other royal. "Now you're going to name something after people who are paying after the fact, but they are paying for the conservation of those species," he says. "Same difference."

In the end, the Blue Auction raised $2,015,000, half a million of which came from a spirited round of bidding over Raja Ampat's walking shark. (An American named Janie Gale bought it and named it *Hemiscyllium galei,* in honor of her husband, Jeff.) This money has translated into direct benefits for Raja Ampat's villagers: a vessel called the MV *Monaco* now patrols the area around Wayag twenty-four hours a day, seven days a week. The region is once again a nursery for baby blacktip reef sharks, and shark finning has disappeared. For Conservation International's chairman and CEO, Peter Seligmann, the auction proceeds amounted to "an enormous shot in the arm for the community that lives in Raja Ampat" and a testimony to the environmental riches CI's scientists have identified in the region's murky waters. "When you go beneath the surface, it's indescribable," Seligmann says. "They're the discoverers."

Having waters teeming with sharks, however, is not an economic asset if they're the sort that can launch deadly attacks. Gregg Oelofse, head of environmental policy and strategy for Cape Town, didn't see sharks as a major part of his portfolio when he started his job in 1999. But Oelofse is an ardent surfer, and he and one of his colleagues at work started picking up word through their surfing and social circles that more great whites were showing up just off the city's shores. One day while he was surfing with three friends in 2001, Oelofse saw it for himself. The group was surfing at a break called the Wedge off the city's harbor wall. A white shark appeared out of nowhere next to one of his friends and then swam at the surface around Oelofse and three friends, about forty-five feet away. As they scrambled to paddle back to the beach, the shark came in front of them, then circled around back before disappearing. "It was really not pleasant," Oelofse says now, in a dry voice.

On November 15, 2004, Oelofse assigned an intern in his office to stand up on the mountain above Muizenberg Beach, in order to do an assessment of how many sharks were in the water. That same day a seventy-seven-year-old grandmother, Tyna Webb, was killed by a great white off a nearby beach, Fish Hoek. All that was left of Webb—who had swum daily at dawn there for nearly two decades—was her red swimming cap, and people began to panic. The incident was one of four fatal attacks in less than two years, and one of fifteen attacks that took place off Cape Town's beaches in the space of four years. Suddenly Oelofse needed to come up with a shark policy.

He convened a task force of experts to examine every possible shark control measure the city could adopt. South Africa has been the world's pioneer in shark nets, first erecting this type of barrier in 1904 around a beach in Durban. Cape Town officials looked at establishing the kinds of mesh nets that ring much of the KwaZulu-Natal coastline to the north, which have protected the area's beaches since a spate of attacks between late 1957 and 1958 that became known as Black December. The KwaZulu-Natal Sharks Board—originally dubbed the Natal Anti-shark Measures Board—is charged with reducing the number of attacks on visitors to the area's popular beaches, and netting has helped achieve its goal. Between 1978 and 2008 these barriers caught close to 33,700 sharks, and the number of incidents involving sharks dropped by 91 percent since the nets were first installed in the 1950s. But this indiscriminate sweeping up of sea life comes at an environmental cost: only 12.5 percent of those nearly 33,700 sharks were released alive, and a number of more beloved marine animals have become entangled and perished in the nets. Every year since 2004, according to the board's chief scientist, Sheldon Dudley, the nets have caught an average of 237 rays, 58 turtles, 53 dolphins, and 5 whales. (It's also worth noting that about a third of the sharks caught in the nets are actually trapped as they're heading out to sea—in other words, the barriers don't prevent every shark from entering the swimming and surfing area.)

For years, the men and women who maintain and manage the nets have tried to fulfill the board's legal obligations while minimizing the nets' environmental impacts. They have been swapping out some of the nets for drum lines, where baited hooks are strung along lines attached to drums that rest on the seafloor, and have explored other forms of deterrence. This approach dramatically reduces the number of animals that are accidentally caught: drum lines replaced half of the nets along the Hibiscus Coast in February 2007, and in the space of two years nonshark bycatch fell by 50 percent. The board also removes the nets during the annual sardine run and warns swimmers and surfers that they face a heightened risk during that time. Still, Dudley knows there's no chance of radically changing the region's shark control policy. Given the board's mission, he says, "there would be resistance to removal of all forms of protection."

Even if Cape Town officials wanted to set netting or drum lines, however, the area's rough seas and the fact that white sharks don't spend all year close to shore make it a less than ideal location for such measures. The 2005 task force rejected outright culling of the area's shark population as well, on the grounds it was inhumane and ineffective and would violate the white shark's protected status under South African law. This is one of the most startling aspects of Cape Town's shark control policy: it is based on the idea that the white sharks have as much of a right to live in the region as people do. "What we were trying to say up front to people is we don't consider it as a problem animal. We don't even want to use that word," Oelofse says. "We see white sharks as an asset and a value."

Oelofse was trained as a conservation biologist, but sounds more like a psychiatrist when he describes his office's campaign to manage the threats great whites pose to residents and tourists who enter the water. Lean and angular, he reclines in his chair as he explains that he is facing a psychological challenge, not just one of public safety. "A lot of what we're trying to drive is a value system," he elaborates, sitting in his cramped, nondescript office in downtown Cape Town. Oelofse and his colleagues must convince people that these animals are an asset, rather than a curse, but they also need to have people take individual responsibility for the very act of entering the water. When it comes to surfing, swimming, and kayaking, he says, "people must realize that taking on those activities is a personal choice, and no matter what we do, there will always be risks."

Part of the problem is that people often have difficulty processing certain kinds of risks, particularly ones associated with activities they don't do on a regular basis. Studies have shown we're very good at calculating the chances of things that we see as quite possible: elderly people know how likely they are to break a hip, while trained equestrians have a good sense of the chance that they'll be thrown from a horse they're riding. It's much easier to contemplate the dangers you can estimate with some degree of accuracy, rather than a murky unknown. Humans accept the risks associated with plenty of mundane and unusual activities—one's daily commute could end in a car accident, while skiing or skydiving can produce a broken leg—because they think they can predict how likely it is.

One of the best examples of this phenomenon occurs among the spearfishing community, the only group of humans that competes directly with sharks for prey. Janette and Jacques du Toit make their living by targeting game and reef fish off the coasts of South Africa and Mozambique, and they're well aware of the danger they face in the water. They've had friends attacked by sharks—a spear fisherman was even killed by a white shark off Cape Town in July 2005—and both of them have faced these predators firsthand. In 2007 a ragged-tooth shark came straight at Janette while she was fishing—when she pushed it away with her spear, it spun around and came at her again. She pushed the animal away a second time, and it slapped her with its tail as it left her. Du Toit escaped without a significant injury. A year later she spotted an eight-foot tiger shark while fishing off the Eastern Cape: she managed to shoot the fish she was after, but when she went to pull it up, the shark "just went berserk, and I thought, 'Okay, you take it.' I just thought, 'I'm not even going to argue.' "

Both Jacques and Janette describe spearfishing as a mind game where practitioners must constantly calibrate their behavior in order to ensure their self-preservation. A twenty-year veteran of the trade, Jacques recognizes what it means to share space with sharks. "You're part of the food chain when you jump in there. That's what makes it so exciting," he says. "You never know what you could encounter." While he tends to adopt a more aggressive stance toward sharks than his wife, du Toit makes just as many underwater assessments as she does and considers swimming with sharks "a calculated risk." He knows diving in dirty water is more dangerous because it's harder to detect what sharks might be swimming there, and if he does encounter one, he looks for any unpredictable or jerky movements. In an odd way, he is applying rationality to the most irrational of situations.

But the average human reaction to the prospect of a shark attack is anything but rational. Alison Kock, a born-and-bred Cape Town native who works for the Save Our Seas Foundation in addition to pursuing her own academic research, sensed the backlash as soon as Webb lost her life in 2004. "I almost didn't want to tell people what

I was working on, because people were so anti-sharks," she says. The following year Kock decided to put her fears aside and hold sessions with local residents to discuss possible responses to the shark threat, but found herself fielding questions on everything from outright shark hunts to the idea of attaching a helium balloon to every shark's tail so that beach visitors could see the animals from shore. "It felt like a witch hunt, people were so scared. When I got home one night, I told my boyfriend at the time that I wouldn't be surprised seeing people running around town with pitchforks." After one incident in August 2006 the city's major paper, the *Cape Argus,* ran a front-page story on the subject every day for three weeks. An article in a South African scientific journal put it best: "Even though shark attacks are a minor cause of mortality for humans, this phenomenon receives an inordinate amount of media cover and interest, probably due to humans' psychological abhorrence of being eaten alive."[1]

The public pressure on the Cape Town task force was enormous. The group reviewed and tossed out all the traditional methods of shark control—exclusion nets that are so finely meshed they keep out all marine animals, physical barriers that create a similar exclusion zone—as impractical. The more innovative methods of shark control, such as erecting some sort of electrical barrier or employing sonar detection, were too expensive and still unproven. City officials were "left with nothing," in Oelofse's words. Which is why they turned to shark spotting.

At nine in the morning, high above Cape Town's Muizenberg Beach, Ethel Tshandu is standing on alert. Muizenberg Beach, a spot one surfing veteran calls "the biggest nursery of surfing in South Africa," is a place that attracts an array of people—swimmers and kayakers, along with aspiring and experienced surfers. And it also lures great whites.

Standing about five feet tall, Tshandu doesn't look imposing, but with her binoculars, polarized sunglasses, and black Windbreaker she's fully outfitted to do her job: shark spotting. Filling out her official data book as she stands watch in a small hut with a corrugated tin roof, the former restaurant cook is all business. She has just noted there are nine surfers, two kayak paddlers, and six bathers in the water, which only boasts 5 percent visibility at the moment. She has instructed her counterpart standing on the beach far below to raise a black flag for everyone to see, so they can know that it's difficult to determine whether any of the great white sharks that frequent False Bay are in their midst. But she is still scanning the sea, methodically working her way from left to right across one horizontal swath after another, to see if she can detect the sharks' black shadows in the water.

For all her precision—Tshandu's careful recording of wind temperature, her refusal to take phone calls from friends while she's at work—the young woman knows her job requires an enormous leap of faith. The men and women who are tugging on their wet suits and heading out to sea are banking on the fact that a single person, perched on a mountain up above them, will keep them safe from a predator whose very survival depends on its ability to commit surprise attacks from below.

"Before I start work every day, I prefer praying and saying, 'God, I put this in your hands,' " she explains. "Sometimes you do get nervous. What if something happens to someone? But I just put it in God's hands."

The shark spotting Tshandu practices started not as a government program but as an informal system surfers employed for self-preservation. When you drive up to Muizenberg Beach, which is also known as Muizenberg Corner or Surfers' Corner, a couple of men are constantly strolling back and forth along the sidewalk eyeing the cars parked in front of them. Known as car guards, the men expect a few coins in exchange for making sure your car remains safe; most people pay them rather than risk any sort of damage to their vehicle. For years surfers had paid the car guards while they went to sea, even leaving their keys behind with them. From time to time they paid them to look out for sharks as well, and in October 2004 Greg Bertish, the owner of a local surfing and travel business, decided to establish a formal shark-spotting operation. Bertish raised money from both corporate and local sponsors, bought some equipment, and made sure the guards got first-aid training.

Now half a dozen beaches surrounding Cape Town all have the same warning system. Every day, regardless of weather conditions, from morning until night, one person stands watch above while another remains on the beach, ensuring the proper flag is flying to signal the current conditions. A green flag means no sharks are in sight and visibility is good; a black flag means while no sharks have been detected, visibility is poor; and a red flag means a shark has been sighted within the last two hours. If a monitor detects a shark in the water, he or she triggers a siren that blasts on the beach below, letting people know they need to come to shore immediately. When the alarm sounds, people move. The whole program, which monitors four beaches seven days a week year-round and another six during peak visiting times, costs the city of Cape Town just under $125,000 a year. In addition to giving beach visitors greater peace of mind, it has provided jobs to more than a dozen underprivileged young people in the area.

Between 2005 and 2008, spotters reported 530 white shark sightings off the city's most popular beaches. This is not even a comprehensive count of the number of great whites that move into and out of False Bay, since scientists have detected many more movements through both aerial spotting and acoustic tagging of individual sharks. Peter Chadwick, who directs the World Wildlife Fund's Honda Marine Parks Program in South Africa, has seen the animals during his scientific missions: "The great whites are swimming amongst the bathers and the surfers. We see it from the air and everyone's blissfully unaware, and quite happy."

In 2005, Kock placed acoustic tags on seventy-eight great whites circling Seal Island near the city's shores. Monitors registered a hit every time a tagged shark swam by them, making it easy to determine where the sharks spent their time during different parts of the year. Yet when Kock started downloading the data from the monitors, she couldn't quite believe it when they revealed they had registered such an immense number of hits. "It was a complete mind blow that over

50 percent of the animals tagged at Seal Island were coming inshore, and they were staying inshore for months," she says. At the very time that people are going to the beaches off Cape Town, the great whites are headed there as well. It's the unintended consequence of the conservation measures South Africa has adopted over the past couple of decades. South Africa was the first nation in the world to protect great whites, in 1991, and its protection of Cape fur seals has helped the sharks as well, by providing the animals with additional prey. As the sharks thrive, their numbers are growing.

Kock's and Chadwick's data also underscore a simple point: if great whites deliberately hunted humans, they would be having a field day every summer off the Western Cape, consuming the many surfers, swimmers, and kayakers in their midst. They don't, but the chances of an accidental shark attack still loom large.

The South African branch of the Save Our Seas Foundation has launched a critically acclaimed advertising campaign detailing the statistics that put shark attacks in perspective—how 652 people died in chair-related accidents in a single year compared with the 4 killed by sharks. It has made Oelofse's job slightly easier, but it is only a start, because when it comes to the public perception of sharks, individuals do not always engage in such coolheaded calculations. (As Oelofse puts it, "When you walk into a room, you're not scared by a chair.")

Knowing that this is the case, Oelofse has a simple mission: keep the sharks and the people apart from each other, to the extent possible. So far the shark-spotting program has done exactly that: for several years it ensured there was not a single deadly attack off Cape Town. But Oelofse has no illusions about the success the project has enjoyed up to this point: the moment a great white takes a beachgoer's life, the public's trust in the shark spotters could evaporate. "We could have two shark attacks in three days next week, and the whole thing could spin back again," he admits. "To the extent we can keep people and the sharks apart, the better for everyone concerned, including the animals themselves. Things could go badly quickly. It's very dependent on what happens in the water."

For decades a cadre of researchers have tried to develop an effective shark repellent, convinced that they were within reach of this holy grail. During World War II, both the American and the British governments had secret programs aimed at developing an elixir that would prevent sharks in tropical waters from savaging the unfortunate pilots and naval personnel who ended up stranded there. (This effort inspired one of the most memorable lines a politician has ever uttered on the subject, when Prime Minister Winston Churchill told the House of Commons, "The British Government is entirely opposed to sharks.") In 1942 the U.S. Office of Strategic Services kicked off a research drive that produced Shark Chaser, a chemical repellent that used copper acetate as a deterrent and included an inky dye that resembled what a squid would spray. The powder, encased in a packet and engineered to smell like rotting shark, was attached to life jackets and included in life-raft provisions; troops were told to open the packet and dissolve it in the water if they found themselves in shark-infested waters. While Shark Chaser produced mixed results at best—experiments showed it worked only in certain instances, and servicemen continued to fall victim to sharks in the Pacific—it provided some degree of psychological comfort to the troops headed to sea.

Still, U.S. federal scientists knew they had not solved the puzzle of how to keep sharks away from humans. In 1958 the Office of Naval Research's Sidney Galler convened a panel of nearly three dozen experts in an effort to devise a more effective repellent.[2] In 1972 one of the nation's most preeminent researchers, Eugenie Clark, determined that the Moses sole, a fish species that lives in the Red Sea, secreted a natural shark repellent. Sonny Gruber, the marine biologist who took me shark diving in Bimini, worked with a team of Israeli and Egyptian scientists in an effort to replicate this milky liquid but found there was a catch: it worked only when they injected it directly into the shark's mouth. So much for the Moses sole solution.

The KwaZulu-Natal Sharks Board has experimented with a range of deterrents over the years, including electrical ones. Since sharks have such sophisticated electroreceptors, the theory goes, a pulsing electric charge surrounding a diver could keep them away. This research has produced the Shark Protective Oceanic Device, or Shark POD, which divers can wear while underwater. In two series of tests conducted on great white sharks off the Western Cape of South Africa, scientists concluded that the probability of an attack within a five-minute period declined from 70 percent to 8 percent when the unit was powered on, and within a ten-minute period the chances dropped from 90 percent to 16 percent. Since the experiments simulated a worst-case scenario—the researchers were offering bait to the white sharks at the very moment they are in their most aggressive predatory state, during their annual pilgrimage to the area in search of Cape fur seals—the chances of facing an attack while wearing a Shark POD are even less likely.[3] However, the Shark POD has its limits: it can't protect an entire bathing area, the unit is not mass-produced, and it's not as if every recreational swimmer is going to take a dip wearing a bulky electrical unit.

A few inventors based in Oak Ridge, New Jersey, have been experimenting with a range of potential repellents since 2001, the so-called Summer of the Shark. Eric Stroud serves as managing partner of Shark Defense Technologies, and he and his colleagues have been trying out their material on Gruber's lemon sharks for years. They discovered by accident that magnets made of neodymium, iron, and boron can rouse sharks from a catatonic state known as tonic immobility and prompt them to flee, but the magnet works only if it's ten inches away from the shark in question. The firm won $25,000 from the World Wildlife Fund's annual International Smart Gear Competition in order to develop magnets that could keep oceangoing sharks from being caught on fishing lines aimed at attracting swordfish and tuna, and they are also exploring the possibility of embedding metals in nets that could repel the sharks instead of having them entangled in the nets and killed.

This work holds considerable promise, though it's yet to be fully realized. A group of scientists have already tested whether electropositive metals could repulse juvenile sandbar sharks in a lab, the first step in proving that electrical hooks could deter sharks from going after unintended bait. The researchers, led by Richard Brill at the

Virginia Institute of Marine Science, determined these types of metals did put off groups of sandbar sharks attempting to feed and altered the swimming patterns of those that were not seeking a meal.[4] Some of these effects were not always long-lived, however, and a team of researchers—which includes Stroud—are still trying to determine what size, shape, and exact metal composite would work best as a deterrent.

Shark Defense has already developed a prototype of a circle hook that could potentially work. The hook, which has a gleaming metal composite wrapped around it, almost looks too gorgeous to sit out at sea on an industrial fishing line. But if it works, the industry could face pressure from environmental activists and regulators to incorporate it into their gear. And these rare earth metals, worn as an anklet, could also help humans avoid shark strikes.

In many ways, the inventors at Shark Defense are using the sharks' own biology to protect them from harm. They are working on a chemical repellent based on the scent of rotting sharks, a closely guarded, slightly sweet-smelling combination of a dozen compounds known as A2. Patrick Rice, a partner in the company and its senior marine biologist, explains they've mixed a more effective version of the repellent, which does not have to be injected directly into a shark's mouth. The fact that this scent repels all types of sharks suggests it stems from a primitive instinct that evolved before sharks radiated into an array of species. At the same time, the scent attracts the very bony fish that sharks seek out as prey. "It's sending a chemical signal to sharks: get out of here," Rice says. "It's sending another chemical signal to bony fish: the predators are gone." They've already packaged the repellent in a number of forms: as a pressurized aerosol spray and as a "pop-pouch," both of which can spurt out underwater at a moment's notice, and as a hard waxy gel that can be injected into bait and seep into the water over time. The latter method would work best for fishing vessels, giving anglers an incentive to keep sharks alive. And while Rice is an unabashed booster of the repellent's powers—"It fires out, and the sharks are gone!"—even he knows these safeguards have their limits. "Just like anything else, nothing's 100 percent effective. If a shark's in a frenzied state, if they're hungry enough, they'll start eatin'.' "

We are often unwilling to acknowledge that experiencing nature carries a risk as well, one that might be a little harder to calculate. Every wild ecosystem operates on a cycle of life and death, and it's naive to assume that one can enter it without, on occasion, falling prey to those forces.

Average citizens in the United States, and most other industrialized countries, have resisted this message for decades. Instead, they tend to blame people in power for not protecting them adequately. In a fascinating piece of electoral number crunching, the Princeton University politics professors Christopher H. Achen and Larry M. Bartels found that voters tend to punish incumbent politicians for natural disasters, including floods, droughts, and shark attacks. "As long as responsibility for the event itself (or more commonly, for its amelioration) can somehow be attributed to the government in a story persuasive within the folk culture, the electorate will take out its frustrations on the incumbents and vote for out-parties," Achen and Bartels write. "Thus, voters in pain are not necessarily irrational, but they are ignorant about both science and politics, and that makes them gullible when ambitious demagogues seek to profit from their misery . . . In most cases, incumbents will pay at the polls for bad times, even in situations where objective observers can find little rational basis to suppose that those incumbents have had any part in producing the voters' pain."[5]

To test this hypothesis, Achen and Bartels analyzed the impact of America's seminal shark attack incident—the killings off the Jersey shore in 1916. The attacks took place just a few months before the 1916 presidential election and generated a spate of negative press for President Woodrow Wilson at the time, including an editorial cartoon in which a black fin titled "defeat" slashed through America's Northeast. Wilson, the former governor of New Jersey, was alarmed enough to call a cabinet meeting in the wake of the attacks, but his advisers were at a loss to offer any preventive policy response. Wilson did command the Coast Guard to patrol and survey the beaches where the attacks had taken place, but at that point the damage was done.

Wilson managed to hold on to the White House in the fall, but he lost New Jersey. More important, he suffered a noticeable dip in the four beach counties—Monmouth, Ocean, Atlantic, and Cape May. Achen and Bartels estimate "the negative effect on Wilson's vote in the beach counties is a little more than 3 percentage points . . . The shark attacks indeed seem to have had an impact—about one-fourth the effect that the Great Depression had on Herbert Hoover's vote in New Jersey 16 years later." He did even worse in two of the townships hardest hit by the shark attacks—with an eleven-point decline in Beach Haven and a nine-point drop in Spring Lake, far more than the negligible changes in the Wilson vote in these townships' broader counties and in the state. As the professors explain:

> Shark attacks are natural disasters in the purest sense of the term, and they have no governmental solution. Yet the voters punished anyway.
>
> Of course, it is possible that the voters did not blame the government for the attacks themselves, but did blame it for not helping them with their economic distress. In that case, retrospection might not be blind. No doubt voters told themselves something like that at the time. Yet in the case of the sharks, it is not clear what the government could have done to help the local economy. The truth could not be covered up. The vacationers could not be compelled to come to the beach, nor could the sharks be forced to stay away.[6]

With every fresh shark strike, politicians often scramble to show voters they are taking concrete action to protect them. Virginia's former Republican governor George Allen formed a shark task force in the wake of the 2001 attacks, in large part to ensure that his state's tourism industry would not suffer a serious downturn. In the end, however, the task force failed to spur any significant changes in state policy. The group did offer commonsense advice in a public report, warning beachgoers who fear being attacked that they should avoid swimming at times when sharks may be feeding: late afternoon, evening, and early morning. But Virginia Institute of Marine Science emeritus professor Jack Musick, the task force's lone scientist, says public officials have to accept the limits of their influence as well. "What the hell are you going to do?" he asks.

Most politicians, and their aides, have a very low tolerance threshold when it comes to sharks. Since I was covering the 2008 presidential campaign for *The Washington Post* at the same time I was writing this book, the idea that I was scribbling about sea monsters in between rallies provided considerable amusement to some of the political junkies riding along with me on John McCain's Straight Talk Express. On April 25 a shark, most likely a great white, killed sixty-six-year-old Dave Martin off San Diego's Tide Beach in a single bite. It was the first recorded attack in Southern California since 1959, and it came on the heels of a report on the most shark-infested beaches in North America. Steve Schmidt, one of McCain's top strategists, e-mailed a news article about the attack to me, and within minutes Mark Salter, another senior McCain adviser, added his own, gently mocking note: "As u can see, this is v distressing to both schmidt and me. Pls reconsider publishing your testimonial to the virtues of these vicious creatures." When the news hit less than a week later that a U.S. surfer in Mexico had fallen prey to yet another shark, Salter kept firing off messages. "Jeez, we settled the West abt 130 years ago. Every place in America should be purged of vicious predators. what kind of country are we?" he wrote in one. Then, in a separate missive, "Holy shit, Juliet. These beasts must go. It's us v. them. Better hurry up and publish. This time next year, they're going to be as rare as a wooly mammoth." While they were joking on one level, their banter also carried a clear message: Why would anyone give a thought to keeping these creatures around?

Just as McCain's aides were firing off these e-mails, some surfers down in Mexico decided to take measures into their own hands. Eager for vengeance, they waded into the water where their compatriot had been killed. And they began murdering sharks.

Fascinated by Schmidt and Salter's preoccupation with sharks, I decided it was worth polling the man they worked for, McCain, on the issue. As one of our bus rides came to a close, and his press secretary, Brooke Buchanan, was doing her best to shoo reporters off the bus, I piped up that the next ride should be entirely devoted to a discussion of shark policy, but in the meantime I wanted to know where the senator stood on the question of sharks.

He looked at me, and the other journalists gathered around me, smiling. Pausing for a moment, he declared his allegiance in the Campaign Shark Wars. "I gotta be pro-shark," McCain said, with a little shrug. "They're important to the whole chain."

Ever the politician, McCain quickly sought to split the difference between the two sides. "But I don't want them eating people," he added. "I'm pro-shark, with the important caveat that I don't want them eating people."

Buchanan—the lone shark supporter among McCain's campaign staff, who happened to be sitting next to Salter at the time—raised her fists in victory. The candidate had spoken.

On South Africa's Eastern Cape, the men and women face the same quandary that McCain fumbled to articulate on the campaign trail: how to tolerate an uncontainable threat for the sake of an abstract ideal. Everyone's got a job to do: Oelofse and Dudley, who want to keep tourists as well as sharks coming to their region in the summertime; the du Toits, who accept the fact that they will cross paths with sharks in the course of their underwater workday; and Tshandu, who composes songs in her head as she stands watch from the mountain above Muizenberg Beach. More than most people in this world, they have learned how to negotiate daily life with the ocean's fiercest predator.

As the car guards make their rounds at Muizenberg Beach, the two veteran surfers pulling on their wet suits in the parking lot take a little comfort that a shark spotter is looking out for them. They know the risks they face, and they're realistic about what they can do to protect themselves. Peter Stride, who has been surfing for nearly half a century, begrudgingly gets out of the water each time the shark alarm sounds. But he's philosophical about what fate might await him in the Atlantic, harboring just one wish should he meet a great white in the water: "If a shark wants to bite me, please heave off and leave me dead." And with that he laughs and heads for the waves crashing behind him.

On January 13, 2010, Oelofse's worst-case scenario transpired. A thirty-seven-year-old tourist from Zimbabwe, Lloyd Skinner, swam by himself off Fish Hoek beach. Though shark spotters were positioned at their usual stations—one on the beach and one at a hut overlooking the water—they could not prevent the lethal attack by a great white shark that took Skinner's life. The entire incident, which involved three separate strikes, lasted roughly three minutes. Within moments the news had gone viral as a nearby resident tweeted about the incident. "Holy shit, we just saw a GIGANTIC shark eat what looked like a person right in front of our house in fishhoek. Unbelievable," wrote a Twitter account user called skabenga.

A confluence of factors contributed to Skinner's demise. He had separated himself from about a dozen other swimmers in the water, making him more vulnerable to an attack. He happened to swim near a school of fish, which attracted the great white to his vicinity. And worst of all, it appears the shark mistook Skinner for a seal, launching a deliberate strike from deep beneath the sea's surface. "All indications are that this attack was predatory in nature," Oelofse and two colleagues wrote in a review after the fact. "The shark's behaviour as described by eyewitnesses and as seen in photographs displayed classic signs of feeding behaviour i.e. thrashing at the surface using its tail to facilitate chewing action." The shark spotter stationed on the beach saw the third pass the shark made at Skinner and immediately radioed his counterpart stationed at the mountain lookout. That spotter, who was looking at an area of water north of Skinner, never witnessed the incident, though he did see the blood in the water once he turned his attention to Skinner's location.

In the end, the reviewers concluded the shark-spotting program hadn't failed. They had raised the black flag to indicate that shark-spotting conditions were poor: the choppy water and intermittent cloud cover made it hard to notice fins breaking the ocean surface. Just as important, the fact that the shark struck from below meant it would have been all but impossible to warn Skinner ahead of time that he was at risk. Still, Oelofse knows that explanation might not be enough to satisfy a skittish public that had expected the shark spotters to protect them from harm. "This time round the reaction has been much tougher than usual as it happened at a beach where our shark spotting programme is," he wrote in an e-mail shortly after the attack. "However, the questions remain the same—the public wants to know why, which, of course, we can't answer as we don't know."

In the end, Skinner's death underscores a harsh reality: there is no way to eliminate the threat the most dangerous sharks pose to us. The best we can hope for is to lessen the odds. If we don't recognize that, there is no possible way we will learn to live with them.

8

FISH FIGHT

As you may know, I was mauled by a shark thought to be a Great White on July 1, 1991 while surfing near Davenport, CA. My experience with the shark convinced me that sharks are an important part of the natural order of things. Any creature which is as well-adapted to its environment as the shark deserves a lot of respect.

—Eric Larsen, writing to California assemblyman Dan Hauser on April 17, 1993, in support of legislation protecting great white sharks off the California coast

Sonja Fordham's colleagues gave her a nickname a few years ago: shark princess. Actually, she and several other women who dedicate themselves to conserving the sharks, skates, and rays that compose the elasmobranchs prefer another moniker to describe themselves: elasmobroads. "More gravitas," she explains.

In the summer of 2006 a coalition of American environmental organizations banded together to form a group called the Shark Alliance, and they sent Fordham—a longtime advocate with the D.C.-based Ocean Conservancy, the kind of person who sports shark earrings as a conversation starter and discusses fisheries management policy with unbridled enthusiasm—to Brussels. The fact that three advocacy groups were funding her job did not mean it was a luxurious overseas posting. Paid in dollars at a time when the euro was rising, Fordham spent years working out of a small Brussels apartment. Many times she trekked to fisheries management meetings in an array of European cities, where officials often looked upon her with disdain as she nagged them to consider clamping down on the shark trade.

While concern about some environmental issues, such as climate change, has steadily intensified in recent years, attention to sharks has waxed and waned. In much of the world, policy makers are now willing to declare the issue merits action, but they are often loath to deliver on their promises. In some cases conservation initiatives have advanced through the political process, only to stall before becoming law. And even within some of the traditional bastions of environmentalism, these efforts can fall short. We may be on the cusp of a new approach to protecting sharks, but it will take a serious political push—and an unprecedented level of global cooperation—to make it work.

When it comes to most green issues, Europeans stand in the vanguard: they drive more compact cars than Americans, live in smaller houses, and rely more on renewable energy. But when it comes to the question of protecting sharks, they're laggards. And that's why Fordham moved from Washington, D.C., to Brussels—a town with not quite as many bureaucrats but much higher quality chocolate.

Until a few years ago, government officials on both sides of the Atlantic didn't accept the concept that any fish could go extinct. Most fishery managers didn't even keep track of shark catches until recent decades, because they did not view the fish as commercially valuable. A handful of marine scientists based in Canada changed that. Coming from diverse backgrounds—one hailing from a small town in Mississippi, another a French-born cosmopolitan of African American descent, and a third a young German—all of these researchers were irreverent, tireless, and willing to defy the conventional wisdom.

One of them, Daniel Pauly, now makes his home as a fisheries scientist at the University of British Columbia. While Pauly grew up and received his doctorate in fisheries biology in Europe, he devoted his early years as a researcher to living in disparate regions including Indonesia, western Africa, and the Philippines, where he examined how fishing activities were reshaping the ocean. The longer overfishing continues, he concluded, the more precipitously the quality of seafood dining will decline. He coined the phrase "fishing down the food web" to capture how our current fisheries system works: we kill off all the big, tasty fish, and when we're through with them, we start pulling out the inferior, smaller fish. Before we know it, he warns, we'll all be eating jellyfish.

Just as Pauly began receiving attention for his dire warning to gourmets across the world, Ransom A. Myers began making his academic mark. Born and raised in Lula, Mississippi, the son of a cotton plantation owner, Myers decided to focus on studying fish after sailing from Africa to the Caribbean in a twenty-eight-foot boat, and settled at Dalhousie University in Halifax, Canada.[1]

Myers—called Ram, a nickname derived from his initials—revolutionized the way researchers calculated the abundance of fish, poring over old catch records to chart massive declines. A quirky academic who padded around campus sporting white socks underneath his sandals, he used numbers to prove his point that fishing fleets were effectively wiping out species after species. He initially focused on cod, one of Canada's most commercially valuable species, showing the collapse of its once-robust cod population stemmed not from seals eating the fish but from overfishing. But then he shifted to top predatory fish such as sharks. In 2003 he published two papers with Dalhousie colleagues that reverberated through the popular press. The first made a small splash: written with Julia K. Baum and four other scientists, it documented that scalloped hammerhead, white, and thresher sharks in the northwest Atlantic had all declined by more than 75 percent in the past fifteen years. That same year Myers and Boris Worm, a charming German who had come to Nova Scotia to work with him, estimated that fishing had eliminated 90 percent of the ocean's top predators, in an academic paper that made the front pages of newspapers across the globe.

In 2004, Baum and Myers published a scientific article that—using data collected by American long-lining vessels in the Gulf of Mexico—calculated the oceanic whitetip shark's demise in precise terms. The shark had ranked as one of the most abundant sharks on earth during the first half of the twentieth century, but after comparing catch rates in the Gulf of Mexico between the 1950s and the

1990s, the two scientists realized the oceanic whitetip shark population had plummeted by more than 99 percent. The silky shark, another commonly caught shark in the region, declined 90 percent during the same period. And while their overall numbers shrank, so did their individual sizes: oceanic whitetip sharks in the 1990s were a third as big as they were forty years earlier, and silky sharks shrank by 83 percent. As a result, they now produce smaller litters.[2] All of this happened, but no one realized it until Baum and Myers crunched the numbers.

"The oceanic whitetip shark may once have been the most abundant large wild animal on earth," surmises Elliott Norse, who heads the Marine Conservation Biology Institute. "If, on land, the most abundant large animal disappeared, everyone would be talking about it. It would be considered an unmitigated environmental disaster. But it happened in the sea, and nobody was looking."

A relentless worker, Myers only stopped producing when he was felled in 2006 by an inoperable brain tumor. He died at fifty-four on March 27, 2007; that week the journal *Science* published his last, groundbreaking paper: it provided convincing evidence that the decimation of sharks in the Atlantic had produced a cascade of unintended effects that were distorting ecosystems up and down the East Coast. He and his colleagues calculated that between 1970 and 2005, the number of scalloped hammerhead and tiger sharks declined by more than 97 percent, and bull, dusky, and smooth hammerhead sharks dropped by more than 99 percent. During that same period nearly all of the sharks' prey species exploded: the cownose ray population off the East Coast expanded to as much as forty million. They became the thugs of the ocean, rampaging and pillaging in their quest to sustain their ever-rising numbers. Cownose rays eat tremendous amounts of bay scallops, oysters, and soft-shell and hard clams, and by 2004 their consumption of nearly all the adult scallops in the North Carolina sounds forced the state to shutter its century-old bay scallop fishery.

Charles H. "Pete" Peterson, a professor of marine sciences, biology, and ecology at the University of North Carolina at Chapel Hill who co-authored the paper, says its findings proved researchers had just "scratched the surface of the implications" of eliminating sharks from a given ecosystem.

Such findings, Elliott Norse argues, show humans have underestimated the extent to which they have changed what goes on beneath the ocean's surface. And as the major fish have disappeared, people are waging battles over smaller fish that they didn't even find desirable a generation ago, as French and Spanish fishermen fight over who has the right to catch more anchovies in the Mediterranean. "What we're doing by removing sharks from the global marine ecosystems is we're producing a massive, onetime uncontrolled experiment on the oceans. All over the world we're seeing jellyfish explosions. We don't know why. Now we're arguing over the anchovies," he says. "We have to live with the consequences, and I don't want to live with the consequences."

Joshua Reichert, managing director of the Pew Environment Group, describes this rapid accumulation of critical statistics as just one more indicator of the fatal flaw in how the world has approached environmental issues since the 1970s. The American buffalo's near demise ultimately came about in the nineteenth century when people on the East Coast acquired a taste for the beast's tongue: in response, hunters for hire slew thousands of them out on the range and left the animals' bodies to rot after ripping out their most valuable asset. In the same way, he says, the growing demand for fins has prompted shark populations to plummet, a phenomenon researchers have documented even as policy makers have failed to act. "We've been steadily driving toward the edge of a cliff," he says, "and taking meticulous notes along the way." Or, as the National Geographic underwater photographer David Doubilet put it as he accepted a conservation award from the Blue Ocean Institute, "We are, in essence, seeing the actions of modern conquistadors: discovery, conversion, destruction."

The extent to which humans can drain the ocean's resources for our own consumption is breathtaking. Whaling provides one of the most vivid examples of this phenomenon. Phillip J. Clapham, a scientist in the National Marine Mammal Laboratory at NOAA's Alaska Fisheries Science Center, describes it in one paper this way: "In terms of sheer biomass, the commercial hunting of whales in the 20th century represents one of the greatest wildlife exploitation episodes in human history."[3] In 101 years fishermen killed more than 200 million whales in the Southern Hemisphere alone. In several cases it took only a matter of decades to wipe out regional whale populations. Humpback whales migrating off New Zealand virtually disappeared after whaling stations operated at full force between 1912 and 1963, in part because Soviet fleets took 25,000 humpbacks in two seasons, between 1959 and 1961.[4] Even back in the seventeenth century, whalers could accomplish similar feats: bowhead whales congregated in the tens of thousands off Spitsbergen in 1610, but by 1670 the landing stations there "were forced to close because of the paucity of whales in coastal waters."[5] Long-lived animals that produce a limited number of offspring are the most vulnerable to collapse due to overfishing, since they lack the kind of resilience other species have. At least with whales, we have the ability to calculate these declines because the animals had a market value and fishermen counted how many they took in. With sharks, we weren't even watching most of the time.

As researchers began to chronicle the rapid decline of sharks off America's shores, U.S. authorities began to take notice. They are still struggling to take stock of exactly where these populations stand at this point: the NOAA fisheries biologist Enric Cortés, who is in charge of assessing every shark species off the East Coast, says bluntly, "When it comes to sharks, we have a long-term lack of data, both biological and in terms of fisheries." But, he adds, no one doubts that they're in trouble. "The general feeling among the community that studies sharks, especially for those who do population dynamics, is that there have been considerable declines."

As with most environmental issues, California pioneered environmental protections for sharks long before any other part of the country. Prompted by studies researchers had been conducting off the Farallon Islands for a couple of decades, a group of activists in 1992 launched a campaign to protect great white sharks off the state's coast. The move was both risky and novel: it had been only a year since South Africa became the first government in the world to decide to afford great whites legal protection. The coalition of scientists and environmentalists approached Dan Hauser, a Democrat who both represented the north coast and chaired the legislature's Joint Committee on Fisheries and Aquaculture, and he agreed to introduce the bill. The group, which included kayakers, surfers, and recreational and commercial fishermen, argued that predators such as great whites helped maintain the coastal ecosystem on which state residents prided themselves. Local papers had long mocked the idea of stopping the killing of great whites—*The San Diego Union-Tribune* ran an article on March 12, 1991, joking that if you're a fierce ocean predator that snacks on humans, "Where do you look for friends? Where else but California, *amigo?*"—and a shark strike against the surfer Eric Larsen off the coast provided plenty of ammunition for the measure's foes. Yet the bill, AB 522, passed four legislative committees as well as the full assembly and senate without a single nay vote.

Still, the bill's backers were unsure whether Pete Wilson, the state's GOP governor at the time, would sign the measure into law. On August 12, 1993, a great white off the Mendocino coast took an abalone diver into its mouth before spitting him out, forcing him to swim nearly ninety feet to shore before his friends could help him out of the water. That incident, supporters of the measure feared, doomed the bill. As the legislative session dragged on, Hauser's staff decided to take advantage of the fact that the assemblyman's office faced Wilson's offices, which lay just across the state capitol's courtyard. The aides drew a poster of a shark fin poking above the waves, along with the message "Please sign AB 522." On October 11—the last day Wilson could sign bills before they expired for the year—his aides posted a sign of their own in one of Wilson's courtyard windows, showing they had noticed Hauser's artistic lobbying efforts. It featured a shark with hot pink sunglasses leaping high above the water, mouth agape, and a message handwritten by the governor, saying, "Dan—Cordially, Pete Wilson." He had signed the bill.[6]

U.S. authorities followed with shark protections of their own, and on December 21, 2000—just a month before leaving office—President Clinton signed into law the Shark Finning Prohibition Act, a landmark law that prohibited finning in U.S. waters. Unless a government demands that boats land sharks with their fins intact, authorities need to make elaborate calculations to ensure these operators aren't taking sharks simply to supply the fin trade. A shark that comes onto shore has typically been "dressed," meaning its head, fins, and guts have been removed. As a result, this dressed weight is half the full weight of a live shark, and the law Clinton signed dictated the fins brought ashore should not account for more than 5 percent of the total dressed weight of sharks on board. These restrictions applied only to ships sailing under the U.S. flag, however, not to foreign vessels in American waters.

Other countries have followed suit, but with varying degrees of success. The tiny country of Palau made history on September 25, 2009, when its president, Johnson Toribiong, declared the first nationwide shark sanctuary, banning shark fishing in all of Palau's waters on the grounds that the activity threatened both the local ecosystem and the nation's tourism industry. Within six months, both Honduras and the Maldives had taken similar measures, creating their own sanctuaries.

Nations including Australia, Brazil, Canada, Costa Rica, Ecuador, El Salvador, Nicaragua, Panama, and Oman have all taken the more modest step of imposing some sort of shark-finning restrictions. But while Ecuador imposed a ban on both shark harvesting and the export of shark fins in October 2004, Asian fishermen regularly catch sharks in areas such as the nationally protected Galápagos, sometimes with the assistance of Ecuadorean naval officers. Roughly 80 percent of Ecuador's shark exports originate in the Galápagos: Wild-Aid estimates that the monthly volume of dried shark fin coming from the archipelago's largest island, Isabela, averages fifteen hundred kilograms, which equates to three thousand dead sharks.[7] Illegal fishing operations continue to poach sharks from Costa Rica's Cocos Island marine reserve and Panama's Coiba National Park. Many of the pledges other countries have made, like signing on to the UN Food and Agriculture Organization's 1999 International Plan of Action for the Conservation and Management of Sharks, have yet to translate into action.

Even well-meaning government officials in many countries often make tentative attempts to curb shark finning, only to encounter fierce political resistance. Yolanda Kakabadse, who served as Ecuador's environment minister between 1998 and 2000, learned shortly after taking office that her plan to eliminate shark finning in the Galápagos had little chance of success. "In the Galápagos, the population is so small that every group is important," she says. Artisanal fishing groups—a faction pitted against Kakabadse's reform proposal—can actually mobilize voters, so she found little presidential support for her plan. Moreover, the fact that scientists have difficulty assessing the exact count of a given shark population made it impossible for her to make her case within the cabinet. "I couldn't get the information I needed to back it up," she explains.

Few activists have fought harder to push their government on the issue than Randall Arauz, president of the Costa Rican shark conservation group Pretoma. Arauz didn't even start out focused on sharks; in the 1990s he and colleagues were monitoring leatherback turtles. In an effort to find out how fishing was damaging endangered leatherbacks, one of Arauz's friends signed up to work on a fishing vessel and brought a video camera, claiming he was simply making home movies. In the process, he captured shark finning on video, and the activists realized that the leatherbacks were, in Arauz's words, "collateral damage" in the drive to kill sharks. An end to shark finning and the twenty-five hundred international flag vessels cruising the eastern Pacific, they reasoned, would save the turtles as well.

In 2001, Pretoma launched a campaign to end shark finning. The Costa Rican fishermen were supportive; they didn't see selling shark fins as an important source of income. In 2003, Pretoma secretly videotaped four boats landing shark fins on private docks, and its public relations campaign exploded, fueled by public outrage. But institutional forces in Costa Rica have thwarted Arauz's efforts for over a decade. Representatives of large fishing interests dominate the workings of the Costa Rican Fishery and Aquaculture Institute, known by its initials, INCOPESCA, prompting regulators to adopt loophole-ridden rules time and time again. Arauz has challenged these regulations on multiple occasions, and he wins, but these court rulings have yet to translate into a sufficiently strong ban on finning. Costa Rica is seen from the outside as a world leader on a host of conservation causes, but Arauz argues his compatriots need to end their schizophrenic approach to fishing policy: "Are we going to be the shark savers of the world, or the culprits?"

International mechanisms to protect sharks remain a work in progress, since the global community has not demonstrated the political will to curb the activities that threaten sharks the most. David A. Balton, who has served as deputy assistant secretary of state for oceans and fisheries under both George W. Bush and Barack Obama, sounds a little rueful when he talks about things like the UN's 1999 International Plan of Action. "It had a lot of good words in it" is the way he puts it. When it comes to dealing with managing sharks in international waters—which, after all, is where most sharks swim—he says, "There aren't that many governments that are hyped up about it, at least until recently. We're a long way from where we need to be." Issuing official statements about the need to preserve sharks is not the same thing as protecting them, especially when governments across the globe will have to collaborate on enforcing fishing restrictions on the high seas.

The Bush administration pressed for further restrictions close to shore, and in 2008 it adopted a rule mandating any shark landed from the Atlantic must have its fins attached—the strictest rule possible. Environmentalists still criticize the federal government for some aspects of its shark management, such as allowing the overfishing of spiny dogfish and sandbar sharks and still permitting the fishing of hammerhead, oceanic whitetip, and porbeagle sharks, but they see the United States as the least of their problems as they push to halt sharks' global decline. In 2010 Hawaii banned the sale, possession, or distribution of shark fins and fin products statewide, and the United States made fins attached the law of the land.

One of the biggest obstacles to adopting any meaningful protections for sharks is that they have to be negotiated in large unwieldy forums, such as the Convention on International Trade in Endangered Species of Wild Fauna and Flora (CITES) and the International Com-

mission for the Conservation of Atlantic Tunas (ICCAT). The fact
that ICCAT doesn't even have the word "shark" in its name gives
a sense of how high they rank on the priority list. These sprawling
international meetings are filled with all the drama and maneuvering
of a high-school model-UN exercise, where delegates from pro-fishing
countries such as Japan, Norway, and Iceland block consensus and
use a variety of techniques to run down the clock as delegates pack
their bags and prepare to leave. Since 2002, CITES has managed to
impose stricter trade rules on three of the most charismatic shark
species: basking, whale, and great white sharks. But when asked to
provide protections for species that have real economic value, the delegates have balked.

Which is why, after spending several years lobbying to strengthen
American laws on shark harvesting, Sonja Fordham decided she
would be better off heading across the Atlantic to deal with the Europeans herself.

Europeans—who crave sharks for their meat rather than their
fins—initially set their sights on their own fishing grounds, but have
expanded these over time as they've depleted one area of the ocean
after the other. Once shark populations took a dive in the North Sea
and the Mediterranean, they turned to waters off America's shores,
but now they're close to decimating those hunting grounds as well.
U.S. authorities have started cracking down on shark catches in recent
years, limiting the number of animals that can be brought to shore
each year. At the moment the European Union is in the midst of a
wrenching debate, as member nations discuss whether to alter the
course of fishing they have pursued for centuries. Spaniards rank
among the most aggressive fishermen in the world, and they have traditionally dictated the European Union's shark-hunting rules. (Spain,
Portugal, Britain, and France make up a fifth of the top twenty
shark-fishing nations that account for 80 percent of the world's catch.)
This puts Spaniards and other Europeans among the world's top suppliers as well as consumers: they now account for nearly a third of
Hong Kong's declared fin imports.

Enric Sala, a Spanish marine biologist who left academia to become an explorer in residence at National Geographic, knows what it's like to live in a country obsessed with catching and eating fish. While he has tried his best to convince his countrymen that the world's oceans are in trouble, they laugh at him. "My friends think I'm crazy, and whenever we go to a restaurant, they say, 'Look, here's all the fish we can't eat.' Not even my mother makes the connection," he laments. Despite all the press about fish stocks running low worldwide, "the mentality in Spain hasn't changed a bit. The problem is they know because we've told them, but they still don't believe it."

A 2008 study by Francesco Ferretti, an Italian who received his doctorate at Dalhousie University, testifies to this mentality. Ferretti and his colleagues examined the toll fishing in the Mediterranean over the past two centuries had taken on sharks, looking at the activities of the twenty-one different countries that use it as their fishing grounds. They were able to come up with comprehensive figures for five large, predatory shark species: the one that fared the best, blue sharks, declined 96 percent during that time. The one that suffered the most, hammerhead sharks, declined by more than 99 percent. Sharks, to put it bluntly, are faring worse in the Mediterranean than anywhere else in the world.

"In Malta, there were places where divers used to be able to see schools of hammerheads. Now it's science fiction," Ferretti says. "The fishing pressure is so intense it makes things hard for sharks to stay around."

It's not that Europeans lack shark-finning regulations: it's just that they contain massive loopholes. In 2003 the EU adopted rules that allow fishing vessels to land fins that account for up to 5 percent of the live weight—rather than the dressed weight—of the total shark catch. Under this policy, member nations can determine how this translates as a percentage of the dressed weight, which is much lower than the whole weight. Spain and Portugal have decided this amounts to between 11 and 12 percent of the dressed weight, a ratio that is twice as lenient as the U.S. standard. On top of that, they can land carcasses and fins separately, which makes any controls meaningless.

Almost no ocean-wide international shark catch limits exist. The

EU has set some restrictions on a handful of species in the North Sea, but these limits regularly exceed the numbers marine scientists recommend. A few people who have grown up on the North Sea, like Struan Stevenson, know exactly what that kind of activity portends for the ocean.

Stevenson was born in Ballantrae, Scotland, and after serving as a councilman in South Ayrshire for nearly a quarter of a century, he now spends much of his time in Brussels, arguing over fish. He is a green Conservative in the mold of the British prime minister, David Cameron, who imbues his environmental crusades with a bit of anti-regulatory rhetoric. First elected to the European Parliament in 1999, Stevenson chaired its Fisheries Committee between 2002 and 2004 while simultaneously holding the title of Conservative front-bench spokesman on fisheries. He remains a senior member on the Fisheries Committee and considers sharks a key part of his policy portfolio.

During the course of his lifetime Stevenson has seen the collapse of small towns that used to thrive on the "Cod is God" philosophy. Cod once filled the North Sea to such an extent, he says, "you could almost walk from Scotland to Norway on their backs." Whole communities sprang up in his country based on fishing cod, but "they're virtual ghost towns now." Now a new phrase is gaining popularity in Scotland, as fishermen struggle with dwindling catch quotas and diminishing fish stocks: "Sod the cod." Having seen Scottish fishermen's livelihoods dry up, Stevenson now adheres to a precautionary approach when it comes to regulating the seas. Roughly translated, it goes something like this: setting fishing limits now will stave off disaster later.

The Spaniards have yet to accept Stevenson's reasoning, arguing that activists are overestimating the risks associated with overfishing and that nations have the right to explore the seas to satisfy consumer demand. Spanish fishing interests have already scaled back their operations and reduced the number of vessels they send out to sea, they point out, so further limits would damage their livelihoods.

Debating rules over shark finning in the European Parliament has a sort of comedic quality. During a debate in September 2006, when the

Spanish delegation was pushing to increase the catch for blue sharks, they circulated an amendment that was only in Spanish. One of the Spanish delegates informed Stevenson it wasn't fair to put strict limits on the fin-body ratio for blue sharks, because the species have "massive fins, great big fins." (This isn't true, anatomically speaking.)

Ultimately, Stevenson's side won a small victory when the European Parliament rejected a recommendation from its Fisheries Committee to weaken the shark-finning rules even further. But the vote was not binding, since it's the European Commission, not the parliament, that sets regulations.

Even as he has made a small bit of progress within parliament, the red-haired Scotsman received a powerful reminder of the market forces driving the shark fin trade when he went to China on an official delegation trip in 2006. At every official dinner, he recalls, the menu included "shark's fin soup, and shark's fin this and shark's fin that . . . It was salty and stringy. It was like thin string, like flat noodles."

Even when Stevenson makes modest strides in Europe, he is faced with the reality that as long as Chinese consumers demand shark's fin soup for every important occasion, sharks are headed off the precipice. It's somewhat akin to the debate Americans and Europeans engage in when discussing what needs to be done in order to curb greenhouse gas emissions linked to global warming: even if the EU and the United States impose strict limits, climate change will accelerate as long as the Chinese build a power plant a week to expand their manufacturing base. Worldwide environmental problems require global solutions, which presents a formidable political and diplomatic challenge. Otherwise, the sharks that escape a European fisherman's nets will simply be trapped by one in Asia.

Armando Astudillo winces a lot when discussing sharks; he is a true European bureaucrat, and a diplomat, and he doesn't like discussing topics that are, in his word, "painful." (This word comes up several times in our conversation.) Moreover, any fisheries discussion constitutes a political minefield for him as a Spaniard.

Astudillo, who used to oversee the EU's fishing fleets before being promoted to head its environment and health unit, is more than willing to acknowledge the EU has not followed up on some of its conservation pledges. "At the end of the day, we didn't do much in terms of a plan of action," he says, referring to the 1999 international UN pact. "We take sharks as a resource."

From Astudillo's perspective, managing sharks poses a political and diplomatic problem for Europeans, since it pits one region of the European Union against another. Nongovernmental organizations have raised "a red flag" about the animals' predicament, which is beginning to resonate with the public. At the same time, agreeing to end shark finning by establishing a ratio of the fin catch to the overall haul "was particularly painful for the Spanish and Portuguese industry . . . The question was very difficult, very painful." And it's impossible not to feel the Spaniards' pain, he reasons. "In this world, the European Union, decisions are made by a majority within the community. The Spanish fleet is the most important one, in terms of fishing in general." And Spanish fishing interests, he adds, continue to complain that they cannot meet the EU's rather laid-back standard when it comes to sharks.

It's not that Astudillo questions the scientific basis for these restrictions: he questions the European Union's political will. "If you are willing to protect sharks, what we know now is sufficient," he says. "The problem is, it is not an easy task. Some people would say, 'Why bother?' " And Europeans, he adds, like their shark. "You can go into any market in Brussels, you can find blue shark, mako shark," he points out. "I have actually tried it. It's not bad at all."

Spending just a few minutes with Javier Garat Pérez, secretary-general of Confederación Española de Pesca, gives one a sense of the delicate task EU officials such as Astudillo face. With 1,450 fishing companies as members, the association Garat heads ranks as the biggest in Europe. These companies own a total of 1,650 vessels, of which 500 are large ships. Garat is not afraid to spend time with environmentalists: he regularly journeys to meetings like the International Union for Conservation of Nature's World Conservation Congress, which took place in Barcelona in October 2008. Garat preaches a message of moderation, saying that his members are just as interested in sustaining shark populations over the long term, because they have become concerned recently about the declining price of shark meat. "They say some species should be prohibited [from being caught]. We are ready to accept that," he says of environmentalists. "What we hope to have is a future with shark fisheries. Now is when we want to take measures, to avoid worse measures in the future."

But while Spanish fishermen are willing to make a few gestures toward conservation, such as reducing the size of their fleet through a buyout program and cutting back on the days the remaining vessels are at sea, Garat and his colleagues balk at the idea of landing sharks with their fins attached, or of tightening the fin-body weight ratio of shark landings to ensure that fishermen are not merely cutting off the animal's fins before tossing it overboard.

"The profits will disappear. If we have to land the fins and body together, that will be the sentence of death to this fleet," he says. "A long time ago, maybe twenty years ago, these long-liners were fishing only swordfish, and through bycatch they caught sharks. But the circumstances have changed over the last few years, and now we have a lot of vessels that are catching sharks. They are not bycatch; they are dedicated fisheries. Now they are very important to the economics of these companies."

While the scientific evidence is mounting that shark populations cannot sustain the sort of fishing pressure they're now under, translating these findings into policy remains challenging. Historically, fishing interests have never recognized the virtue of restraint, and instead relied on exploiting different species in succession in order to support their trade. Despite public pressure, the Spaniards are not ready to declare defeat when it comes to shark fishing.

Just over a year after Astudillo and I had a chance to talk, the EU published a "consultation document" aimed at finally producing an action plan for sharks. It contains many of the goals Fordham and her allies have been fighting for, including a fin-to-meat ratio of 5 percent of a shark's dressed weight and a call to adhere to catch limits based on scientists' recommendations. Now that the EU has released the document—which not only needs to be approved by EU officials but also must pass muster with Europe's Council of Ministers and its parliament—fishing interests and environmentalists are hashing out the details in front of key decision makers.

While Sonja Fordham relocated to be in the fight, much of it takes place behind closed doors, where she can exercise little control over the outcome. "It's so much more transparent in the U.S.," she says. "At least you can go see the sausage being made." In the United States, federal fisheries officials issue a public notice for a hearing and wait for anyone to show up. In Europe, policy makers hand out personal invitations.

Fordham finds herself making pilgrimages to hostile territory in Spain and France—provided she gets an invite. "I go and make a presentation. It's not really welcome," she acknowledges. "They sort of start out as gentlemen . . ." Fordham's voice trails off. The fact that she usually ends up being pilloried goes unsaid.

But Fordham remains undaunted. She's fine being seen as "the glaring American" at times, crusading for sharks. On occasion, she even passes as European, even if not as Mediterranean. "I got called a British woman the other day," she recounts gleefully. In Fordham's world, that's progress. Rather than being considered a total outsider, she's beginning to be accepted as a legitimate participant in the European debate over sharks.

In December 2008, the EU Council of Fisheries decided to ignore most of the shark catch recommendations made by the European Commission and independent scientists. Rather than abolishing the porbeagle and spurdog shark fisheries, the ministers just reduced the catch limits by 25 and 50 percent, respectively. France, which held the EU presidency at the time of the decision, engineered the outcome, because France operates Europe's one remaining porbeagle fishery and was unwilling to shut it down. The vote marked a serious setback for Fordham, who had thought before the negotiations began that Europe was prepared to adopt strict fishing limits for the region's most imperiled sharks. While the ministers agreed during the same meeting to fully protect angel sharks, a species that's been decimated in Europe, Fordham remains convinced she and her allies aren't making progress fast enough. "It really can be too late for sharks."

But by April 2009, the EU Council of Fisheries appeared to be listening more closely to the concerns of Fordham and other environmentalists. It issued a document titled "Council Conclusions" endorsing a new EU Commission Shark Plan, which aims to broaden knowledge about sharks, ensure more sustainable catches, and reconcile the policies the EU espouses abroad and what it does at home. Even Spain is modifying its approach: in October 2009 it banned fishing eleven species of hammerhead and thresher sharks in its waters, making it the first EU member nation to do so. Spain doesn't have a perfect record—its vessels continue to scour the high seas for commercially valuable sharks, and they're still hauling illegally caught basking sharks onto land at Galicia and Asturias. But sharks' allies are slowly making inroads in the halls of power.

Fordham had to pack up her bags in the summer of 2009—the funding for her post disappeared when the global recession hit, and she relocated to Washington to launch a new group, Shark Advocates International. Since then, shark conservation campaigns have only attracted a higher profile. Lesley Rochat runs the Save Our Seas Shark Centre in Kalk Bay, South Africa, within walking distance of where surfers brave the bay's shark-infested waters. Rochat, a photographer and filmmaker with a university degree in the dramatic arts, has taken an unorthodox approach to shark conservation. Sometimes it amounts to a performance art routine; other times it's more like a Madison Avenue advertising campaign. But Rochat is focused on winning over her audience, and more often than not she succeeds.

Rochat's career trajectory changed one day when she was photographing an exhibit at Cape Town's Two Oceans Aquarium, which featured a ragged-tooth shark named Maxine. Maxine had been caught in one of the shark nets that surround Durban but survived and was released, only to be caught again near Cape Town. The shark was scarred in the process, and Rochat, intrigued by the backstory, launched a fund-raising campaign that eventually got Maxine released from captivity in 2004 with a satellite tag that tracked her initial movements.

While Maxine's release attracted plenty of attention, Rochat decided she needed to enlist the aid of a professional ad firm in order to reach a broader audience. The Cape Town branch of Saatchi & Saatchi devised a clever set of advertisements under the banner of "Rethink the Shark," an ironic take on the classic beach scene from *Jaws*. While the initial shots resemble the movie—a pleasant day at the beach that quickly devolves into a scene of panic—the scary object jutting out of the water in the end is not a shark's fin. Instead, it's an ordinary object that takes many more lives worldwide each year than sharks: a toaster, a kite, or a chair, depending on the commercial. It's an effective ad, partly because the inanimate objects are so banal. As the toaster floats, seemingly harmless, the tagline reads, "Last year 791 people were killed by defective toasters. 4 by sharks."

Rochat didn't stop with a single ad campaign. She's come up with a slew of different ways to challenge popular perceptions of sharks. The shark tank in Two Oceans Aquarium now has a warning label posted on its inside stating, "Warning: Predators Beyond This Point." The implication: humans are the predators, not the fish. In another public awareness stunt, Rochat littered a couple of South African beaches with shells that carried a recorded message from the sea, followed with messages in glass bottles from different creatures (Greg the Great White wrote, "Now I realize we have a BAD reputation because of that DAMN MOVIE, but we're not like that") and finally a coffin that washed ashore with a brass plate detailing the number of dolphins that drown each year in fishing nets. While Rochat's main message is pretty grim, she does her best to leaven it with a bit of creativity. She chose to work with trained marketers because they think about how a message can infiltrate the public consciousness.

"Their skill is to take this complex subject and put it in a way that's simple but powerful," she explains as she pulls out sketches for the next ad campaign she and Saatchi & Saatchi are cooking up.

Groups across the globe have their respective pitchmen: the Pew Environment Group has got shark attack survivors to make the case for shark preservation, while Oceana enlisted January Jones, a Hollywood actor who has made her mark as the long-suffering suburban housewife Betty Draper on the television series *Mad Men*. In each case, the appeal is the same: we pose the real danger to sharks, not the other way around.

Oceana's chief scientist, Michael Hirshfield, feels confident his group has gotten the right person to make its case. "It's the surprise factor. It's not your big macho surfer dude. It's a petite actress, who instead of being afraid of sharks is afraid for them."

There's no question that Jones—a striking blonde who sported a formfitting black dress and high heels as she made her congressional rounds—is an effective lobbyist. A South Dakota native, she has gotten the state's one Democratic senator, Tim Johnson, to co-sponsor a measure banning the finning of sharks in U.S. waters. Not only that, she has so endeared herself to McCain (who declined to press for shark conservation measures once he returned to the Senate in 2009, despite his campaign trail declarations) that he not only signed on to the same bill but gave her a thirty-minute tour of the Capitol and walked her to her car.

The day Jones launches her Capitol Hill charm offensive—September 30, 2009—Hirshfield is triumphant. "You heard it here first, it's the turning point for sharks," he says. "The day January Jones came to Washington."

About six months later, representatives from 175 nations demonstrated that Hirshfield might be a little premature in declaring victory. The delegates who gathered at the Convention on International Trade in Endangered Species of Wild Fauna and Flora considered four separate proposals to protect eight species of sharks: scalloped hammerhead, smooth hammerhead, great hammerhead, dusky, sandbar, oceanic whitetip, porbeagle, and spiny dogfish. The small island nation of Palau—which created its shark sanctuary just days before January Jones was paying her courtesy calls at the Senate—had joined forces with the United States and the European Union to press for the trade measures, which would have monitored international sales of these species to ensure they were sustainable. Palau's president, Johnson Toribiong, sent a message to delegates explaining that while he's banned shark fishing within two hundred nautical miles of his country's coasts, an area roughly the size of France, "Palau cannot protect our environment alone." Advocates came armed with plenty of statistics on how fishing has wiped out as much as 99 percent of some of these sharks' populations, hoping that alone would secure the two-thirds majority they needed for passage.

But a cadre of coastal nations, along with major fish consumers such as Japan and China, beat back the proposals. Grenada's chief fisheries officer, Justin Rennie, who pushed for a secret ballot on some votes, called the decision to protect hammerheads "arbitrary." In an interview the day before the final day of voting, Rennie explained that while countries like his are willing to take some responsibility for their use of the ocean, Americans and Europeans can't expect them to relinquish their economic claim on the sea altogether. For many of them, he explained, their exclusive economic zone in the ocean is fifty times larger than their country's land area: "We have very little opportunity on the land. That is why we look toward the sea."

For a short while it looked as if activists had scored at least one victory when delegates adopted the proposal to monitor the trade of porbeagle sharks, which have declined by at least 80 percent in the northeast and southwest Atlantic Ocean. But the convention has a quirky rule: delegates can revote on any proposal on the last day of the conference, and the result of that balloting is the one that carries the day. So just hours before the gathering ended, opponents called for one more vote on the porbeagle protections. The measure failed to get the two-thirds majority it needed by a margin of two votes, as members of the Japanese delegation stood at the back of the room, shaking each other's hands in congratulations. The delegates to the world's largest wildlife-trafficking conference, which occurs only every three years, left sharks swimming on the high seas exactly where they've always been, with no international catch limits whatsoever.

John Scanlon, the Australian who took over as secretary general of CITES after that meeting in Doha, has a soft spot for sharks. He hopes a report from a joint U.N. Food and Agriculture Organization– CITES workshop held in the wake of the failed votes—which focused on how shark species that might face new trade restricitions are faring and what such curbs would look like—might help broker a future compromise on the issue. "The issue has not gone away, by any stretch," Scanlon says. "Sharks will definitely come back."

Scanlon was right. Delegates to the International Commission for the Conservation of Atlantic Tunas had resisted the idea of limiting shark fishing for years. But in November 2010 the commission banned the catch, retention, and sale of seven species in the Atlantic Ocean—oceanic whitetips and six types of hammerheads: great, scalloped, scoophead, smalleye, smooth, and whitefin. But member nations balked at protecting the species fueling the bulk of shark fin trade, rejecting catch limits the United States proposed on shortfin makos.

Shark conservation, it turns out, is only partly a matter of finding the exact sales pitch and the right person to deliver it. While activists have finally mastered the science and the message, it takes time to shift the mind-set of both the public and policy makers. The question is how much time the sharks have left.

9

GAWKING AT JAWS

I am very grateful to the sea because for the little I have, it was given to me from the sea.

—Luis "Meli" Muñoz, La Paz fisherman

Shark fishing in Mexico is a matter of economics and tradition. This nation has been catching sharks since the time of the Aztecs and the Olmecs, gloried civilizations that made distinctions between the different shark species swimming in the Gulf of Mexico. Even now Mexico remains one of the top shark-fishing nations in the world: men on the Pacific and Atlantic coasts troll for sharks that will primarily go for domestic consumption, whether it's a dry, shredded jerky many Mexicans love or meat for fish tacos or for the Chinese restaurants in Mexico City that offer shark's fin soup. But Mexico—like a handful of other nations, such as South Africa—represents the crossroads we find ourselves at when it comes to our relationship to sharks. It embodies our past, but could offer us a very different future.

One of the Mexican areas that still sustains a lively shark trade is La Paz, a major city on the Baja California peninsula, and the small towns that surround it. Now boasting roughly 200,000 residents, La Paz no longer embodies its name, which means "Peace" in Spanish. Its downtown waterfront promenade features an Applebee's as well as multiple realtors' offices, and is usually clogged with cars regardless of the time of day. As the capital of Baja California Sur, La Paz is the state's economic center, the biggest of several fishing towns scattered up and down the peninsula. John Steinbeck traveled there in 1940 with his friend Ed "Doc" Ricketts, a marine biologist, aboard a seventy-six-foot sardine boat dubbed the *Western Flyer,* and the two men translated their six-week, four-thousand-mile expedition into the book *Sea of Cortez: A Leisurely Journal of Travel and Research.* Later, Steinbeck paid homage to La Paz in his novella *The Pearl,* describing how divers there sought out what they hoped would be the "Pearl of the World."

Baja still banks on its marine resources to generate commercial, as well as tourist, dollars. Partyers flock to Cabo San Lucas (immortalized in the 1970s television series *The Love Boat* in well-worn lines such as Captain Stubing's remark to Julie, "Do you like my sombrero? I picked it up in Cabo San Lucas!") to the south, while ecotourists head farther north to see the gray whales, which congregate there in the late winter and early spring. The hardiest visitors usually opt for kayaking trips to the island of Espíritu Santo, which lies fifteen miles from La Paz. Steinbeck described the somewhat forbidding island as standing "high and sheer from the water."

But when it comes to defining Baja's cultural identity, fishing still dominates. The practice sustains tiny outposts like Las Barrancas, a Baja town five hours north of La Paz. Getting there is arduous. While there is technically a highway stretching from La Paz to a turnoff not far from Las Barrancas, this "highway" is more like a series of cratered potholes, strung together by small stretches of dirt. Driving there in a tiny rental car with my future husband, Andrew, and two researchers from the Mexican conservation group Iemanya Oceanica, we careen wildly from side to side on the road. Our assumption: skidding off the highway's edge is a safer bet than dipping into one of the potholes, at which point our rental compact will surely crumple in on itself. We were right.

Far removed from either the state's whale-watching center or its cruise ship ports, Las Barrancas is composed of a handful of shacks with corrugated metal roofs, the biggest of which have a beaten pickup truck standing out front. For most of the day, Las Barrancas is pretty much silent. At around 2:00 p.m., however, the fishing boats come in, and the entire town—about a dozen people—troops down to the beach to meet the fishermen and help process the fish.

One spring afternoon—the day we come to visit—Francisco and

Armando Bareno, two brothers, manage to haul in nearly two dozen mako and blue sharks. The brothers have left their nets out for two days due to bad weather, so by the time they drag in their catch, the sharks are glassy-eyed and lifeless. In addition to having dull expressions, the sharks are less than formidable in size: all of them are clearly juveniles, about three or four feet long.

Standing in the shallow water, the Barenos methodically dismember the animals, always in the same order, in a process that takes less than sixty seconds per shark. After cutting off the head, they slice off the fins—the most valuable part of the body—and place them into one set of brightly colored plastic crates. Then they gut the animal, cut off the tail, and throw the remaining meat into a separate set of crates.

Just yards away on the beach, an aged white truck idles, waiting to take the Barenos' haul to Mexico City. Unlike countries such as Indonesia, Mexico consumes an estimated 90 percent of its shark catch, mostly as a dried, shredded jerky. The Barenos couldn't sell the fins right away, since they needed to dry them first: once dry, they fetch 1,000 pesos, or about $100, per kilo. By contrast, they hand over the fresh shark meat to the wholesalers waiting with their Mexico City–bound truck for just 15 pesos, or $1.50, a kilo. (As another Baja fisherman put it, "The fins are what bring the money.")

Francisco Bareno leans against the truck as I ask him in Spanish whether he enjoys shark fishing. "Not much," he replies, "but I have to live."

One of the reasons Mexican shark fishermen are less than enthusiastic about their trade nowadays is there are fewer fish to catch. Mexican authorities have little idea of how many sharks their fishermen catch each year, so on Valentine's Day 2007 they passed a law requiring observers on larger shark-fishing vessels and satellite tracking of these ships. The law, which also prohibits large commercial shark fishing within twenty miles of Mexico's shores and grants special protection for great white, whale, and basking sharks, aims to provide regulators with an overview of how many sharks are killed in their waters.

Many Mexican fishermen are skeptical of the law. Manuel Espinoza Álvarez, who lives in La Paz and has spent thirty of his forty-four years working at sea, resents the fact that the government lets some large vessels scour the region's depths for fish while he and other fishermen struggle to make a living. Like Francisco, he works with his brother, and he suspects the additional regulations will undermine his already-precarious standard of living along the shore. "Where's the benefit for us?" he asks.

Paul Ahuja is one of the people who spend their time trying to convince Espinoza that protecting sharks is a smart economic move. A lanky, bearded six-foot-five-inch New Yorker, Ahuja stands out in a crowd when he walks the streets of La Paz. (He likes to say he resembles "Gulliver among the Lilliputians.") Now in his mid-forties, Ahuja came to Baja by a circuitous route: he joined the U.S. Army before heading to grad school in California, and initially came to La Paz not to track sharks but to study the giant mantas that swam in the Sea of Cortez. Within a couple of years the giant mantas—huge, flapping creatures that look like bats or aliens, depending on your perspective—disappeared. But Ahuja stayed on as Mexico research director for Iemanya Oceanica, in an attempt to make sure Mexican sharks do not go the way of his beloved mantas.

Ahuja has a dark sense of humor, which serves him well in his line of work. Most days he heads out from La Paz's waterfront in his small motorboat, named for an ex-girlfriend (his current one wants him to rename it, of course), to survey the fishermen's wreckage. Just a few minutes' ride away sits El Mogote, a narrow strip of land where La Paz fishermen fillet their catch and discard body parts with no value before heading to port. Ahuja and his colleagues, armed with cameras and vials for collecting DNA evidence, descend on El Mogote like a forensics team.

As we disembark, Ahuja scans the water for castoffs: he digs into the muck just offshore, and within moments he has begun pulling up the heads of hammerhead and angel sharks, as well as plenty of remains of *mobilas,* a species of ray protected under Mexico's shark law, and whip rays. He pulls up the rays two at a time, by their skinny tails, as other researchers use their scalpels to extract small pieces of flesh to conduct DNA tests.

"There must be a manta taco special today," Ahuja mutters, the rays hanging down behind him.

Ahuja holds out some hope that Mexico's 2007 regulations will give federal officials enough information to correct the worst shark-fishing abuses—"For the first time we will have data," he says—but he places more faith in the ability of Luis Muñoz to convert his fellow shark fishermen into conservationists. It's a wise bet, since Muñoz—a La Paz fisherman who goes by the nickname Meli—is as charismatic as it gets.

Meli was born the same year Steinbeck and Ricketts journeyed to his home city. He remembers the very first day he began fishing at the age of twelve: June 5, 1952. At that time, he recalls, "the seas were full of sharks."

Sitting in front of his house, with his shiny blue pickup truck behind him, Meli can hardly contain his enthusiasm. His face is wrinkled and dark after spending so many years in the sun, but he has the energy of a man decades younger: he freely gesticulates as he speaks, leaning forward intently to convey his points. He can divvy up shark species according to how serious a threat they pose—"There are some shark species you have to respect, like the mako shark; blue sharks are a little aggressive"—and can't say enough good things about shark meat, which he describes as "delicious." In many ways Meli sees sharks as willing partners in his fishing expeditions who have helped pay for the house in which he lives and the truck he drives.

"I love the sharks very much. I've been living with them. I've captured hundreds and hundreds of sharks; none of them have attacked me," he says. "I feel a great love and affection for the sharks because the sharks have for many years given me food. For me, the sharks are my life."

Meli doesn't go out fishing anymore. For years he has belonged to a fishing labor cooperative, and now he takes the fish his fellow cooperative members catch in Todos Santos, a small town on the Pacific Coast a couple of hours away, and sells it in La Paz. The son of a fisherman, around 1992 Meli started getting concerned that he and his cooperative buddies had to go farther and farther out to catch sharks compared with a few decades earlier. It's a complaint you hear often on the beaches of Baja: Jesús Orozco, a Todos Santos fisherman who goes by the nickname of Lobo, or Wolf (all Baja fishermen seem to have a nickname; it's like a CB handle or something), says he spends the bulk of his days trolling the waters in search of sharks, rather than battling them from his boat. "It's not difficult to fish the sharks," he says. "It's difficult to find them."

Meli told his three sons they would be better off staying in school than following his example, but they opted to hunt sharks as well. "I'm studying and studying, when am I going to earn money?" one of his sons asked him. Meli had no answer, so he let his sons leave school.

But at this point, Meli spends much of his time worrying about "the future of sharks, and of our children and grandchildren and great-grandchildren." So he has teamed up with the researchers at Iemanya Oceanica, and when he shows up on the Punta Lobos beach in Todos Santos on Saturday afternoons, he talks to his fellow cooperative members about whether they might want to ditch fishing for whale shark guiding.

Many cooperative members are open to the idea of starting a new tourism venture. José Mesa, who caught two hammerhead sharks and one mako shark on a day when Meli showed up, says he looks forward to the moment when he and other local fishermen will be shuttling visitors across local waters rather than foraging for sharks. "Economically, it would be better than fishing," he reasons. "It would be easy to do, because we know the sea. The only thing that's hard is the English." Shark fishing, by contrast, is "too much work. It's difficult work. We don't have medical insurance, and it's dangerous work."

Everyone acknowledges Baja fishermen will have to overcome some logistical obstacles before they start bringing Americans down for sightseeing. The waters right off Punta Lobos are rough, so the cooperative needs a loan to build a marina with a proper deck from which to launch. As Ahuja puts it, "When the waves are big, if you get five overweight Americans in a boat, they're not going to be up for it."

Orozco fears building an adequate marina, from which whale shark–watching guides can push off their boats farther at sea, will cost "many thousands of pesos." But a fisheries professor from a local university gave a lecture on ecotourism to the Todos Santos fishermen in August 2006, and cooperative members have been plotting a career switch ever since.

Todos Santos fishermen have done the math: on many days Jorge Cambillo Zazueta spends 500 pesos, or $50, on fuel—along with extra money on ice and bait—and he catches about 350 pesos' worth of sharks.

Even the researchers who support the idea of whale shark–watching operations, however, worry about whether Baja will adopt adequate regulations. Deni Ramírez, a Ph.D. student at Centro de Investigaciones Biológicas del Noroeste who has been studying whale sharks in both Baja and Isla Holbox, an island off the Yucatán, says environmental rules in Mexico often come down to a question of nationalism.

"The gray whales have a lot of protection because they are Mexican; they are born here," she says. No one knows exactly where the whale sharks swimming along the Baja peninsula are born, so they lack the same Mexican imprimatur. "It's amazing in Mexico—in one area they protect the sharks, and when they move to another area in Mexico, they have trouble."

Ramírez spends a decent amount of time underwater photographing whale sharks in Baja, since each animal has a separate coloring pattern that allows researchers to identify them. Much of the time she can spot propeller marks on their bodies, vestiges of the many run-ins the fish have had with commercial and tourist boats. While some high-end cruise lines focused on conservation, such as Lindblad

Expeditions, take safety precautions, most do not. "It's not fair," she complains. "You're making money with these whale sharks, and the whale sharks are getting hit by propellers."

Ahuja harbors his own concerns about whale shark watching in Baja, fearing that the sharks one day might become like bears in Yellowstone that have become dependent on humans for food, or the stingrays in the Cayman Islands that have reversed their nocturnal feeding patterns to maximize their take from tourists.

"I have a problem with saying tourism is the way to go," he says, right after detailing how his group has devoted much of its time to evangelizing about its virtues to local fishermen. "But I don't see another road on which to go. So does everyone in Mexico. That's all they talk about."

The place the Baja fishermen are talking about is Isla Holbox (pronounced OHL-bosh, reflecting its Spanish and Mayan roots), a small Yucatán community that has successfully made the ecotourism leap. Rafael de la Parra, who is research coordinator for the conservation group Proyecto Dominó and splits his time between Cancún and Holbox, is confident it can serve as a model for Mexico and other developing countries. De la Parra is an unabashed ecotourism booster: in an effort to woo locals, his group printed up placards depicting a whale shark trailed by a bunch of dominoes (as a play on the shark's nickname) and a slogan in Spanish reading, "Conserve the whale shark, it's your best game." It's a mantra, he argues, that has finally begun to sink in here.

Sitting on the beach with hotels arrayed behind him and whale shark–watching boats tied up at the dock in front of him, de la Parra is satisfied with the transformation he has witnessed in Holbox over the past few years.

"This originally was a shark-fishing village. They were using mantas as bait till last year, and a long time ago they used dolphins," he says, peering out at sea. "Now everything turns around the whale sharks."

Back in 2002, Isla Holbox resembled Las Barrancas more closely than the holiday destination it's become. Lying roughly ninety miles northwest of Cancún, Holbox has never managed to lure American frat boys the way its better-known neighbor has. (Perhaps this is because getting to Holbox, on the very northern tip of the Yucatán, involves riding over rocky dirt roads for two and a half hours and then taking a noisy, water-soaked ferry ride.)

But a few years ago a small cadre of scientists from Mexico, the United States, and Belize started making an annual pilgrimage to this narrow, twenty-five-mile-long island in order to observe the whale sharks that flock in the hundreds to its shores each summer in search of plankton-rich water. For decades researchers had paid little attention to whale sharks: as filter feeders with tiny, vestigial teeth, they did not hold the same scientific or popular appeal as murderous great whites or the other fierce predators roaming the seas.

In a world of shrinking shark populations, however, this summertime whale shark aggregation intrigued scientists: there is a higher concentrated number of whale sharks here than anywhere else in the world. The whale sharks have picked the Yucatán as their annual vacation spot, and researchers want to know why. Even better, whale sharks—hulking but harmless creatures with polka dots and stripes on their backs—are the kinds of animals a kid can love, making them a sort of conservation poster child.

As David Santucci, who trekked to Holbox to see this phenomenon for himself when he worked as a spokesman for the Georgia Aquarium, puts it, "There is no better species to represent sharks than whale sharks. They're gentle giants, they're awe inspiring, they're magnificent creatures."

And this is how, in just five years, Holbox transformed itself from a sleepy island into a whale shark ecotourist mecca.

Founded 150 years ago, Holbox is the type of place whose official history includes phrases such as "according to legend" and "the locals say" before any fact is given. Most people agree the former pirates' hideout got its name from a small dark lagoon on the southern part of the island: Holbox means "black hole" in Mayan. A different, freshwater lagoon named Yalahau was the island's real draw: the Maya viewed it as a fountain of youth, and around 1800 Spanish Armada ships stopped by to get their drinking water from the pristine source.

Despite its attractive lagoons, Holbox has remained a backwater for centuries. Even now its official tour guide describes islanders as "descendants of pirates, mestizos of several races, fishermen by trade." Jungle mangroves divide the island, which is less than two miles across at its widest point, into three parts; only the smallest section is inhabited.

For years Holbox had one business: fishing. In the 1980s the town's inhabitants started earning a decent living for the first time by exploiting the local lobster fishery in earnest, moving them solidly into Mexico's middle class. That initial prosperity, however, sowed the seeds of class conflict in the mid-1990s as some of the town's residents began dealing in real estate. By 2000, Holbox was divided between those who could afford to own property and those who could not, and with the lobster fishery depleted, villagers were left wondering what to do next.

Willy Betancourt Sabatini was one of the first Holboxeños to realize how the residents could benefit from the massive whale sharks that congregated near the island from May to September. Like most of the other men in Holbox, Betancourt worked as a fisherman, but he knew the sea was an unreliable seafood supplier. So when the scientists started coming to the island—and meeting with Betancourt's sister Norma, a local environmentalist who now serves as the project director for the Yum Balam National Protected Area just off the island's shores—Betancourt wanted in.

Whale shark tourism had just begun to take off in nearby Belize, since researchers had figured out the animals tended to congregate around an area known as Gladden Spit during the full moon in spring. But some scientists there, including Rachel Graham, a D.C. native who had made Belize her home, became concerned that overenthusiastic divers were disturbing both the sharks and the red snappers whose eggs the whale sharks coveted. Graham started working with whale sharks in Belize in 1998, and by 2002, she says, tour operators told her they had "noticed if a lot of people jumped in the water and grabbed the shark's tail, the behavior of this animal was evasive or elusive." Graham wanted to make sure Holbox did not repeat these same mistakes.

So as Holbox began to establish its own marine tourism standards, Norma Betancourt and others made it clear they wanted a plan developed and enforced by members of the community, so that cheaters would face their neighbors' wrath. Few Holboxeños have as much social standing as Norma, a direct descendant of one of the town's founding families.

"I have Holbox everywhere," she likes to say, in Spanish, with a smile.

A petite woman with a broad Mayan face, Betancourt brooded at first that the burgeoning whale shark–watching business "was going to end in disaster." But in the spring of 2003 researchers and local entrepreneurs—including Norma's brother Willy—worked to devise an ethical code that established the ground rules for frolicking with the polka-dotted giants. At any given time only two divers and one guide can be in the water with a single shark, and they must snorkel, rather than dive, so it's obvious how many swimmers are in the water. Flash photography and touching of the sharks are forbidden. Any given boat can only have up to ten tourists in it, and each whale shark operation must apply for a permit.

"People said we were crazy, that we couldn't do it," Betancourt recalls. But she and her allies had made an apt calculation: the fishermen had learned enough from the 1980s lobster debacle to know they needed to set limits when it came to dealing with the sea. "They know if we don't take care, all of us are going to lose."

The economics of shark tourism are pretty clear: the fish are worth much more alive than dead. In Belize tourists flock to the small town of Placencia to gawk at whale sharks in the Gladden Spit Marine Reserve, and a 2002 study estimated they brought $3.7 million to Placencia over a six-week period. In the Donsol region of the Philippines, the number of whale shark tourists mushroomed from 867 to 7,000 over the course of five years, bringing $620,000 to the country's economy in 2005. A third of all diving activity in Spain's Canary Islands is linked to sharks and rays, according to a recent study by the Institute of Social and Political Sciences at the University of La Laguna, accounting for nearly $25 million a year of the region's tourist economy. While shark tourism is not yet on par with whale watching, which generates roughly $2 billion a year worldwide, it has started to generate significant revenues. As Maldives president Mohamed Nasheed puts it, "We think that you can make more money by looking at a shark than by making it into a soup."

From Willy Betancourt's perspective, sacrificing fishing for tourism was a fair deal. "It's simple and more predictable than fishing," he explains, adding that the twelve men who now work for him as boat operators and guides earn as much in half a day as they used to earn fishing for an entire day. "We respect the rules. People understand it very well."

Graham is not entirely convinced that Holbox is as much of a paradise as some of its residents think. A member of the Wildlife Conservation Society's Ocean Giants Program, Graham is as physically imposing as Paul Ahuja: the word "Amazonian" best describes her nearly six-foot, broad-shouldered frame. Equally at ease in English, Spanish, and French, Graham is adept at convincing local fishermen to confide in her about their activities, which is why she knows that some of them still fish some shark species, out of the tourists' sight. Even more important, they've told her some of the whale sharks swimming off Holbox have begun to shy away from people the same way they do in Belize. This isn't a coincidence: Graham has been tracking these whale sharks for years, and it's quite likely that the same individuals are making their way from Belize to Mexico and Honduras, in search of the best available food as tourists gawk at them.

"This is the same population," Graham says. "Along the Mesoamerican reef they're being hit up in three locations. That, to me, is a worry." It is, she suggests, akin to autograph seekers bothering you in a restaurant each time you begin to approach the buffet line.

The fact that now some tour operations in Cancún are bringing visitors in on fast boats to see the sharks, and that fishermen at nearby Isla Mujeres are also angling to become whale shark tour guides, only exacerbates Graham's concern. Maybe the whale sharks can handle it. Or maybe they'll give up on the buffet and head somewhere else.

There are still a few vestiges of the fishing village Holbox used to be, like the faded and cracked mural on the edge of the town square that touts the failed 2006 presidential candidate from the Institutional Revolutionary Party (PRI), Roberto Madrazo. "More Support for the Fishermen," the mural reads. "Roberto, Yes We Can. President Roberto."

But while those allusions still resonate somewhat—the once-powerful ruling authoritarian party is making a bit of a comeback from Mexico's political sidelines—fishing no longer defines Holbox. The town's Main Street now bears the name of the animal that has brought money to Holbox: Calle Tiburón Ballena, or Whale Shark Street. Every few yards boasts a storefront that is serving tourists one way or another, whether it's the Cyber Sh@rk Internet café or the McRústico hamburger and sandwich shop, serving "the best subs on the island." Images of whale sharks dominate the entire town, and every hotel offers sightseeing trips to see the famed fish in action.

Francesca Golinelli is a Holbox hotel operator whose parents, Greta and Johnny, came over from Italy in 1999 to build a vacation home. By 2001 they had enlisted their daughter in their plan to start a small hotel on the island, and a year later Casa Las Tortugas opened on the same skinny stretch of sand that houses the rest of Holbox's accommodations. Casa Las Tortugas is pretty mellow: guests can eat their breakfast at a table planted in the sand, and air-conditioning in one's room costs an extra $10 a night. Much of the building is made out of local wood, and each bathroom sports all-natural artisanal soaps from nearby Mérida.

Golinelli had been working in the Italian fashion business before her parents started extolling the wonders of Holbox. "They just fell in love with the island, the environment," she recalls. "It was so beautiful and so pure." Tired of having other people telling her what to do in her previous job, Golinelli came to live on the island devoid of motorized vehicles, robberies, and tchotchkes.

Several years after her arrival, Holbox has changed. Even with the serious setback of Hurricane Wilma, which pummeled the island in October 2005, the place has exploded with business enterprises. There are at least a dozen hostels and more than fifteen hostels and posadas crammed into the island's one inhabited section; restaurants offer everything from Italian fare to Cuban food. While cars remain scarce, golf carts have become ubiquitous, offering visitors fresh off the ferry a cheap ride from the dock to their hotel of choice. While Holbox's full-time population hovers just below two thousand, registered tourist visits have increased exponentially in recent years: six thousand came in 2004, ninety-five hundred in 2005, and twelve thousand in 2006. And all that was before *The New York Times* and *The Washington Post* wrote about the place.

At times, Golinelli—like most people who live in Holbox—waxes nostalgic for the early days. As she flips through the pile of travel magazines featuring Holbox that are stacked up on the main table in her hotel's reception area, she recalls, "When I came here there were not any golf carts. For me this was amazing, because I hate the golf carts . . . The thing that has changed the most was the Holboxeños. Money came to the island. The tourists arrived, we arrived, and the whale sharks arrived."

Locals now stroll across the plaza wearing hip, angular glasses and brightly colored Crocs. As Willy Betancourt puts it, "There have been changes in the way people dress because we imitate the Europeans. We see orange Crocs, and we think, 'Ooh, we should get those.' "

To a large extent the local government has yet to catch up with this proliferation of people and services: the island's roads are still all sand, not asphalt. Residents question how that sort of rudimentary infrastructure, along with the unchecked growth in golf cart traffic and lack of decent sanitation, can support an ever-expanding visitor population. Vultures hover over piles of trash in the town dump, located right next to the village cemetery. There's no school beyond junior high and no town hospital—only a clinic where a doctor occasionally shows up to see patients.

But despite this, the number of whale shark–watching permit applications increases every year, and it's unclear whether officials will ever place a limit on them. "It's so important for the hotels, the restaurants, the stores," says Norma Betancourt. "Whale sharks are an opportunity. It's good luck and we shouldn't lose it."

Or, as her brother Willy reasons, they've simply traded in lobsters for whale sharks: "We live off the fish."

While Holboxeños may understand the economics of whale shark watching, nobody really understands whale sharks. They are, quite literally, the biggest fish in the sea. Many whale sharks weigh well over a ton; some grow as long as forty feet. Their common name stems from their superficial similarity to whales, since they are enormous and spend much of their time filter feeding on plankton at the ocean's surface. Unlike whales, whale sharks don't need to breathe air, and they have a different internal mechanism for gulping down the tiny creatures that sustain them. A group of a dozen researchers led by University of South Florida biologist Philip J. Motta have determined that whale sharks spend between eight and twelve hours a day cruising the ocean with their mouths agape and angled upward at roughly 13 degrees, swallowing more than 162,000 gallons of water an hour to get the small crustaceans and worms that sustain them. They estimate a whale shark measuring twenty feet long takes in 6,721 calories per day, twice what U.S. dietary guidelines suggest for a six-foot, two-hundred-pound, moderately active thirty-year-old man.[1]

Until researchers learned about the group of whale sharks congregating in the Caribbean and Gulf of Mexico, even most marine biologists had never seen them. (Officials at the Georgia Aquarium, which is the only facility outside of Asia to house whale sharks, like to brag that ocean explorers such as Sylvia Earle and Philippe Cousteau never saw a whale shark until they visited the aquarium, which opened in downtown Atlanta in the fall of 2005.) Even the hundreds of thousands of dollars scientists have spent researching them in recent years has just begun to pin down some basic facts about whale sharks, and much of this remains speculation.

"There are a lot of unanswered questions out there," says Ray Davis, the Georgia Aquarium's former senior vice president of zoological operations. "Everyone's admitting they don't know the answers, and everybody's working together to get the answers."

So far, in fact, many of the answers have come from dead whale sharks rather than live ones. It wasn't until 1995, when some scientists got a look at a whale shark fished off Taiwan, that they determined the sharks were oviparous, meaning they could reproduce young from eggs. "Up to that point everything was conjecture," Davis says.

But as with other elements of shark scientific inquiry, that's pretty much where human understanding of whale shark reproduction ends. When scientists say whale sharks can produce three hundred eggs at a time, all they're doing is referring to that one shark that had the misfortune to find itself on a Taiwanese wharf in the mid-1990s, since no one's ever gotten another peek inside a pregnant whale shark's belly.

Even the death of a male whale shark can spark an academic boomlet, as when two of the Georgia Aquarium's whale sharks died in succession in 2007. Shark scientists from across the country rushed to Atlanta to take part in the necropsy of first Ralph and then Norton, the two males the aquarium had imported from Taiwan in June 2005.

Scientists focus on whale sharks for a couple of reasons: the critters eat constantly, and this, in turn, makes them enormous. Mote Marine Laboratory's Robert Hueter, who has been coming to Holbox since 1994 and tracking whale sharks there since 2003, compares them to cows. "You come out here and here's these big beasts who are only about eating," Hueter explains one afternoon as we are cruising the Gulf of Mexico tracking whale sharks from the yacht of Jim Jacoby, a major real estate developer and Georgia Aquarium board member. "It's their own equivalent of the great grassland."

In the same way that cows are straightforward feeding machines, so are whale sharks. Thanks to the Georgia Aquarium's necropsies, scientists discovered a whale shark's massive body contains a brain smaller than the size of a human fist. But whale sharks do something infinitely more interesting than cows: they dive. And they dive deep.

Eugenie Clark, the founding director of the lab where Hueter works, encountered a whale shark off the coast of the Baja peninsula while diving there decades ago. Jacques Cousteau got most of the hype in the 1950s for surveying the underwater world, but women like Clark and Sylvia Earle were just as adventurous explorers, if not more so. Clark is in her late eighties now, but she is still a pixie, a diminutive researcher who relates her most daring adventures and shows off her latest scientific discoveries with relish. At one point, as we sit in her office at Mote Marine Laboratory, she casually mentions how deep she has gone diving recently and then realizes she needs to shush me before her colleagues find out. "Don't mention how deep I went," she cautions me, suddenly stern. "I'm not supposed to do that anymore." Then she explodes into laughter.

The first time Clark ever encountered a whale shark, she grabbed on to a fold in the animal's skin under its first dorsal fin, using it as a sort of handle as the fish cruised by. She zipped along with the shark for a while even though her air tank slid off her back; holding on to the tank, she went even deeper underwater. The shark was a massive pregnant female, so it was undisturbed by the lady on its back, but at some point it occurred to Clark that she had been going for some time.

"It was incredible," Clark says now of her ride. "When I finally came up, I could barely see the boat, I was so far away."

At the time Clark went on her whale shark ride, marine biologists had no idea how far these animals plunged below the surface. Rachel Graham, the first scientist to put satellite tags on whale sharks, determined that one of the nearly two dozen sharks she tagged in Belize between 2001 and 2002 dived as deep as 4,921 feet below the surface.

Hueter, whose team from the Mote lab has worked with Mexican scientists from the research group Proyecto Dominó, has also devoted much of his time to monitoring how whale sharks dive throughout their travels. One of his sharks has surpassed Graham's poster shark by going 6,194 feet deep, more than a mile underwater. (Initially, scientists were limited by the fact that the satellite tags they attach to these fish would break off at 5,905 feet to ensure the tags' computer circuitry remained viable, but as the gadgetry advanced, so did their findings.) As the sharks descend to these formidable depths, they move without trouble from balmy sea surface temperatures in the high seventies to water as chilly as thirty-nine degrees Fahrenheit. They don't stay down for long, according to tagging data, but instead begin to rise once they've gone far down.

Graham sees this flexibility as one of whale sharks' best assets: "Their ability to adapt to all sorts of different environments is an important part of their survival."

But this deep diving also raises an obvious question: Why do the whale sharks go that deep? Even after several years of study, Hueter falls back on the process of elimination in order to answer the query. At first, researchers thought the animals were seeking food down below, but the plankton is pretty thin at those depths. Then they thought these dives might serve to regulate the sharks' body temperature, but they haven't found particular evidence to support that in the data they've collected. So now they're leaning toward the theory that diving allows whale sharks to rest, as they engage in a sort of harmless free fall toward the seafloor. But they are still trying to figure out why whale sharks, along with basking sharks, dive in a number of distinct patterns, such as V-shaped spikes, a W-shaped sawtooth, and oscillatory staircasing.

Whale sharks are a hot property, scientifically and academically speaking: in 2002 the world's governments decided to protect the species through CITES, one of only a handful of sharks to receive such protection. No one knows how many whale sharks are out there, though Proyecto Dominó and its partners have estimated that at least a thousand—and perhaps as many as fifteen hundred—of them come to Holbox each summer.

"There's no question they have gotten attention because of their gargantuan size, and they're polka-dotted animals people are attracted to," Hueter says. "Does that mean they're more important? I don't think so. Does that mean they're threatened or endangered? Not necessarily. They've been treated sort of royally because of the warm-and-fuzzy factor."

In fact, Hueter and his Mote colleagues had been studying blacktip sharks in Holbox for close to a decade when local researchers mentioned in passing that each year, just after the Floridians left, whale sharks came to the island in droves.

"Why did they start paying attention?" Hueter asks, referring to the Holboxeños. "Because the outside world was telling them how special this is."

In other words, the market—rather than some abstract environmental ideal—is what has driven conservation in Holbox. Once researchers from the United States and elsewhere in Mexico conveyed to locals that these animals—if kept alive and accessible—have an economic value, area residents started using it to their advantage. And that was the best possible thing that ever could have happened to the whale sharks. Other species, including several kinds of reef sharks, serve as viable tourist attractions across the globe. Once a community manages to turn live sharks into a commodity, they have a better chance of staying underwater instead of being hauled ashore to die.

In fact, whale sharks in the wild make for a stunning sight. Early one morning in August 2007, I headed out to sea with Hueter, de la Parra, and a few other scientists. One of the things locals (and scientists) know about whale sharks is they're easiest to spot between 7:00 and 11:00 a.m., while they're surface feeding. Around lunchtime they descend, at which point people don't have much of a clue as to what they're doing.

It took an hour to reach the sharks' usual gathering place. At first the ocean was absolutely smooth: the reddish plankton in the water was so thick it was nearly impossible to discern anything underneath the surface. Then one of the researchers cried out, "There's one of them!" pointing to a large, shiny dorsal fin poking out of the water. We pulled the boat alongside it, and I found myself gazing at the largest shark I had ever seen.

At twenty-three feet, it really was as big as a school bus. (The researchers have a very straightforward way of measuring the animals: they use a ruler to mark off feet on the side of the boat and then wait until the tail is aligned with the back of the boat to assess its proper length.) Its skin was dark gray and shiny, glinting in the sunlight, with mottled white dots on its back.

All of a sudden it seemed as if there were whale sharks everywhere. It was not as if they were out of the water entirely. Often we could see only a fraction of their massive bodies: their gently curved mouths, agape as they sucked in volumes of water, or the tips of their tails, flicking back and forth as they glided through the water. But more often than not, we could spot their first dorsal fins jutting out of the sea from dozens of yards away.

After the researchers had made some of their basic measurements, I donned my mask, snorkel, and fins and prepared to jump into the water. This should be easy, I thought to myself. The shark does not appear to be moving so fast—Hueter estimates they move between one and two miles an hour—so I should be able to keep up. I've watched de la Parra hop over the boat, with his bright yellow plastic tag and slingshot pole in hand, and come back empty-handed, with the tag firmly attached to the shark's skin. Surely, I can swim alongside this animal.

Wrong.

I made a cardinal mistake: I jumped in near the shark's tail. From that point on, I was furiously swimming to try to catch up with the fish, an impossible task.

I tried again, with a different shark. Same problem: by the time I swam out to it, the shark had turned and I was out of luck.

Finally, I managed to plunge into the water near the animal's head. Within seconds, I found myself facing an enormous, blunt-nosed creature, heading toward me at what seemed like a shockingly rapid rate. While I marveled at its massive nostrils and the eyes tucked on either side of its head, I was also cognizant of the fact that I was set for a head-on collision with a three-thousand-pound shark. It doesn't matter that it didn't boast sharp teeth, since I was simply going to get smushed. I ducked.

The whale shark cruised by, seemingly unperturbed by my last-minute bailout. It was on its way, and I was now on the sidelines.

By the time I scrambled back onto the boat, everyone was ready with their quips about my sudden evasive maneuver. I did not care. I had seen a whale shark, face-to-face. And I began to think that maybe whale shark tourism in Mexico has a future after all.

To get a sense of what this sort of sightseeing looks like when it becomes truly big business, one must travel thousands of miles away from the Yucatán Peninsula to South Africa. It has capitalized on shark tourism better than almost any other country, in part because it serves as a part-time home for the iconic great white. While scientists can predict when the white sharks will show up—they congregate around areas such as Dyer and Seal islands during June, July, and August and come closer inshore during September through December—it remains slightly unclear what draws them to the area. Food is the most obvious explanation: young seal pups are just beginning to venture out into the water during South Africa's winter months (what is the summer for the Northern Hemisphere), making them vulnerable to predation.

The improbable idea of charging tourists for jumping into the water with lethal animals began on February 5, 1976, when the underwater filmmakers Valerie and Ron Taylor agreed to guide four Americans on an expedition to Port Lincoln, South Australia, to see white sharks in what Valerie Taylor later described as "their natural element." The trip—organized by the U.S.-based See and Sea Travel—cost $4,000 a person, plus airfare, and generated significant publicity. Judging from Taylor's diary of the trip, it's miraculous that everyone emerged unscathed from the adventure. As she wrote on February 8 at 7:30 p.m. of the first great white the group encountered, "That poor shark. He must have wondered what kind of creature this wall of black eyes looking at him belonged to. Every pass of the boat was heralded by the excited cries from the Americans and a dozen clicking cameras. Never was a shark so photographed . . . The shark rammed into the far cage. Everyone yelled and cheered. From our boat, it looked chaotic and probably was. But the visitors were so happy it made us natives happy just watching them."[2] The events on Dangerous Reef were captured on film, not only by Ron Taylor, but also by some of the Americans, and sparked an unexpected backlash. Shark hunters flocked to the reef and killed at least twelve sharks, while some members of the public recoiled at the idea that great whites were that accessible. A similar trip planned for the following year was canceled.[3]

For years, cage diving was the exclusive preserve of the very rich and the occasional adventure-documentary filmmaker. But around 1989, Kim Maclean—who at the time was earning extra money on weekends taking people out fishing on a small jetty—was strolling along the harbor in Hermanus, South Africa, when she saw a little Afrikaner boy fishing with a rod and reel. He happily plunked one fish after another into his bucket, until he reeled in a small sand shark. That one he tossed aside and left to die on the sand.

Maclean—who had grown up "shark mad," as she describes it, with shark posters covering her bedroom walls—was horrified. "This little boy had been trained the only good shark is a dead shark," she thought to herself. And she decided there was a straightforward way of convincing people to think otherwise. It just meant getting them into water with great whites.

Maclean is a blunt-spoken, stocky bleached blonde who's spent years taking on the fishing boys' club. She started Shark Lady Adventures in 1992, and she's still the only woman running her own great white diving operation on the Eastern Cape. Maclean can operate in every position on a ship, and isn't shy about saying so. But while she's not above a bit of self-promotion, she also is a genuine conservationist. There's a visible divide among the eight cage-diving operators who work out of Gansbaai, the impoverished town two hours away from Cape Town. Several of them have brochures that picture a great white with its mouth agape (the typical shark money shot), with phrases like "The JAWS . . . of LIFE." While nearly every operator touts its eco-friendly credentials, several highlight the scarier aspects of getting in the water with white sharks.

Shark Lady Adventures, by contrast, appeals to the higher-end, tree-hugger crowd. With catchphrases like "We care, protect and educate" and "This time, it's you in the Zoo," the operation navigates the line between typical thrill-seeking tourism and environmental protection. Maclean has established strict rules for the dive master, including making sure the bait is at least six feet from the boat so that the sharks don't come into contact with the divers. In 2009 she constructed the White Shark Embassy, an attractive building right on the water that includes educational panels on sharks prepared by the Save Our Seas Foundation as well as plenty of stuffed animals, sweatshirts, and beaded wire sculptures. Maclean has little patience for backpackers, or the tourists who have put cage diving on their to-do list, right after bungee jumping and skydiving. "I'm not there to entertain people who just want to tick it off their list," she says. "They want to see the gory blood, and want to see the fierce teeth."

That said, everyone who decides to cage dive with a great white is looking for thrills. And all of them are at least a little bit scared when they show up at the Shark Lady's launching point.

Gansbaai—the so-called White Shark Capital of the World—is a grim town. The largest local commercial establishment appears to be Dit and Dat Trading, and the most cheerful roadside signs all feature sharks. There are none of the usual trappings of a destination spot: small bed-and-breakfasts, restaurants, or curio shops. Tourists come first thing in the morning to head out to sea, and they depart in the afternoon for either Hermanus or Cape Town. Maclean tried to put on a white shark festival one year, to generate a little income for the town, but her competitors weren't interested in cooperating. While cage diving might support more than half a dozen tour businesses, it's done little to lift the standard of living for these operations' departure site.

By the time I arrive at the White Shark Embassy—a freshly white-washed building with clipper ship chandeliers and ocean views—a small group has begun to assemble on the building's second floor, where there's a hot breakfast being offered. It's an eclectic mix of people: a professional South African cricket player and his girlfriend; a Scottish business consultant and his daughter, fresh out of university; a Brazilian sales representative for Caterpillar, his wife, and their nine-year-old daughter; and a Malay-British couple with two teenage sons.

"It was his idea," Jeanne Kietzmann says bluntly. Kietzmann's boyfriend, Dale Steyn, is one of the South African national cricket team's star players. After seeing a show about great whites on a sports channel, he decided they needed to go. "I'm just being dragged along," Kietzmann offers, glancing out the window at the boats docked below. "I've actually got a massive shark phobia. So it's going to be interesting."

Lance Coetzee, the dive master, is a cheerful sort, sunburned all over his face except for the strip of white skin protected by his sunglasses. He gives a decent lecture on the white shark basics—their anatomy, different senses, feeding habits—and does his best to reassure the most jittery customers. "It will not come up on the boat and attack it just because you're afraid and your heart is beating," he lectures, just after describing how the sharks can detect the heartbeats of other creatures underwater. "These animals have been portrayed by the movie *Jaws* as bloodthirsty monsters. They're not." (Later, Coetzee confides, "I'm sure *Jaws* sells the product for us. I'm sure it helps, sensationalism. But sensationalism isn't going to keep the sharks here.")

Then we're off, with Coetzee shepherding us gently on the boat. Stuart Richardson, the Scottish businessman, relishes the idea of crossing paths with a dangerous animal underwater: "The ultimate is swimming with something like that. It's almost a religious thing. If God wants to meet you, he's going to meet you." This is what sustains the cage-diving industry—the idea that one is doing something theoretically dangerous, even though every possible precaution is taken to minimize risk.

After motoring for fifteen minutes, we're within reach of Dyer Island, a well-known congregating spot for sharks. Several other boats have already made it out there, and from the cries we can hear nearby, they've presumably found what they're looking for. As one of the mates starts chumming the water with a reddish fishy soup, Coetzee lowers the cage into the water. It doesn't look anything like what I had envisioned: black rubber covers the metal contraption, which has four separate chutes divers can lower themselves into simultaneously. And only the most rudimentary gear is required—a hooded wet suit and snorkeling mask—since once in the cage, divers keep their heads above water until a shark comes close enough to observe.

Before heading out, Coetzee warned that great whites don't just circle in the water with their fins jutting out. But within minutes of our anchoring and throwing out bait, an ominous, nearly black fin appears just yards away from the boat. The shark we had been anticipating—and fearing—had arrived.

By the time I manage to get an underwater look at a great white, my fear has dissipated. Maclean isn't exaggerating when she says, "It's you in the Zoo." The cage is a solid piece of equipment, an assemblage of firm, crisscrossing bars that show no sign of failing. As Coetzee shouts, "Divers, look left," I draw a deep breath and push myself down, whipping my head around to catch a glimpse of the shark heading for the tuna head Coetzee is dangling on a rope before it. The shark moves slowly, making lazy figure eights in and out of range of the cage. While there are plenty of whites in the area, they never congregate. One fish will come in for the bait, give up after a few attempts, and swim away. Then another will do the same.

The great whites that parade before us are elegant despite their size. They lack the hulking mass of the whale shark, along with the cartoonish markings. There is a seriousness to the torpedo-shaped bodies that slice through the water, a wedge of muscle ready to flex when necessary. And then the moment comes: a white lunges for the fish head, its teeth bared. While much of the diving experience smacks of being in a glorified aquarium, this is the one time when it feels, for an instant, as if we're witnessing nature in its element. The shark's teeth are jagged, and it manages to snatch a bit of the head before shoving off. It's the money shot.

Everyone makes it into the cage but Kietzmann, who is held back not by fear but by seasickness. And the tourists go away with exactly the impression Maclean had predicted they would: reverence, and affection. It's an odd sort of adventure tourism, whose proprietors depend on long-held stereotypes to lure customers but harbor a hidden agenda to unravel them at the end of the day.

Boarding a flight out of Cape Town a few days later, I happen to run into Richardson as he and his family are embarking on the same plane. "I loved it," he reminisces about our dive. "It was surreal. There you were, in with the shark. You felt like you could reach out and tickle its tummy."

Climbing up the stairs on the Jetway, he pauses to contemplate why sharks have such a terrible reputation. But even if it's unjustified, he notes, it's what brought him to Gansbaai. "Of course, if they didn't demonize it, we wouldn't have come. Now I get to go back and tell my friends, 'I've been with a shark,' and they'll think, 'What a man.'"

And with that, he makes his way with his wife and daughter to their designated seats, headed home to tell his fish tale. He has managed to conquer a formidable predator while allowing the animal—like himself—to live another day.

CONCLUSION: SHARK NIRVANA

I know the human being and fish can coexist peacefully.
—George W. Bush, campaigning as a presidential candidate
in Saginaw, Michigan, September 29, 2000

I am still optimistic about sharks.
—Peter Klimley, professor at the University of California at Davis

The northern Line Islands are, quite literally, in the middle of
nowhere. It is a place where sharks rule.

A series of Pacific atolls lying roughly one thousand miles south of
Hawaii, the Line Islands remind us of what the sea used to look like.
To get there from Honolulu, you must ride on a motorboat or ship,
on open ocean, for five days. Its uninhabited Kingman Reef is pristine; the other islands are slightly more populated in quick succession
until you reach Kiritimati, or Christmas Island, with a population of
fifty-one hundred.

National Geographic's Enric Sala led an expedition to the atoll in
2005 and returned in 2006. What he saw was something unlike anything he had ever seen: a reef so dominated by sharks and other top
predators that other fish were nowhere to be seen, since they know
that to be seen is to be eaten.

"There is a landscape of fear," he tells me as we sit on a beach in
the Dominican Republic. He is drawing in the sand, to try to give me
a sense of how bit by bit humans have degraded the world's oceans.
The other fish are elusive at Kingman, he explains, because they know
the risks if they come out.

Sharks make up 75 percent of the fish biomass at Kingman Reef. At

Kiritimati, by contrast, top predators make up just 19 percent. While diving at Palmyra, an island not quite as unpopulated as Kingman, Sala witnessed firsthand what it meant to exist in a perfectly honed predatory system. In an effort to conduct a comprehensive survey of the marine organisms on the reef, he caught a damselfish and tucked it into a Ziploc bag, which he in turn deposited into the nylon mesh bag he was holding at his side. Then he reached for a grouper about half a foot long, hoping to fit it into another Ziploc bag. During the course of this tussle the fish began to shake, and suddenly—whoosh—a couple of blacktip sharks came along, aiming for the grouper. "They started biting at it," he recounts. "Then a whitetip and gray reef shark came." At this point Sala decided to abandon the mesh bag with the two fish still inside it and swim away to a safe distance where he could observe the scene. "They destroyed the mesh bag and ate the fish, right through the Ziploc. These guys were really hungry. There's a lot of competition. Everything that is injured or sick is eaten within seconds there."

Kingman Reef looks like few other atolls in the world: the only ones that rival it are those that help compose the Phoenix Islands, another Pacific archipelago that, like the Line Islands, is split between the American and the Kiribati government. Not only is Kingman Reef supremely healthy, with corals covering the seafloor to such an extent that it's nearly impossible to see the sand, but the fish have been so sheltered from human beings that they view them as a curiosity. When Sala and his colleagues began diving there, the snappers and groupers appeared to be fascinated by the strange sight of these alien creatures, checking out the Spaniard's ponytail and the other scientists' equipment.

"I bet it was the same feeling Darwin had when he stepped on Galápagos for the first time," Sala says. "It was a totally new experience."

There's just one problem: as soon as you add humans to the mix, the sharks start disappearing.

Sala and his collaborators published the results of their expedition on February 27, 2008, in the online edition of *Public Library of Science*

Biology. It is the most comprehensive analysis ever of what they call "reefs without people." That same edition included a commentary from Nancy Knowlton and Jeremy B. C. Jackson, coral experts affiliated with the Scripps Institution of Oceanography and the Smithsonian Institution, saying the study has redefined the way we should view corals worldwide. Examining coral reefs without taking into account what they were like before humans degraded them, they analogized, was like "trying to imagine the ecology of tropical rainforests by studying environmental changes and interaction among the surviving plants and animals on a vast cattle ranch in the center of a deforested Amazon without any basic data on how the forest worked before it was cleared and burned."

When you imagine the coral reefs of old, or even the sea just a hundred years ago, sharks play a starring role. We think of oceans, and wild landscapes in general, as a neat pyramid in which there are a small number of big predators on top and many small predators below. The study Sala and his colleagues have published suggests just the opposite: an undisturbed ecosystem resembles an inverted pyramid with plenty of large predators on top and fewer small predators below. The animals at the top clear out the weakest animals in the population and keep the midsize predators in check. Without the top predators, the waters begin to look completely different.

Ransom Myers provided the first evidence that it was worth keeping sharks around, and his students continue to build the case for it. Boris Worm, one of Myers's closest collaborators, co-authored a 2008 paper in the journal *Trends in Ecology and Evolution* that elaborated on this phenomenon. Worm and his colleagues identified how the "landscape of fear" that Sala talks about reverberates throughout ecosystems worldwide. In Prince William Sound, Alaska, harbor seals are so scared of Pacific sleeper sharks that they forage in shallower areas, which in turn keeps the walleye pollack population intact. The tiger sharks in Shark Bay, Australia, intimidate large herbivores such as sea turtles and dugongs enough that these prey species shift their distribution depending on the season: that keeps the area's sea-grass habitat from being overgrazed.[1] Sharks, Worm explains, "have a huge impact on the ecosystem because they were there before everything else. When everyone came into the system as an evolutionary baby, sharks were already there and had figured it out." Nowadays sharks keep other, smaller predators in check. "Sharks are being kind of 'the cop on the street' in the ecosystem," Worm analogizes.

Rachel Graham makes the identical pitch when she lobbies local officials in Belize to put protections in place for sharks. "Think about what would happen to your town if there was no rubbish collector," she tells them. That would be a problem, they respond. "Now imagine in a month's time nobody's arrived in a month, and the rubbish's piled up," she continues. "And the policeman hasn't arrived." Graham's point is clear: sharks may not perform the most glamorous function in Belize's waters, but their role keeps the marine ecosystem humming. Take out the sharks, and the species that Belize's citizens really care about—the ones that make up the bulk of the commercial fish trade—will suffer.

In the same way that scientists now use computers to predict how climate change will reshape the planet by the end of the century, researchers are modeling the implications of taking large sharks out of the ocean. One group found that a simulated decline of tiger sharks in Hawaii's French Frigate Shoals would boost the numbers of seabirds, turtles, monk seals, and reef sharks, thereby triggering a rapid decline in tuna and jacks. A similar exercise showed that taking sharks out of Floreana Island in the Galápagos would harm several commercial reef fish species, since the ranks of toothed cetaceans, sea lions, and other predators would swell accordingly. Just as we are conducting an uncontrolled experiment on the earth by emitting an unprecedented amount of carbon dioxide into the atmosphere, we are altering the sea with the same sense of abandon, by yanking out what Francesco Ferretti and his colleagues call "a relatively stable force in ocean ecosystems over evolutionary time."[2]

Researchers have recently discovered this same behavioral ripple effect in the northern Rockies. When Americans wiped out gray wolves in Yellowstone and the surrounding areas in the late 1920s, the willow and aspen trees stopped reproducing. Then, after the Fish and Wildlife Service reintroduced wolves to the region in the mid-1990s, the willows and aspens began to reappear: in time songbirds and beavers came back as well. It wasn't just that the wolves were eating the elk, but the elk became sufficiently frightened of wolf attacks that they stopped grazing all winter on the banks of streams, where the aspens and willows grow. Even local mountain lions changed the way they roam, and often take longer routes on rougher ground so if a wolf comes along, they can climb up a tree for shelter. Ed Bangs, who heads the U.S. Fish and Wildlife Service's gray wolf recovery program in the northern Rockies, explains that all the other animals in the ecosystem recalibrated their behavior once one of the top predators returned. "Everyone was like, 'Oh, yeah, wolves, I remember how to deal with that.' "

A few months before Worm's paper came out, a group of nineteen scientists, led by Benjamin S. Halpern at the National Center for Ecological Analysis and Synthesis, published an article and map in *Science* capturing the extent to which humans have left a footprint on the sea. They culled seventeen global data sets for twenty marine ecosystems and came to a stunning conclusion: "No area is unaffected by human influence." None. Nearly half of all coral reefs experience "medium high to very high impact" from humans, they concluded, with areas in the Mediterranean, the South and East China seas, and the North American Eastern Seaboard ranking among the hardest hit.[3]

Sometimes humans' impact on the sea is visible, like in the aftermath of the April 20, 2010, explosion of the Deepwater Horizon in the Gulf of Mexico. The massive oil spill that spewed out of BP's doomed exploration well not only covered brown pelicans and northern gannets but also soaked sharks swimming well below the ocean's surface. While it will take years to assess the full extent of the accident's toll, there is no question that sharks—possibly some of the most imperiled ones, such as bigeye thresher, dusky, and oceanic whitetip—suffered along with other wildlife in the region. Two months after the accident ten whale sharks showed up just twenty-three miles southwest of Sarasota, Florida, raising the possibility that these animals had been forced to seek refuge in a different part of the ocean as pollution contaminated the Gulf of Mexico.

We attack sharks in subtle ways, and in blunt ones. In one of the most telling incidents of just how dramatically the "man bites shark" story has evolved in recent years, a Coney Island lifeguard had to come to the aid of a juvenile shark—most likely a sand tiger shark—that was being attacked by a crowd of Labor Day beachgoers in 2007. As New York's *Daily News* put it, "Tender-hearted muscleman Marius Mironescu rescued a 2-foot sand shark from a mob of panicked swimmers, grabbing the wriggling fish in his arms and—in a neat reversal of the usual scenario—swimming out to sea with the stunned animal." Mironescu estimated that between seventy-five and a hundred people had encircled the small creature and begun attacking it. "They were holding on to it and some people were actually hitting him, smacking his face. Well, I wasn't going to let them hurt the poor thing," he told the *Daily News*. In the end the shark proved less forgiving than the lifeguard who came to its rescue: while it played dead during the attack, as soon as Mironescu began doing a backstroke with the fish in one hand, it revived and tried to bite him.[4]

Figuring out where the sea is in the most trouble is not terribly complicated: any decent marine biologist can tell you if you want to see the ocean at its most vulnerable, go to where the people are.

Bimini, to which I journeyed around the same time Sala and his colleagues first visited the Line Islands, used to be a place where sharks and other big fish ruled. Years ago, Ernest Hemingway used to spend weeks on end here: when he wasn't writing novels such as *The Old Man and the Sea,* he spent his days struggling to bring in the massive sport fish exerting overwhelming strength on the end of his fishing line. Pictures of the trophy fish he lured in and showed off at the Bimini Big Game Club used to be on display here, until fire destroyed the museum a few years ago.

Now the fish aren't so gigantic, and Bimini isn't much of a vacation spot. There are a couple of Caribbean bars—the kinds with sand on the floor and women's underwear hanging from the ceiling—and a few unimpressive condo developments. But Rafael Reyes, president of the Bimini Bay Resort and Marina, and his business partner Gerardo Capo want to change all that. For about a decade the two developers have been building a golf resort that aims to bring as many as five thousand tourists a day to an island with a year-round population of just sixteen hundred residents. In order to do so, they need to rip up the island's mangroves and replace them with golf turf.

That dredging and destruction is eroding the vegetation that local lemon sharks depend on for survival. Sonny Gruber, who has spent more than three decades studying lemon sharks in Bimini, has been driven to despair by the development. Based on an eleven-year study started in the mid-1990s, he and his colleagues determined that after March 2001, during the heaviest dredging of the seafloor for the resort, the first-year survival rate for lemon sharks fell 23.5 percent, and it hadn't fully rebounded by the time the study concluded in 2006.[5] The dredging could have hurt the sharks in several ways, including the fact that toxins were introduced to the water, and the fact that the sharks now had to compete for more limited resources within a degraded habitat.

In Bimini, Gruber and I also headed out in his motorboat to observe Reyes and Capo's bulldozers do their work. Gruber slipped into despondency as the yellow machines mangled the mangroves, alternately muttering and yelling at me for not expressing more outrage at this environmental travesty.

"At the end of my career, I get to document the destruction of the species I've been documenting for twenty years," he declared as the machines toppled the vegetation and scattered the remains into the ocean. "Wonderful." As soon as we returned to the biological station where Gruber resides, he slipped away to his room and remained there for the rest of the afternoon, too depressed to talk.

But an avalanche of bad press, coupled with elections that have placed the former opposition party in power, ended up turning the tide against the developers. Bahamian officials have rewritten the rules for the project multiple times, seeking to contain the number of units and compelling the developers to set aside land on East Bimini, one of the island's most ecologically valuable areas. On December 29, 2008, the Bahamian government announced it was creating a new marine reserve on Bimini's North Sound in an effort to preserve the mangroves on which the lemon sharks and nearly a hundred other species depend. The new protections will make it much harder to build a golf course as part of the Bimini Bay Resort. When I call Gruber at his Miami office to discuss the news, he seems stunned at the turn of events. "It's a damn miracle," he says repeatedly.

Still, the resort's developers haven't given up. At the time of the marine reserve announcement, the complex already boasted 250 housing units, three restaurants, two pools, and the Bahamas' two largest marinas, as well as approval to build a ten-thousand-square-foot casino. Allison Robins, Bimini Bay's public relations manager, says the creation of a protected area amounts to "a step forward . . . Basically, they'll put up a bunch of buffer zones and we'll develop around that."

It remains unclear what will happen to sharks in Bimini, as well as elsewhere around the globe. Sala believes the only way these predators will survive is if international officials impose "a global, indefinite moratorium on shark fishing. Otherwise sharks and humans cannot exist together." And in the places where sharks have been hardest hit, such as in the Mediterranean, he adds, they will never come back.

In some cases an ecosystem can come back, though it can take decades. Scientists and tourists alike have spotted more great whites off the East Coast, a trend that has led to temporary closings in locales ranging from Brooklyn's Rockaway Beach to Cape Cod's Chatham Harbor. While a number of factors may have prompted this trend, including warmer sea temperatures and better observation systems, there's a clear driving force: more seals for the sharks to eat. There is now a steady increase in the number of gray seals and a growing resident seal population off the coast of Chatham and Monomoy Island, Massachusetts, largely because the state phased out its bounty on seal "noses" in 1964, and protections the federal government put in place in the 1970s. And there still hasn't been a deadly shark attack off New England since 1936.[6]

This sort of recovery will require an extraordinary act of global cooperation. While individual nations can protect the waters within a couple hundred miles of their coasts—right now, 4 percent of the world's continental shelves enjoy some level of protection[7]—the high seas are unpoliced when it comes to sharks. Until they are, sharks will remain vulnerable. It has taken humans centuries to create the bizarre turn of events we now face. As the State Department's David Balton puts it, "For most of human history, sharks have been seen as a threat to us. Only recently are we beginning to see we're a threat to them."

As policy makers continue to postpone taking meaningful shark conservation measures, they may want to consider the historic debt we owe to these animals. With their rituals of ancestor worship, the shark callers of Papua New Guinea may seem quaint to outsiders. But their religious belief is rooted in scientific fact: sharks are our actual evolutionary ancestors. The physical characteristics we've inherited from them have helped shape the way we hear, and even swallow. It's something to think about the next time you gulp down a mouthful of shark's fin soup.

Peter Klimley has a sunnier outlook than most marine biologists. Humans are beginning to understand how perfectly sharks have adapted to their marine environment, and they are willing to pay money to observe them underwater. Since sharks congregate in some of the most ecologically diverse regions of the sea, he reasons, government officials could protect them if they wanted and stave off the most dire effects of overfishing and habitat destruction. And with ecotourism, "you have a competing financial incentive to save the sharks."

Perhaps Klimley is right, and we will end up saving these fish so we can sell whale shark tchotchkes like the ones on Isla Holbox, and squeeze pudgy tourists into metal cages off Guadalupe Island in Baja. Having swum with sharks a couple dozen times, I can attest to the allure of watching their perfectly adapted bodies glide through the water, giving just a hint of the power they could unleash at any moment.

But the best example of how we should treat sharks came from perhaps the unlikeliest conservation hero of them all, George W. Bush, in June 2006. For years environmentalists had been pressing the White House to fully protect the Northwest Hawaiian Islands. Another remarkable series of Pacific atolls stretching fourteen hundred miles long and a hundred miles across, the uninhabited chain boasts more than seven thousand marine species, at least a quarter of which are found nowhere else on earth. In the sea the Northwest Hawaiian Islands serve as home to species such as the endangered Hawaiian monk seal and threatened green sea turtle; on land they provide a rookery for fourteen million seabirds.

President Theodore Roosevelt first recognized the atoll's value in 1909, when he established a bird sanctuary there and provided federal protections. Bill Clinton used executive orders to create a coral reef ecosystem reserve in the area during the final months of his administration, but stopped short of making it a permanent federal sanctuary. Eight Hawaiian fishermen held licenses to fish in the area, and several of these men, along with their powerful political allies, had blocked efforts to preserve the reef even though it was a minor fishery that required a two-day boat journey from Honolulu to reach. (One of the permitted commercial anglers, Zenen Ozoa, broke with the others and lobbied to shut down the fishery on the grounds that it was too environmentally harmful to the region.)[8]

Ocean advocates waged a tireless campaign to convince Bush that he could burnish his green credentials by making the islands a marine reserve, lobbying not just his top environmental adviser, James L. Connaughton, an avid diver, but First Lady Laura Bush, an enthusiastic bird-watcher. The filmmaker Jean-Michel Cousteau, son of the renowned explorer, spent a month and a half filming on the archipelago and produced two one-hour documentaries on the subject. He showed one of them to the president in the White House movie theater. In the end Bush surprised even his own advisers by declaring the islands the Papahānaumokuāwakea Marine National Monument, making it the largest marine protected area in the world, one that will remain untouched for generations. Tourists as well as fishermen will not be able to make the trip out there; federal enforcement officers will ensure only a handful of scientists will be able to conduct research on the reef. (Less than three years later the British government snatched the record of the world's largest marine reserve away from the Americans when it afforded protections to the Chagos Archipelago, a string of fifty-five islands in the middle of the Indian Ocean.)

Just two weeks before leaving office on January 6, 2009, Bush made one last offering to conservation activists by creating three separate marine monuments in the Pacific that will protect some of the most pristine parts of the sea. The three reserves—which include the islands Sala has chronicled in the central Pacific and a long stretch along the world's deepest underwater canyon, the Mariana Trench—total 195,280 square miles, an area that even surpasses the Papahānaumokuākea Marine National Monument. The waters surrounding the Mariana Trench and those at Kingman Reef boast some of the highest densities of sharks on earth. And while the new monuments, like the one in Hawaii, didn't amount to a very heavy political lift, it meant Bush had to defy Vice President Dick Cheney and the U.S. recreational fishing lobby. These groups, and the vice president, argued the president had no right to deny American citizens the right to take their rod and reel to the farthest corners of U.S. territory. In the end Bush decided that he did.

I have wanted to visit the Northwest Hawaiian Islands and the northern Marianas for years: now I will likely never go. But that's beside the point—the sharks will be there. They were here long before we arrived, they are unlike anything else on earth, and they, more than any other living thing, embody what is profound and beautiful about the sea.

In 1858, Lieuenant Joseph Christmas Ives, the first American official to visit the Grand Canyon, made a comment about the vista before him that seems quaint in retrospect. "The region last explored is, of course, altogether valueless," he said. "It can be approached only from the south, and after entering it there is nothing to do but leave. Ours has been the first, and will doubtless be the last, party of whites to visit this profitless region. It seems intended by nature that the Colorado river, along the greater portion of its lonely and majestic way, shall be forever unvisited and undisturbed." Ives was terribly wrong about the idea that the Grand Canyon would be "forever unvisited and undisturbed." But perhaps those words can still be applied to places like the Northwest Hawaiian, the northern Mariana, the Phoenix, and the Chagos islands.

Boris Worm, a child of the 1970s, grew up in Hamburg. When he went scuba diving, he had a simple choice: dive in either the Baltic or the North Sea. Both had been degraded in the centuries before he was born. As Worm puts it, "I just grew up with these really low expectations of the ocean." He lives in Nova Scotia now: while it's the New World, so to speak, its seas have been plundered as well. But Worm has traveled to places like the Line Islands, diving deep until the sharks surround him in the way that they encircled Enric Sala.

"It's like growing up in a really poor neighborhood, and then you begin to see what else is out there," he says now. "You're being continually surprised by how rich the world can be."

Even some of the most remote areas of the ocean have come under assault. Scientists have determined the abundance of sharks in the Chagos Archipelago declined 90 percent between 1975 and 2006, mainly due to illegal poaching.[9] The area has not been tightly patrolled, historically, and the incentive to steal sharks will stay high as long as the price for shark fins continues to hover at exorbitant levels. But the area is still relatively pristine, and experts estimate that the new protections will save at least sixty thousand sharks a year. So it stands a real chance of recovering.

At the time of the Papahānaumokuākea monument designation, Ed Case was the Hawaii congressman whose district encompassed the archipelago: he lobbied hard to save the place even though he hadn't had a chance to venture out there. I spoke to Case the day before the president made his official announcement, because I had gotten a tip it was going to happen. The House Democrat had criticized Bush on plenty of occasions, but this time he gave him full credit for performing what Case described as "the most revolutionary act by any president, any administration, in terms of marine resources."

Toward the end of our conversation, Case and I chatted about how neither of us had traveled to the atoll. It was a rare moment in politics, he noted, when policy makers could agree to protect something without a specific payoff. Bush's decision would not usher in a new era of ecotourism; the Northwest Hawaiian Islands would never become a catchy, picturesque symbol for America like the Grand Canyon or Yellowstone. It simply would exist, undamaged, with all of its wondrous creatures swimming below the surface.

"We are all going to have to take it on faith that it's that special, because . . . most of us will never see it, and we never should see it," he told me. "We're just going to have to let it go."

But even this doesn't capture the full complexity of what we must do for the ocean. We are changing the natural world through our actions at such an unprecedented rate that we will have to recalibrate them in order to restore some sort of balance. The remedy Bush provided with Papahānaumokuākea was just a partial answer, after all, because on his eight-year watch America's greenhouse gas emissions rose unchecked by any national limits. At the current rate we are increasing carbon concentrations in the atmosphere at a hundred times their historic rate, and the warmer and more acidic seas that come in the wake of these emissions may no longer be hospitable to coral reefs within a matter of decades. If these reefs disappear, so will the sharks and the other marine creatures that depend on them. And a team of scientists from Dalhousie University has calculated that warmer sea temperatures account for a 40 percent decline since 1950 in the microscopic marine algae known as phytoplankton. Since phytoplankton forms the basis of the ocean's food chain, this climate-related trend has tremendous implications for both sharks and their prey.[10]

Any significant environmental issue involving humans—climate change, habitat destruction, overfishing, name the problem—comes down to a question of choices. In almost every question, there's a cost either way: you can produce cheap energy but simultaneously exacerbate global warming, and the rise of industrial fishing methods has caused fisheries across the globe to crash. Advocates on both sides of these issues often gloss over these questions to bolster their cause, by implying that pursuing a particular course is inevitable, rather than an act of will.

The best way to pierce through these skewed arguments is to look at the evidence, recognize that our actions have consequences, and weigh the costs and benefits of our current course of action versus an alternative path. While sometimes environmental trends are difficult to identify—the fact that fishery managers used to not count what shark species were landed on their shores complicates these estimates—researchers have become increasingly sophisticated about calculating the state of sharks today. And the fact is they're in trouble. The average species exists on this planet for six million years. For millennia, sharks have outcompeted their rivals and defied these odds. Now their survival is uncertain.

Deciding to save them entails a choice, and it is not a pain-free option. For many in Asia, it means finding substitutes for a delicacy that allows them to impress their business partners, relatives, or friends. For some of the world's poorest fishermen, whether they live in Baja or Indonesian Papua, it necessitates another source of income, be it ecotourism or a different, sustainable fishery. Curbing global warming—which could devastate both coral reefs and the sea's smallest creatures in the decades to come—will entail putting a price on carbon, most likely, which will drive up energy prices in the near term, and perhaps for good. And for the men who head out on monster fishing tours with Mark the Shark, it translates into discovering some other sort of activity to bolster their sense of manhood.

Saving sharks, it turns out, requires that we both confront one of our most primordial fears and reevaluate the way we envision the world around us. This is not to say that we must become environmental extremists and place the fish that roam the sea above our own species. It is to recognize that sharks are among us, and while we are radically different creatures, we are about to decide whether we will coexist or not. Despite the occasional strike sharks launch at humans, the choice is ours, not theirs.

Acknowledgments

When I was young, my father suspected I had a secret life as a fish.

While I learned to swim at an early age under my grandmother's watchful eye, I never really mastered the proper strokes as other children did. Instead, I dived as deep as I could into whatever body of water I found myself in, only surfacing when I was nearly out of air. The simple act of swimming always paled in comparison to what I could find beneath the surface, whether it was a tadpole in Maine's Kezar Lake or a sea star in the Atlantic.

For whatever reason, I found myself spending less time swimming in—and thinking about—the ocean as I grew older. Four people changed that once I started covering the environment for *The Washington Post* in the spring of 2004. Roger Rufe, who headed the Ocean Conservancy at the time, told me I'd better hurry up and take a refresher scuba-diving class if I wanted to interview him about marine issues. Ellen Pikitch, who now directs the Institute for Ocean Conservation Science at Stony Brook University, persuaded me to ignore my better judgment and jump into a sea teeming with sharks off the coast of Bimini. Joshua Reichert, the Pew Environment Group's managing director, convinced me that the ocean ranks as one of the most compelling environmental stories of our time. And the *Post*'s former science editor Nils Bruzelius, a skilled sailor, helped show me how I could cover marine life in a rigorous and thoughtful way for a daily newspaper. I'm grateful to all of them.

It took the dogged persistence of my agent, Brettne Bloom, to convince me I should write a second book, and her willingness to listen patiently to my ideas (over ice cream and cocktails, depending on the locale and time of day) helped me realize that I should choose sharks as my subject matter. Andrew Miller, my editor at Pantheon, had faith in this project from the outset and pushed me to write a better book. His colleague Andrew Carlson provided helpful suggestions toward the end of the writing process, for which I am grateful, and Josefine Kals started promoting it with enthusiasm before it ever hit the shelves.

The institutions that provided travel grants for the book, the American Littoral Society and Stanford University's Bill Lane Center for the American West, deserve my profound thanks. The Lane Center's executive director, Jon Christensen, has been unfailingly supportive over the years—meeting him in Big Sky, Montana, years ago counts as one of my lucky breaks.

I would also like to thank my current and former *Post* colleagues who gave me the time and freedom to pursue this book, as well as guidance and support in my day job: Don Graham, Marcus Brauchli, Liz Spayd, Kevin Merida, Marilyn Thompson, Len Downie, Phil Bennett, Susan Glasser, Rajiv Chandrasekaran, Frances Sellers, Kathryn Tolbert, and the entire science pod, especially Marc Kaufman and David Fahrenthold, who cared enough about environmental news to cover it when I had to duck out of the newsroom. A few of the paper's amazing researchers were willing to pitch in at critical moments, including Lucy Shackelford, Magda Jean-Louis, Eddy Palanzo, Alice Crites, and Madonna Lebling, and did so with aplomb.

More than any other single group, the Pew Marine Fellows have helped educate me about the ocean. My thanks go to all of them, as well as to the program's manager, Polita Glynn, and the Pew Environment Group's director of marine science, Rebecca Goldburg. I would like to single out the Pew fellows whom I harassed most frequently for this book: Barbara Block, Wen Bo, Mark Erdmann, Sarah Fowler, Les Kaufman, Jane Lubchenco, Tim McClanahan, Elliott Norse, Stephen R. Palumbi, Daniel Pauly, Yvonne Sadovy, Carl Safina, Enric Sala, and Greg Stone. Nancy Baron deserves the credit for introducing me to these scientists, along with other talented marine biologists such as Boris Worm and Andrew Rosenberg. Moreover, Nancy has done more to bridge the chasm between journalists and scientists than anyone else I know, and I can't imagine how I would have covered the environment if we hadn't met in 2004. Boris Worm was even willing to read over key parts of this manuscript, and they emerged sharper as a result. I would also like to thank Mahmood Shivji, a rare scientist who is both brilliant and unafraid of the media, for sharing his shark expertise with me.

It was during my first Pew fellows session that I had the privilege of meeting the late Ransom Myers. His work profoundly influenced this book, and it is one of my great regrets that I cannot hand him a copy of it now that it's done. I am also sorry that Peter Benchley will not read this book, but I cannot thank his widow, Wendy Benchley, enough for the generosity she displayed in discussing her husband's legacy with me.

Since I traveled far and wide to research this book, I would like to thank the people who helped me overseas by location. In Baja California, Mexico, I relied on John O'Sullivan, Michael Sutton, and Ken Peterson from the Monterey Bay Aquarium to introduce me to scientists working on the ground in Baja and guide me through the scientific literature once I returned; once I arrived, Paul Ahuja and Arturo Elizalde of Iemanya Oceanica served as invaluable guides. On Mexico's other coast, I had a team of researchers who helped me see whale sharks up close off Isla Holbox, including Mote Marine Laboratory's Robert Hueter and John Tyminski, Rafael de la Parra from Proyecto Dominó, University of South Florida's Phil Motta and Kyle Mara, and David Santucci from the Georgia Aquarium. Nadine Slimak in Mote's communication department—and later Hayley Rutger—lent a helping hand from Florida, along with Eugenie Clark. Liza Boyd served as a fantastic traveling partner in the Yucatán. In Belize, Ellen Pikitch was on hand to teach me, as well as Vera Agostini, Beth Babcock, Demian Chapman, Archie Carr III, and Norlan Lamb. The Wildlife Conservation Society's Stephen Sautner provided help from his perch at the Bronx Zoo, and Rachel Graham was willing to talk about Belize's sharks with me days after giving birth to her second son, for which I'm grateful. In Hong Kong, Yvonne Sadovy not only shared her knowledge with me but lent me three of her most talented students—Vivian Yan Yan Lam, Allen Wai Lun To, and Shadow Ying Tung Sin—to serve as my translators. I appreciate how Charlie Lim afforded me access to the world of shark fin trading, and both Candice To and Paul Hilton helped provide me with an excellent lay of the land. Two Papua New Guineans living in the States initially helped introduce me to their amazing country: the UN ambassador Robert Aisi and Papua New Guinea's former U.S. ambassador Meg Taylor. I'm grateful to both of them for their advice and friendship. Once I got there, several Papua New Guinea residents provided me with help, including Paul Vatlom and Ange and Dietmar Amon. Laura "Tiny Fins" Berger provided critical moral support and companionship in both Papua New Guinea and Indonesia. In Indonesia, Mark Erdmann, Max Ammer, and the entire staff of Papua Diving did their best to help me navigate Raja Ampat, both underwater and through muck-filled swamps, while Eva Claudio and Bruno Fortin provided me with an idyllic respite at their home in Bali. I also want to thank Conservation International's CEO, Peter Seligmann, and CI's former spokesman Marshall Maher for helping educate me on the region, to say nothing of letting me slip into the most glamorous fish auction I have ever attended, in Monaco. Later, CI's Katrin Olson and Kim McCabe were happy to pitch in from the group's headquarters. In South Africa a cadre of researchers from the Save Our Seas Foundation helped educate me, including Cheryl-Samantha Owen, Alison Kock, and Lesley Rochat. The indomitable Shark Lady, Kim Maclean, and her staff made it possible for me to witness great whites in their native habitat, while Gregg Oelofse, Peter Chadwick, and Markus Burgener shared key insights with me based on their experience studying sharks. My Japan journey would never have happened without the support of Japan's ambassador to the United States, Ichiro Fujisaki, as well as his amazing career staff: Izumi Yamanaka, Hideo Fukushima, and Tomofumi Nishinaga. Once I arrived in Tokyo, Sumiyo Terai served as an enthusiastic translator and guide to her country's fishing traditions. Both Kasumasa Murata and Shigeo Sugie generously shared their knowledge of the shark trade with me, and the Ministry of Foreign Affairs' Yutaka Aoki and Hiroshi Yamasaki also made time for me in the midst of their busy schedules.

In Shanghai, Professor Xu Hongfa and his two students, Xie Zhigang and Xu Xun, helped me navigate the city's shark fin trade. And I never would have made it to the city in the first place without the inspiration of the Institute for Education's CEO Kathy Kemper.

In Florida, Mark Quartiano hosted me on his fishing boat twice, even after I told him I would be scrutinizing the impacts of recreational shark fishing.

In Washington, the staff of Oceana and the Ocean Conservancy were always on hand to answer my questions. Dianne Saenz and Dustin Cranor—and, before them, Bianca DeLille—tapped into Oceana's considerable international network to keep me informed, while the group's senior scientist, Michael Hirshfield, freely shared his thoughts and personal contacts to help further my research. Not only did the Ocean Conservancy's press team, Tom McCann and Kelly Ricaurte, help me out, but the group's president, Vikki Spruill, never tired of talking about the sea with me. A team of folks at the Pew Environment Group, including Matt Rand, Dave Bard, Jo Knight, Gerry Leape, Sue Lieberman, Dan Klotz, and Karen Sack, have provided me with invaluable assistance on all things fish related, including shark research, for years. Shark Advocates International's president, Sonja Fordham, peppered me with updates whether she was in Brussels, London, or a fisheries management meeting in the Seychelles. Jim Toomey, the creator of the cartoon strip *Sherman's Lagoon,* and the Nature Conservancy's M. A. Sanjayan also shared important insights with me. At the National Oceanic and Atmospheric Administration, Justin Kenney, Connie Barclay, Monica Allen, and Teri Frady all helped connect me with key NOAA officials, researchers, and resources. Susan Povenmire at the State Department helped me regardless of what political party occupied the White House, proving that shark policy might actually transcend partisan politics. While I thought I had mastered American electoral politics with my first book, Milan Vaishnav proved me wrong by showing me that politicians pay a political price for shark attacks. The staff at the Library of Congress's Science, Technology, and Business Division were always willing to help me track down ancient ship logs and obscure books, providing invaluable sources of information. I am also grateful to three Washington wise men who have weighed in on international environmental issues for years—Thomas E. Lovejoy, Roger Sant, and Timothy E. Wirth—for sharing their insights and connections with me. And through his own example, Chuck Savitt of Island Press has shown me how publishing fine environmental writing can make an impact.

Once I finished the manuscript, I relied on some fellow journalists to give it a close read. Nils Bruzelius pored over every single line of my first draft, and three of my favorite nonfiction authors, Eric Roston, Tom Zoellner, and Sasha Issenberg, also examined it in detail. As thanks, let me recommend that anyone reading this book buy these writers' amazing work—*The Carbon Age, The Heartless Stone* and *Uranium,* and *The Sushi Economy,* respectively—as soon as possible. My dear friend Mark Allen makes documentaries, but he asks all the right questions when you're in the midst of writing a nonfiction book.

A group of talented photographers and generous institutions have allowed me to reprint their images, and also deserve my appreciation: Conservation International, Edith Blake, Neil Hammerschlag, Grant Johnson, and Dos Winkel.

On a personal note I would like to thank my friends and family, not just for their constant support, but for their greatest gift to me: an ever-expanding brood of little ones. I especially appreciate how so many of these children—including Sam and Nate Fox-Halperin; Noa, Jacob, and Gideon Rosinplotz; Io, Violet, and Clover Demos; Nava and Tatum Parker Mach; Edith Sklaroff Carey; Alexandra Duncan; Jennifer Jurkowski; Grace Sutherlin; Ayden Light; Alexander and Liana Raguso; Zora Citerman; Theo Baker; and Anya Morrison Biggs—have shown such interest in my shark stories. Collectively, their existence has improved my life immeasurably.

Finally, I want to thank my own environmental ethicist, Andrew Light. Andrew, I might have met you under the mistaken assumption that you would be a source for this book, but at least I was smart enough to figure out by the end of the evening that I would be better off marrying you instead. To help me research and write this tome, you've navigated cratered Mexican highways, suffered through exploding glass bottles in Surabaya, and plunged to the depths in Raja Ampat. On top of that, you agreed that there was nothing wrong with me taking our son, Miloš Eilperin Light, during my maternity leave to three different continents to see sharks firsthand. For all of this and a hundred other things, I love you beyond words.

Notes

INTRODUCTION: SHARK

1. WildAid and Oceana, *The End of the Line? Global Threats to Sharks,* 2nd ed. WildAid, San Francisco, 2007, p. 12 (http://www.wildaid.org/PDF/reports/EndOfTheLine2007US_Oceana.pdf).
2. Interview with Dalal Al-Abdulrazzak, Watson fellow, Dec. 10, 2007.
3. Jeffrey C. Carrier, *Discovering Sharks* (St. Paul: Voyageur Press, 2006), pp. 9–10.
4. Tom Vanderbilt, "When the Great White Way Was the Hudson," *New York Times,* May 29, 2005, sec. 14, col. 1.
5. ReefQuest Centre for Shark Research Web site, Biology of Sharks and Rays.
6. EurekAlert! press release, July 15, 2005.
7. Mote Marine Laboratory, "Sharks Smell in Stereo: Mote Research Explores Shark Senses as Never Before," press release, June 11, 2010.
8. Jennifer L. Molinar, ed., *The Atlas of Global Conservation: Changes, Challenges, and Opportunities to Make a Difference* (Berkeley: University of California Press and the Nature Conservancy, 2010).
9. "Nature conservation has become one of the most important human endeavors on the planet, and the area under protection now exceeds the total area of permanent crops and arable land." Stuart Chape, Mark Spalding, and Martin Jenkins, eds., *The World's Protected Areas: Status, Values, and Prospects in the Twenty-First Century* (Berkeley: University of California Press, 2008).

I THE WORLD-FAMOUS SHARK CALLER

1. Glenys Köhnke, *The Shark Callers: An Ancient Fishing Tradition of New Ireland, Papua New Guinea* (Boroko: Yumi Press, 1974), p. 15.
2. Ibid., p. 16.

2 AN ANCIENT FISH

1. Nicholas H. Barton et al., *Evolution* (Cold Spring Harbor, N.Y.: Cold Spring Harbor Laboratory Press, 2007); Eric Roston, *The Carbon Age* (New York: Walker, 2008).

2. Skomal, *Shark Handbook,* pp. 16–22.

3. "Origin of the Egyptians: Petrie Derives Them from the Stock Whence the Phoenicians Come," *New York Times,* Aug. 9, 1894.

4. Xavier Maniguet, *The Jaws of Death: Shark as Predator, Man as Prey,* trans. David A. Christie (New York: Skyhorse Publishing, 2007), p. 21.

5. Oppian, *Halieutica* 5.20ff., at www.theoi.com/Ther/Ketea.html.

6. From the collections of the National Archives in Waltham, Massachusetts, and Washington, D.C., the Peabody Essex Museum in Salem, the Marblehead Historical Society, and smaller collections in other archives. These logs have been rediscovered and collated by Dr. William Leavenworth at the University of New Hampshire under the aegis of History of Marine Animal Populations (HMAP), the Gulf of Maine Cod Project, and other organizations doing research in the environmental history of the sea.

7. Louis Agassiz, "On the Method of Copulation Among Selachians," *Proceedings of the Boston Society of Natural History* 14 (1871), p. 340.

8. Matthew T. McDavitt, "Cipactli's Sword, Tlaltecuhtli's Teeth: Deciphering the Sawfish & Shark Offerings in the Aztec Great Temple," *Shark News: Newsletter of the IUCN/SSC Shark Specialist Group* 14 (March 2002).

9. Matthew T. McDavitt, "The Cultural Significance of Sharks and Rays in Aboriginal Societies Across Australia's Top End," *MESA's SeaWeek* (2005), pp. 3–4.

10. Martha Warren Beckwith, "Hawaiian Shark 'Aumākua," in *Nanaue the Shark Man & Other Hawaiian Shark Stories,* ed. Dennis Kawaharada (Honolulu: Kalamaku Press, 1994), p. 2.

11. Ibid.

12. Leighton Taylor, *Sharks of Hawai'i: Their Biology and Cultural Significance* (Honolulu: University of Hawaii Press, 1993), p. 20.

13. Young, *Shark! Shark!* p. 93.

14. Beckwith, "Hawaiian Shark 'Aumākua," p. 15.

15. Pa'ahana Wiggin, "Mikololou," in *Nanaue the Shark Man,* pp. 71–72.

16. "Ka'ehikimanō-o-pu'uloa," in *Nanaue the Shark Man,* pp. 75–83.

17. Emma M. Nakuina, "Kahalaopuna," in *Nanaue the Shark Man,* p. 41.

18. Emma Nakuina, "Nanaue," in *Nanaue the Shark Man,* pp. 19–32.

19. Martha G. Anderson and Philip M. Peek, *Ways of the Rivers: Arts and Environment of the Niger Delta* (Los Angeles: UCLA Fowler Museum of Cultural History, 2002), p. 153.

20. Matthew T. McDavitt, "Cultural Significance," in: *Sharks, Rays, and Chimaeras: The Status of the Chondrichthyan Fishes,* ed. Sarah L. Fowler et al. (Gland, Switzerland, and Cambridge, U.K.: IUCN, 2005), p. 31.

21. McDavitt, "Cultural Significance of Sharks and Rays," pp. 2–3.

22. Ibid., p. 3.

23. Gerald L. Crow and Jennifer Crites, *Sharks and Rays of Hawai'i* (Honolulu: Mutual Publishing, 2002), p. 147.

24. Brent M. Handley, "Role of the Shark in Southern New England's Prehistory: Deity or Dinner?" *Bulletin of the Massachusetts Archaeological Society* 57, no. 1 (1996), pp. 27–34.

25. McCormick and Allen, *Shadows in the Sea,* pp. 137–40.

26. McDavitt, "Cultural Significance," p. 30.

27. Tom Jones, "The *Xoc,* the *Sharke,* and the Sea Dogs: An Historical Encounter," in *Fifth Paleugue Round Table, 1983,* ed. Virginia M. Fields (San Francisco: Pre-Columbia Art Research Institute, 1985), pp. 211–220.

28. Oxford English Dictionary Online, shark, n., 2nd ed. (1989).

29. Ibid.

30. *Dampier's Voyages,* ed. John Masefield (New York: E. P. Dutton, 1906), vol. 1, p. 107.

31. Ibid., vol. 2, pp. 426–27.

32. McCormick and Allen, *Shadows in the Sea,* p. 148.

33. Marcus Rediker, *The Slave Ship: A Human History* (New York: Viking, 2007), pp. 37–38.

34. Ibid., pp. 38–40.

35. Marcus Rediker, "Slavery: A Shark's Perspective—a Strange Text Sheds New Light on the True Roots of Abolition," *Boston Globe,* Sept. 23, 2007.

36. Julius L. Esping, *Adrift and at Anchor: A Sailor's Experience Among Sea Dogs and Land Sharks: With an Account of His Conversion and Labors as a Missionary Among Seamen* (Boston: H. L. Hastings, 1870), pp. 112–23.

37. George Barker, *Thrilling Adventures of the Whaler* Alcyone: *Killing Man-Eating Sharks in the Indian Ocean, Hunting Kangaroos in Australia* (Peabody, Mass.: George Barker, 1916), pp. 33–34.

38. Capuzzo, *Close to Shore,* pp. 88–103.

39. Ibid., pp. 141–246.

40. Ibid., pp. 168–79.

41. Young, *Shark! Shark!* p. 78.

42. Ibid., pp. 18–19.

43. Ernest Hemingway, *The Old Man and the Sea,* excerpted in *Great Shark Writings,* ed. Taylor and Taylor, p. 317.

44. Zane Grey, *An American Angler in Australia,* excerpted in *Great Shark Writings,* p. 234.

45. McCormick and Allen, *Shadows in the Sea,* p. 31.

46. Mitchell Landsberg, "Roy Scheider, 75, 'Jaws' Star Excelled in Tough-Guy Role," *Los Angeles Times,* Feb. 11, 2008.

47. As National Public Radio's Cory Turner reported in his excellent June 2, 2010, piece, "Hunting Bruce; or, On the Trail of the 'Jaws' Shark," the head of the mechanical shark measured six feet eight inches and weighed four hundred pounds. There were three mechanical sharks, nicknamed Bruce, since one was pulled by a boat to replicate swimming while two sat atop a metal arm in order to leap onto the deck of the *Orca.* All three Bruces were destroyed and the mold was lost, but a fourth shark, which was likely cast from the same mold, now looms above Aadlen Brothers Wrecking in Sun Valley, California.

48. Benchley, *Jaws,* p. 94.

49. Erich Ritter, Kai Lutz, and Marie Levine, "When Humans and Sharks Meet," in *New Developments in the Psychology of Motivation,* ed. Filip M. Olsson (New York: Nova Biomedical Books, 2008), pp. 45–52.

50. EurekAlert! press release, Aug. 28, 2003.

51. Klimley, *Secret Life of Sharks,* pp. 195–215.

52. Ibid., p. 185.
53. WildAid and Oceana, *The End of the Line? Global Threats to Sharks*, 2nd ed. pp. 13 and 40.

3 A DEMON FISH

1. John D. Stevens, Terence I. Walker, Sid F. Cook, and Sonja V. Fordham, "Threats Faced by Chondrichthyan Fish," in *Sharks, Rays, and Chimaeras: The Status of Chondrichthyan Fishes,* ed. Sarah L. Flower et al. (Gland, Switzerland, and Cambridge, U.K.: IUCN, 2005), pp. 48–57.
2. www.st.nmfs.noaa.gov/st1/fus/fus07/03_recreationa12007.pdf.
3. Ibid.
4. George Vancouver, *A Voyage of Discovery to the North Pacific Ocean and Round the World, 1791–1795,* ed. W. Kaye Lamb, 4 vols. (London: Hakluyt Society, 1984).

4 DRIED SEAFOOD STREET

1. Piamsak Menasveta, Sombat Inkong, and Pimporn Charoensri, "Mercury Contents in Dried Shark Fins in Bangkok Markets," *Journal of the Royal Institute of Thailand* (2002).
2. Oceana, "The International Trade of Shark Fins: Endangering Shark Populations Worldwide," March 2010.
3. Shelley Clarke, "Shark Product Trade in Hong Kong and Mainland China and Implementation of the CITES Shark Listings," *TRAFFIC East Asia, Hong Kong, China* (2004).
4. Jim Tharpe, "Gov. Perdue Welcomed, State Will Open Trade Office in Beijing," *Atlanta Journal-Constitution,* March 31, 2008.
5. David Barboza, "Waiter, There's a Celebrity in My Shark Fin Soup," *New York Times,* sec. 4, p. 3.
6. Neil Ray, "Shark Fin Demand Sinks," SeafoodSource, March 30, 2009.
7. World Briefing, "Japan: Princess Becomes Fair Game," *New York Times,* Feb. 5, 2008.
8. TRAFFIC, *The World Trade in Sharks: A Compendium of TRAFFIC's Regional Studies* (Cambridge, U.K.: TRAFFIC International, 1996).
9. O. W. Barrett, "Shark Fishing in the West Indies," *Scientific Monthly* 27, no. 2 (Aug. 1928), pp. 125–33.
10. McCormick and Allen, *Shadows in the Sea,* pp. 182–87.
11. Gary K. Ostrander, Keith C. Cheng, Jeffrey C. Wolf, and Marilyn J. Wolfe, "Shark Cartilage, Cancer, and the Growing Threat of Pseudoscience," *Cancer Research* 64 (2004), pp. 8485–91.
12. Mock Joya, *Things Japanese* (Tokyo: Tokyo News Service, 1960), p. 261.
13. Ibid.

5 THE SHARK SLEUTHS

1. Carol Vogel, "Swimming with Famous Dead Sharks," *New York Times,* Oct. 1, 2006, sect. 2, p. 28.

2. Arifa Akbar, "A Formaldehyde Frenzy as Buyers Snap Up Hirst Works," *Independent,* Sept. 16, 2008.

3. ENDCAP, Exotic Pet Trade Fact Sheet.

4. Plea Agreement No. CR06-0051CW, *United States of America v. Ira Gass,* U.S. District Court for the Northern District of California, Oakland Division.

5. Robert Gammon, "The Man v. Moon," *East Bay Express,* Jan. 31, 2007.

6. Plea Agreement No. CR06-0051CW, *United States of America v. John Newberry,* U.S. District Court for the Northern District of California, Oakland Division.

7. Demian D. Chapman, Danillo Pinhal, and Mahmood S. Shivji, "Tracking the Fin Trade: Genetic Stock Identification in Western Atlantic Scalloped Hammerheads Sharks *Sphyrna lewini,*" *Endangered Species Research* 9, no. 3 (2009), pp. 221–28.

8. Robert D. Ward et al., "DNA barcoding Australian Chondrichthyans: Results and Potential Uses in Conservation," *Marine and Freshwater Research* 59 (2008), pp. 57–71.

9. Demian D. Chapman, Beth Firchau, and Mahmood S. Shivji, "Brief Communication: Parthenogenesis in a Large-Bodied Requiem Shark, the Blacktip *Carcharhinus limbatus,*" *Journal of Fish Biology* 73 (2008), pp. 1–5.

10. Malcolm P. Francis, "Observations on a Pregnant White Shark with a Review of Reproductive Biology," in *Great White Sharks: The Biology of* Carcharodon carcharias, ed. A. Peter Klimley and David G. Ainley (San Diego: Academic Press, 1996), pp. 157–72.

11. Harold L. Pratt Jr. and Jeffrey C. Carrier, "A Review of Elasmobranch Reproductive Behavior with a Case Study on the Nurse Shark, *Ginglymostoma cirratum,*" *Environmental Biology of Fishes* 60 (2001), pp. 157–88.

6   SHARK TRACKERS

1. Francesco Ferretti et al., "Patterns and Ecosystem Consequences of Shark Declines in the Ocean," *Ecology Letters* 13, no. 8 (2010), p. 1056.

2. Camhi, Pikitch, and Babcock, *Sharks of the Open Ocean,* pp. 27–30; Clark, *The Lady and the Sharks,* p. 90.

3. MacQuitty, *Eyewitness Shark,* pp. 16–17.

4. Mary M. Cerullo, *The Truth About Great White Sharks* (San Francisco: Chronicle Books, 2000).

5. Stephen Wroe et al. "Three-Dimensional Computer Analysis of White Shark Mechanics: How Hard Can a Great White Bite?" *Journal of Zoology,* 276 (2008), pp. 336–42.

6. Edith A. Widder, "A Predatory Use of Counterillumination by the Squaloid Shark, *Isistius brasiliensis,*" *Environmental Biology of Fishes* 53 (1998), pp. 267–73.

7. Jeffrey C. Carrier, *Discovering Sharks* (St. Paul: Voyageur Press, 2006), p. 18.

8. John Maisey, Randall Miller, and Susan Turner, "The Braincase of the Chondrichthyan *Doliodus* from the Lower Devonian Campbellton Formation of New Brunswick, Canada," *Acta Zoologica* 90, suppl. 1 (May 2009), pp. 109–22.

9. Personal communication with John Maisey, Division of Paleontology, American Museum of Natural History, Aug. 23, 2010.

10. EurekAlert! press release, Apr. 9, 1999.

11. Shubin, *Your Inner Fish,* pp. 90–93.

12. Ibid., pp. 193–96.

13. J. Craig Venter Institute, "Of Jaws and Men: Initial Decoding of Elephant Shark Genome Helps Uncover Ancient DNA in Human Genome," press release, Dec. 21, 2006.

14. Klimley, *Secret Life of Sharks,* p. 19.

15. Jayne M. Gardiner and Jelle Atema, "The Function of Bilateral Odor Arrival Time Differences in Olfactory Orientation of Sharks," *Current Biology* 20, no. 13 (2010), pp. 1187–91.

16. Carrier, *Discovering Sharks,* p. 24.

17. Lisa Cook and Joel Simonetti, *Why I Care About Sharks: Will Sharks Survive This Century?* (Hong Kong: Big Fish Press, 2003), p. 8.

18. MacQuitty, *Eyewitness Shark,* p. 23.

19. Salvador J. Jorgensen et al., "Philopatry and Migration of Pacific White Sharks," *Proceedings of the Royal Society,* doi:10.1098/rspb2009.1155. Published online Nov. 4, 2009.

20. Personal communication with Stanford University professor Barbara Black, January 4, 2011.

7 LIVING WITH SHARKS

1. C. F. Smit and Vic Peddemors, "Estimating the Probability of a Shark Attack When Using an Electric Repellent," *South African Statistical Journal* 37 (2003), pp. 59–60.

2. Baldridge, pp. 11–14.

3. Smit and Peddemors, "Estimating the Probability of a Shark Attack," pp. 59–78.

4. Richard Brill et al., "The Repulsive and Feeding-Deterrent Effects of Electropositive Metals on Juvenile Sandbar Sharks (*Carcharhinus plumbeus*)," *Fishery Bulletin* 107 (2009), pp. 298–307.

5. Christopher H. Achen and Larry M. Bartels, "Blind Retrospection: Electoral Responses to Drought, Flu, and Shark Attacks," paper presented at the annual meeting of the American Political Science Association, Boston, Sept. 2002, pp. 1–9.

6. Ibid., p. 20.

8 FISH FIGHT

1. Kenneth R. Weiss, "Obituaries; Ransom A. Myers, 54, Warned That Overfishing Posed Sweeping Threat," *Los Angeles Times,* March 29, 2007.

2. Julia K. Baum and Ransom A. Myers, "Shifting Baselines and the Decline of Pelagic Sharks in the Gulf of Mexico," *Ecology Letters* 7 (2004), pp. 135–45.

3. Phillip J. Clapham et al., "Determining Spatial and Temporal Scales for Management: Lessons from Whaling," *Marine Mammal Science* 24, no. 1 (2008), p. 184.

4. Ibid., pp. 183–88.

5. Ibid., pp. 190–91.
6. Burr Heneman and Marci Glazer, "More Rare Than Dangerous: A Case Study of White Shark Conservation in California," in *Great White Sharks: The Biology of* Carcharodon carcharias, ed. A. Peter Klimley and David G. Ainley (San Diego: Academic Press, 1996).
7. WildAid, "At Rock Bottom: The Declining Sharks of the Eastern Tropical Pacific" (San Francisco: WildAid, 2005).

9 GAWKING AT JAWS

1. Philip J. Motta et al., "Feeding Anatomy, Filter-Feeding Rate, and Diet of Whale Sharks *Rhincodon typus* During Surface Ram Filter Feeding off the Yucatan Peninsula, Mexico," *Zoology*, 113: 4 (August 2010) pp. 199–212.
2. Taylor and Taylor, *Great Shark Writings*, pp. 48–49.
3. Ibid., pp. 45–46.

CONCLUSION: SHARK NIRVANA

1. Michael R. Heithaus et al., "Predicting Ecological Consequences of Marine Top Predator Declines," *Trends in Ecology and Evolution* 23, no. 4 (2008).
2. Francesco Ferretti et al., "Patterns and Ecosystem Consequences of Shark Declines in the Ocean," *Ecology Letters* 13, no. 8 (2010), pp. 1065–71.
3. Benjamin S. Halpern et al., "A Global Map of Human Impact on Marine Ecosystems," *Science*, Feb. 15, 2008, pp. 948–52.
4. Helen Kennedy and Alyssa Giachino, "One Fin Fellow: Coney Is. Lifeguard Rescues Shark to Cap Crazy Summer," *New York Daily News*, Sept. 4, 2007.
5. David E. Jennings et al., "Effects of Large-Scale Anthropogenic Development on Juvenile Lemon Shark (*Negaprion brevirostris*) Populations of Bimini, Bahamas," *Environmental Biology of Fishes*, Dec. 2008.
6. "Great White Shark Sightings on the Rise on the East Coast," National Public Radio, August 13, 2010, and personal communication with Larry Selzer, president, Conservation Fund.
7. Jennifer L. Molinar, ed., *The Atlas of Global Conservation: Changes, Challenges, and Opportunities to Make a Difference* (Berkeley: University of California Press and the Nature Conservancy, 2010), p. 155.
8. Juliet Eilperin, "Hawaiian Marine Reserve to Be the World's Largest: Bush to Designate National Park in Pacific Waters," *Washington Post*, June 15, 2006.
9. Nicholas A. J. Graham, Mark D. Spalding, and Charles R. C. Sheppard, "Reef Shark Declines in Remote Atolls Highlight the Need for Multi-faceted Conservation Action," *Aquatic Conservation: Marine and Freshwater Ecosystems* 20, no. 5 (2010).
10. Daniel G. Boyce, Marlon R. Lewis, and Boris Worm, "Global Phytoplankton Decline Over the Past Century," *Nature* 466 (2010), pp. 591–96.

Bibliography

Benchley, Peter. *Jaws.* New York: Doubleday, 1974.

Camhi, Merry D., Ellen K. Pikitch, and Elizabeth A. Babcock, eds. *Sharks of the Open Ocean: Biology, Fisheries, and Conservation.* Oxford: Blackwell Science, 2008.

Capuzzo, Michael. *Close to Shore: A True Story of Terror in an Age of Innocence.* New York: Broadway Books, 2001.

Clark, Eugenie. *The Lady and the Sharks.* Sarasota, Fla.: Mote Marine Laboratory, 1969.

Klimley, A. Peter. *The Secret Life of Sharks: A Leading Marine Biologist Reveals the Secrets of Shark Behavior.* New York: Simon & Schuster, 2003.

MacQuitty, Miranda. *Eyewitness Shark.* New York: DK Publishing, 1992.

Matthiessen, Peter. *Blue Meridian: The Search for the Great White Shark.* New York: Penguin Books, 1997.

McCormick, Harold W., and Tom Allen, with William E. Young. *Shadows in the Sea: The Sharks, Skates, and Rays.* Philadelphia: Chilton Books, 1963.

Shubin, Neil. *Your Inner Fish: A Journey into the 3.5-Billion-Year History of the Human Body.* New York: Vintage Books, 2008.

Skomal, Greg. *The Shark Handbook: The Essential Guide for Understanding the Sharks of the World.* Kennebunkport, Maine: Cider Mill Press, 2008.

Taylor, Valerie, and Ron Taylor, with Peter Goadby, eds. *Great Shark Writings.* Woodstock, N.Y.: Overlook Press, 2000.

Young, William E. *Shark! Shark! The Thirty-Year Odyssey of a Pioneer Shark Hunter.* London: Kegan Paul, 1934.

Index

ABOUT THE AUTHOR

Juliet Eilperin graduated from Princeton University. She works as *The Washington Post*'s national environmental reporter, covering science, policy, and politics in areas including climate change and oceans. She lives with her family in Washington, D.C.

A NOTE ON THE TYPE

The text of this book was set in Sabon, a typeface designed by Jan Tschichold (1902–1974), the well-known German typographer. Designed in 1966 and based on the original designs by Claude Garamond (ca. 1480–1561), Sabon was named for the punch cutter Jacques Sabon, who brought Garamond's matrices to Frankfurt.

Composed by North Market Street Graphics
Lancaster, Pennsylvania

Printed and bound by Berryville Graphics,
Berryville, Virginia

Designed by M. Kristen Bearse